THE PEN͟
DICTI͟   ͟NCE

Graham Bannock is a graduate of the London School of Economics
and author of several books on finance and business. He has worked in
market research for Ford and Rover and in economic research at the
OECD and the Economist Intelligence Unit, of which he was
managing director. He is now with Graham Bannock & Partners, an
economic research and consultancy company in London. He is also the
co-author of *The Penguin Dictionary of Economics*.

William Manser is a graduate of Cambridge University and read
International Law and Economics at Geneva University. He is an
economic and financial author and consultant, working at the moment
inter alia with the Economic Intelligence Unit and Graham Bannock &
Partners. He has been Economic Adviser to Baring Brothers, the
British Institute of Management, the British Civil Engineering Federation and the International Iron and Steel Institute. He is a Fellow of
the Royal Society of Arts and Commerce, the Royal Statistical
Society and the Institute of Management Consultants. His other books
include *Britain in Balance* (Penguin 1973), *The British Economic Base*,
The Financial Role of Multinational Enterprise, *Control from Brussels* and
many other works.

THE PENGUIN
INTERNATIONAL
DICTIONARY OF
FINANCE

Graham Bannock and
William Manser

PENGUIN BOOKS

PENGUIN BOOKS

Published by the Penguin Group
Penguin Books Ltd, 27 Wrights Lane, London w8 5tz
Penguin Books USA Inc., 375 Hudson Street, New York, New York 10014, USA
Penguin Books Australia Ltd, Ringwood, Victoria, Australia
Penguin Books Canada Ltd, 10 Alcorn Avenue, Toronto, Ontario, Canada m4v 3b2
Penguin Books (NZ) Ltd, 182–190 Wairau Road, Auckland 10, New Zealand

Penguin Books Ltd, Registered Offices: Harmondsworth, Middlesex, England

First published by Hutchinson Business Books,
in association with The Economist Books, by arrangement with Penguin Books, 1989
Published in Penguin Books 1990
Second edition 1995
3 5 7 9 10 8 6 4 2

Typeset by Datix International Limited, Bungay, Suffolk
Printed in England by Clays Ltd, St Ives plc

FOREWORD TO
THE SECOND EDITION

This new edition has been brought up to date and greatly enlarged. Hundreds of new terms have been added especially in the fields of commodity markets, derivatives, emerging markets, institutions, insurance, pensions, venture capital and foreign language terms. The full term for all abbreviations will now be found in alphabetical order at the appropriate point in the dictionary. Definitions and explanations, where they are considered necessary, will still be found under the full term to which the abbreviation is cross-referenced. We have been helped and encouraged by the response we have received from our many readers. We hope they will continue to write to us with any errors or omissions.

GB, WM
London, November 1994

FOREWORD TO
THE FIRST EDITION

This book is intended as a source of reference for all those concerned with finance. It is entitled 'International Dictionary of Finance', rather than 'Dictionary of International Finance', because it is concerned not solely with transnational finance, but also with domestic financial matters in the major countries, particularly in the United Kingdom and the United States. No one involved in business finance, savings and investment or public finance can now neglect the international dimension.

Money markets, commodity markets, securities markets, banking and *insurance*, the five principal subjects of the book, have always involved international connections. Some or parts of these markets have always been fully international, but we are now well on the way to the globalization of virtually all financial markets, as barriers to entry fall with the abandonment of exchange controls and the deregulation of these markets in the United States, Europe and Japan. These developments are now being given additional impetus by the adoption of the Single Act of the European Community, which is intended to bring about by 1992 the full integration of the capital markets of the EC member states. Just as the regulation of markets following the Second World War led to innovation in finance – notably the development of the Euromarkets – so too has deregulation stimulated further innovation. Each phase of change has generated new terminology, which has been further enriched by the cross-fertilization of languages, business cultures and electronic technology.

The specialized terminology of finance is vast and expands daily, and we have had to be highly selective, even within the five core areas mentioned above. We have attempted to include all the more common terms which market operators and those in financial institutions are likely to encounter in English-speaking countries.

We have also included key terminology in accounting, business finance, investment appraisal, public finance, savings and investment, statistics and technology. We have not assumed much prior knowledge of the subject, and the dictionary is specifically directed at businessmen, students and the investing public as well as at financial professionals who may need to verify terms outside their own specialized field.

Happily for English speakers, their language is dominant in international finance, but we have been careful to note where US and British terminology differs. Where a term is not generally common to both countries we have indicated this by (US) or (Br.) after the entry. We have also included a large number of the key foreign-language terms, including institutional terms, with an indication of their national reference thus: (Aus.) Australia; (Bel.) Belgium; (Den.) Denmark; (Fr.) France; (Ire.) Ireland; (It.) Italy; (Jap.) Japan; (Neth.) Netherlands.

All terms, even where commonly abbreviated (for example, SEAQ), are defined under the full term to which the abbreviation is cross-referenced thus: See **Stock Exchange Automated Quotation System**. Cross-referencing is elaborate, both in the interest of avoiding repetition and to enable the reader to pursue subjects in greater depth and in their wider context. All cross-references are shown in **bold**. Where a cross-reference is given in parentheses, it refers only to the phrase or sentence immediately preceding it and not to the whole entry.

While we, as authors, though professionally experienced in research on financial matters, cannot be expected to be expert across the whole of such a broad field, we have sought advice and help from many people and published sources, too numerous to mention. We do, however, wish to thank our editor, Andrew Franklin, for his enthusiasm and support through a lengthy task.

GB, WM
London, September 1988

'A' day (UK) 29 April 1988, when the **Financial Services Act** came into force.

à la criée (Fr.) **Open outcry**; one of the three methods of quotation on the French **stock exchange**, the others being **par casier** and *par opposition*. Normally used in the **marché à terme**.

'A' shares See **share**.

ABI See **Association of British Insurers**.

Abschlag (Ger.) **Discount**.

absolute liability See **strict liability**.

accelerated accrual Use of a denominator less than 60 in the **accrual rate** applied in the calculation of an employee's pension (see **pensions**). If the denominator is, e.g., 40, then an employee having served for 40 years would receive 100% of their final salary as pension.

accelerated depreciation See **capital allowances**.

acceptance The act of accepting, i.e. agreeing to honour, a **bill of exchange**. By extension, the document itself.

acceptance credit A use of **acceptances** whereby a set **credit** period is accorded the buyer by means of a documentary letter of credit, or **documentary credit**. A bank or **accepting house** is itself the drawee of the bill, subject to **clausing** and to the documentary credit. The bank or accepting house normally **discounts** the bill and remains responsible for payment of the bill at **maturity**, making arrangements with the buyer for the latter's payment in turn. Should the buyer fail to pay, the bank's liability to pay remains, contrary to the practice for a simple acceptance.

accepting house A **merchant bank** originally belonging to the Accepting House Committee (now the British Merchant Banking and Securities Association), a category historically entitled to smaller, or finer, rates of **discount** on accepted **bills of exchange** at the **Bank of England**. All accepting houses are major merchant banks, and in 1986 they numbered 16. Their discount privileges with the Bank of England now extend to all banks on the **eligible list**. Accepting houses are so named because they initiated the practice of bill **acceptance**.

accommodation bill (Jap.) A **bill of exchange** accepted by a bank (a **bank bill** or **banker's acceptance**) based on a number of **trade bills**.

account 1. A record of financial transactions as in a bank account (**current account**; see **banking**) or **balance sheet**. 2. An arrangement between a seller and a buyer under which a period of **credit** is allowed before payment, e.g. the period in which **London Stock Exchange** transactions take place and after the end of which **settlement** must be made. Up to the end of the account, transactions are made without payment, and account dates are thus of vital importance to speculators. Until recently there were 24 account periods in a year. Other countries have different systems for settlement. See also **account day**.

account day (UK) The day on which all transactions made during the previous **account** at the **London Stock Exchange** must be settled (see **settlement**). It is normally a Monday, 10 days after the last day of dealings on the account. In the USA markets use rolling accounts which are settled a fixed number of days after the transaction. The London Stock Exchange announced that from 18 July 1994 a rolling account system would be adopted. Initially accounts need to be settled within 10 days of dealing, and from the beginning of 1995 the rolling settlement period will fall to five days.

accounting equation, basic See **balance sheet**.

accrual rate The rate, i.e. the number of years of service, at which an employee's rights to a pension (see **pensions**) accumulate throughout their period of employment. Normally this number is expressed as a fraction of 60 and then applied to the employee's final salary to arrive at the pension. Thus a person who has served 40 years will receive 40/60ths of their final salary as their pension.

accruals accounting Where expenses have been incurred, or income is due, but not paid or even invoiced at the time accounts are drawn up but are nevertheless included in the accounts. For example, accountancy fees or the cost of electricity consumed in an accounting period can be included in the accounts as liabilities even though these costs have not been paid and invoices have not yet been received.

accumulation units See **unit trust**.

acid ratio The ratio of current **assets** minus **stock** to current **liabilities**. Used as a crude test of **solvency**.

acquis communautaire (Fr.) 'Community attainment'. A term in common use in **European Union** (EU) circles to refer to all that has been achieved by the Union (formerly the European Community) to date – invariably as part of a statement that past successes should not be allowed to go to waste.

acquisition accounting See **consolidated accounts**.

Act-only policy Motor **insurance** that offers the strictly minimum cover required by law.

actif (Fr.) **Asset**.

action group A group of **names** on certain heavily loss-making **syndicates** taking joint action, including litigation, against alleged fraud or negligence on the part of the market operators.

actionnaire (Fr.) **Shareholder**.

actions (Fr.) Shares in the **equity** capital of a business. See **ordinary share**.

active underwriter The **working member** authorized by the **managing agent** to underwrite on behalf of the members of a **syndicate**. An active underwriter is usually assisted by up to 10 working members.

actual A **commodity** immediately or very quickly available for delivery, sold on a **commodity market**. Also termed *physical* and *cash*. See also **forward**, **futures**, **option**.

actual price The price of a **commodity** available for immediate sale and delivery. Also known as *cash*, *physical* or *spot* price. See also **forward**, **futures**, **option**.

actuary A senior **insurance** company official, expert in statistics and particularly in those of **mortality** and loss incidence, responsible for estimating future **claims** and disbursement requirements and for calculating necessary fund and **premium** levels. Actuaries may not call themselves such unless they have passed the examinations of the Institute of Actuaries. Actuaries are also employed in **savings banks** and may in any case move from insurance companies and savings banks to positions elsewhere, particularly in the financial services industry.

ad valorem 'By value'. An *ad valorem* tax is a tax (see **taxation**) on the price of a good or service. The *ad valorem* principle is used, e.g., in import **tariffs** and **value added tax**.

adaptive expectations hypothesis (US) A theory of **rate of interest** prediction based on the assumption that the future course of a target variable can be discerned from previous patterns.

ADEF (Fr.) See **Agence d'Evaluation Financière**.

adjustable rate mortgage (ARM) (US) A **mortgage** loan in which the **rate of interest** is adjusted in line with market interest rates at predetermined intervals. **Floating rates** are, of course, common practice in the UK and elsewhere.

adjustable rate preferred (ARP) stock (US) A form of **preference share** for which **dividends** are linked to the **rates of interest** on **Treasury bills**. ARPs carry a 'collar' that sets the minimum and maximum dividend rates that will be paid. ARPs may be convertible into common **stocks** at a fixed price at a specified date or dates.

adjustment credit (US) **Loans** of a few days' duration only from the US **Federal Reserve** to banks and other **deposit**-taking institutions for the purpose of meeting a shortage of **reserves**.

ADR See **American depository receipt**.

adventure A legal term referring to a project or venture, as distinct from an item of property or other consideration, that is the subject of an **insurance** policy.

AFBD Association of Futures Brokers and Dealers. See **Financial Services Act**.

Affärsvärlden General Index The Stockholm Stock Exchange share index.

affiliate See **subsidiary**.

after-hours trading See **24-hour trading**.

aftermarket Dealing in **securities** immediately after a **new issue**.

AG (Ger.) See *Aktiengesellschaft*.

age admitted A phrase in a **life assurance** policy indicating that the assured has provided evidence of their age, no further proof being needed when a claim is made.

Agence d'Evaluation Financière (ADEF) (Fr.) The French **rating agency**.

agency (US) Of a **security**, one issued by an agency of the US government. Most are in the form of **bills** and are issued mostly by Eximbank (see **Export–Import Bank**), the **Government National Mortgage Association**, the **Federal home loan banks** and farm credit banks.

agency bill A **bill of exchange** drawn on a local branch (e.g. in London) of a bank based abroad.

agency loan A loan of the **European Investment Bank**, available only to public bodies, which may be subdivided into smaller components for various purposes.

agent A person authorized by another person (a **principal**) to carry out transactions with third parties on their behalf, e.g. a **broker**.

agent de change (Fr.) **Stockbroker**; an official member of the French **stock exchange**, or *bourse*.

agente de cambio y bolsa (Sp.) **Stockbroker**. See also **Madrid Stock Exchange**.

agente di cambio (It.) **Stockbroker**.

agio A turn or **spread**, usually in the sense of a banker's return on the difference between the **rate of interest** they pay on **deposits** and that on the **loans** they extend.

AGM See **annual general meeting**.

agreed value policy An **insurance** policy in which the sum of money to be paid in the event of loss or damage is specifically stated.

AIBD See **International Securities Market Association**.

AIM, See **Amsterdam Interprofessional Market**.

Aktie (Ger.) **Share**.

Aktiengesellschaft (AG) (Ger.) Public limited company. See **incorporation**.

Aktionär (Ger.) **Shareholder**.

all or nothing A theory of money measurement in which all money forms are regarded as equal. Also known as the *simple sum theory*.

All Ordinaries See **Australian Stock Exchange**.

All Ordinaries Index The main Australian **share index**.

all risks insurance Insurance covering a generality of **risk**, i.e. loss or destruction, rather than one confined to specific **perils**, such as theft or flood.

Allfinanz (Ger.) **Insurance** and **banking** operation within the same institution. See also **bancassurance**.

ALM See **Association of Lloyd's Members**.

allocated capacity That part of the **overall premium limit** of a member of **Lloyd's of London** that is allocated to **syndicates**.

alpha coefficient A statistical measure of the price volatility of a

share against the volatility of all shares or selected risk-free shares. It identifies the price fluctuations inherent in the **security** as distinct from those in the market as a whole (*systematic risk*), which are measured by the *beta coefficient*. These terms are used in **portfolio theory**.

alpha securities, stocks (UK) A discontinued classification of some 130 **equity shares** most actively traded on the **London Stock Exchange** by at least 10 **market makers** of which at least six had to quote on SEAQ (see **Stock Exchange Automated Quotation System**) firm **bid** and **offer prices** in a minimum quantity of 1,000 shares. Details of transactions in alpha stocks had to be notified and were displayed on SEAQ within five minutes of the trade. The term was part of a three-category classification of shares. *Beta stocks*, of which there were some 550, required only six market makers of which at least four provided firm prices on SEAQ. *Gamma stocks* (1,500 in number) required two market makers quoting at least indicative prices on SEAQ that had to be firmed up on inquiry. *Delta stocks* (130 in number) were the least actively traded stocks, for which market makers quoted prices only on inquiry so that prices were not shown on SEAQ. Trading volumes were shown on SEAQ only for alpha stocks. This classification system was replaced on 14 January 1991 by a new system called **normal market size**.

alphabet brokers (US) A popular term applied to the dominating **insurance brokers** in the USA, commonly known by their initials, e.g. Marsh McLennan (M.M.), Alexander & Alexander (A.&A.), Johnson & Higgins (J.&H.).

alternative investment market (AIM) Proposed in 1994 by the **London Stock Exchange** to replace the **unlisted securities market**. The AIM would operate with minimum entry requirements under Rule 4.2 (formerly **Rule 535(2)**).

American depository receipt (ADR) (US) A **certificate** registered in the holder's name or as a **bearer security** giving title to a number of **shares** in a non-US-based company deposited in a bank outside the USA. These certificates are traded on US **stock exchanges**.

7

American Stock Exchange (AMEX) (US) The smaller of New York's two **stock exchanges**, listing mainly smaller and younger **companies** than those listed on the **New York Stock Exchange** (NYSE). Also referred to as the Little Board and the Curb Exchange.

American style An **option** that may be **exercised** at any time up to expiry.

AMEX See **American Stock Exchange**.

AMEX Major Market Index (MMI) A **share index** measuring the average prices of 20 major industrial **stocks** quoted on the **New York Stock Exchange**. **Futures** based on the **AMEX MMI** are traded on the **Chicago Board Options Exchange**.

amortize, amortization See **sinking fund**.

amount at risk The real **liability** of the insurer in a life policy, given that reserves against the sum payable increase steadily through the duration of the policy. At any one time, therefore, the amount at risk is the balance of the sum payable not covered by **reserves** and thus potentially falls on the *net worth* (see **net assets**) of the company.

Amsterdam Interprofessional Market (AIM) A method of transacting large business at negotiated **commission**, initiated on the **Amsterdam Stock Exchange** in 1986, between banks and commission houses, and institutional investors. The method dispenses with the services of **brokers**, or *hoekmen*.

Amsterdam Stock Exchange The 35 or so members of the Amsterdam Stock Exchange, the world's oldest exchange, are known as *hoekmen* or *hoeldieden*. These members act as **market makers** specializing in **single-capacity** dealing in particular **stocks** on the **trading floor** through a screen-based **quotation** system set up in 1990. **Block** trading is carried out off the floor in the **Amsterdam Interprofessional Market** (AIM). The second-tier market (see **unlisted securities market**) known as the *parallel markt* was closed to new entrants in 1993.

anbei kabunushi (Jap.) An inter-company shareholding rarely traded on the **stock exchange**.

Anlage (Ger.) **Investment**.

Anleger (Ger.) Investor.

Anleihe (Ger.) Borrowing, **bond**.

annual depreciation allowance See **capital allowances**.

annual general meeting (AGM) All public limited companies (see **incorporation**) in the UK are required by law to invite all **shareholders** to a general meeting with directors each year. (US = *annual meeting, annual stockholders' meeting*.) Among other things the meeting elects directors, appoints **auditors** and fixes their remuneration.

annual percentage rate (APR) The true statement of the annual cost of financial charges levied on **consumer credit**, as required by the **Consumer Credit Act** in the UK and the **Truth in Lending Act** in the USA. The lender's administrative costs, profit margin and interest charges on the loan are normally incorporated in an added charge payable throughout the term of the contract and expressed as a percentage of the value of the transaction. Until legislation was adopted, the percentage was often shown as a rate per month, a figure clearly smaller than the rate per year. The legislation made annual quotation compulsory.

annuitant Person in receipt of an **annuity**.

annuity 1. A regular annual payment of money. 2. A future stream of guaranteed annual income purchased by an immediate lump-sum payment. The lump sum is calculated by **discounted cash flow** and varies according to the **rate of interest**. Annuities can be *certain* or **terminable** life, **immediate**, **deferred** or **perpetual**. Some annuities offer protection against the erosion of the real value of income at higher cost, e.g. by a guaranteed increase of 5% or some other percentage each year, or the income may be tied to the profits of a life fund. See also **life assurance**.

ANRPC See **Association of Natural Rubber Producing Countries**.

anti-trust legislation See **trust**.

APCIMS (UK) Association of Private Client Investment Managers and Stockbrokers.

appreciate To rise in value, as of a **security** on the **stock exchange** or a **currency** against other currencies in the **foreign exchange** market.

APR See **annual percentage rate**.

arbitrage. Use by arbitrageurs (see **ARBs**) of the difference between the value of, or return on, **assets** in order to obtain a profit, namely: **1**. The purchase of a currency or **money-market** asset **forward** at three months and the sale of the same asset forward at six months, with the intention of securing a profit on the immediate cost, as against the contracted subsequent price, of the asset. **2**. The sale and purchase of matching assets in different currencies in order to obtain a profit on an anomaly in exchange rates. **3**. The switching of funds between money-market assets in order to obtain a profit on the differences in the yield or the **discounted** value of the assets. **4**. A **swap** of **securities**. **5**. The purchase and sale forward of **commodities** or the purchase and sale of these in different **commodity markets**.

ARBs Arbitrageurs (see **arbitrage**) who buy **shares** in companies subject to **take-over** bids.

arithmetic average See **average**.

arithmetic mean See **average**.

ARM See **adjustable rate mortgage**.

arm's length As between financially unrelated parties.

ARP See **adjustable rate preferred stock**.

Article 65 See **Securities and Exchange Act**.

articles of association See **memorandum of association**.

articles of incorporation See **memorandum of association**.

as-you-like option An **option** in one form that, at the choice of the holder, can, within a specified time limit, be changed into another form. Also known as a *chooser* or *call-or-put* option.

Asian option See **average rate options**.

asked price See **offer price**.

asset Something that has value or earning power. On the **balance sheet** of a company the following categories of assets are distinguished: *current assets* – cash, bank deposits and bills receivable; **trade investments**; *fixed assets* – land, buildings, plant and machinery, vehicles and furniture; *intangible assets* – **goodwill**, patents, etc. Financial assets are titles to cash such as a **bank deposit** or income and/or **capital gains** such as **ordinary shares**.

asset-backed security An **issue** whose **security** or **collateral** is the return on a financial **instrument**, e.g. a **mortgage**, **credit card receivables** or a **currency hedge**.

assignment A transfer of the right to receive payment from the original beneficiary (the *assignor*) to another (the *assignee*); e.g. a person may assign the rights under an *endowment assurance* (see **life assurance**) to a bank as **collateral** for a **loan**.

associate company (UK) A company over which another company has some influence, normally through a minority shareholding of less than 50% but more than 20%. See also **consolidated accounts**.

Association of British Insurers (ABI) A trade association formed in 1985 by a merger of the British Insurance Association (BIA) with a number of other representative bodies in the insurance industry.

Association of Futures Brokers and Dealers See **Financial Services Act**.

Association of International Bond Dealers See **International Securities Market Association**.

Association of Lloyd's Members (ALM) A voluntary and non-official association of **external members** of **Lloyd's of London**, formed to inform and advise members on Lloyd's issues, and to represent the views of members to the market's authorities. The ALM has some 9,000 members and has been acknowledged by the market authorities as making a useful contribution to the formulation of policy. It is not to be confused with the various 'action bodies' formed to pursue loss-making members' grievances against syndicates and agents.

Association of Natural Rubber Producing Countries (ANRPC) An intergovernmental organization, comprising India, Indonesia, Malaysia, Papua New Guinea, Singapore, Sri Lanka and Thailand, formed in 1970 to bring about co-ordination in production and marketing, to promote technical co-operation among member countries and to achieve fair and stable prices. The member countries account for approximately 90% of world supply. In 1982 a Standing Committee on INRO Matters (see **International Natural Rubber Organization**) was formed to co-ordinate members' position on subjects discussed at that body. The association consists of an assembly and an executive.

Association of Tin Producing Countries (ATPC) A market grouping of tin-mining countries (Australia, Bolivia, Indonesia, Malaysia, Nigeria, Thailand and Zaire) accounting for 60% of world production, formed after the collapse in 1985 of the International Tin Council and the release on to the world market of buffer stocks of 100,000 tonnes. The aims of the ATPC are to reverse the resultant fall in price (from $12 per kg in 1981 to $5 per kg in 1993) by means of export quotas. However, economic decline in industrialized countries and increased exports from non-ATPC sources (Brazil, Burma, China, Peru, Portugal, the former Soviet Union, the USA and Vietnam), often at lower prices, largely nullified the quota scheme.

ASX See **Australian Stock Exchange**.

at best An instruction to a **broker** to buy or sell a **security** at the best price they can get at the time of the **order**.

at call See **call money**.

at-the-money The **exercise price** of a **derivative** that is closest to the market price of the underlying instrument.

Athens Stock Exchange Like **stock exchanges** in many countries, the Athens exchange (the only one in Greece and founded in 1876) is in the process of modernization. Following a major expansion in activity in 1986–7, a draft law for the reform of the stock exchange was published in December 1987 that included provision for an **unlisted securities market**. At the end of 1992 there were 156 companies listed on the Athens Stock Exchange and a further eight on the second-tier market.

ATPC See **Association of Tin Producing Countries**.

ATX Index (Austria) The main Vienna Stock Exchange **share index**.

au jour le jour (Fr.) **Overnight money**.

auction system See **order driven**.

audit trail An important advantage of the **market maker** or **quote-driven** system of **securities** dealing is that computer files can be maintained of price quotations and transactions so that irregularities may be investigated along the audit trail, which is the name given to the successive entries in this system, which when necessary are followed through by an investigator or auditor. Checks may be made, e.g., to ensure that when dealers buy or sell from their own account from or to a client they have done so at a price that is fair in relation to the prices being made by other market makers at the time.

auditor An accountant or firm of accountants appointed by the directors on behalf of the **shareholders** of a company (see **annual general meeting**, **incorporation**) to verify that the accounts of the company present a 'true and fair view' of its financial affairs. Audits are a legal requirement for all companies in the UK but only for those registered with the **Securities and Exchange Commission** in the USA.

Aufgeld (Ger.) **Premium**.

Aufsichtsrat (Ger.) Supervisory board of a company.

Auftrag (Ger.) **Order**.

Ausgabe (Ger.) **Issue**.

Ausland (Ger.) Abroad.

Auslandskassenverein (Ger.) The **Kassenverein** for foreign **securities**.

Auslandsobligation (Swiss) A **foreign bond** (8 to 15 years' **maturity**) or **note** (3 to 8 years) issued in Switzerland.

Austraclear The Australian clearing house for **commercial paper**.

Australian Associated Stock Exchange See **Australian Stock Exchange**.

Australian Ratings The **rating agency** set up in Australia.

Australian Stock Exchange (ASX) There were six stock exchange **trading floors** in Australia: in Adelaide, Brisbane, Hobart, Melbourne, Perth and Sydney. The formation of the national stock exchange in April 1987 amalgamated the six state exchanges, loosely federated in the Australian Associated Stock Exchange (AASE), into one body. Floor trading ceased in 1990 when the new Stock Exchange Automated Screen Trading System (SEATS) came into operation (see **automated screen trading**). The exchange is regulated by the Australian Securities Commission. The barometer for the Australian Stock Exchange is the All Ordinaries Share Price Index, a weighted **share index** of 250 companies. There is a second board market in shares in **unlisted companies**.

authorized capital (UK) The amount of share **capital** fixed in the **memorandum of association** and the articles of association of a company as required by the Companies Acts (see **incorporation**). US = *authorized capital stock*.

authorized capital stock (US) See **authorized capital**.

authorized foreign exchange bank (Jap.) A bank licensed by the Ministry of Finance to lend and borrow in foreign **currencies** at **short term**. Such licences are granted to most commercial banks, as well as to **long-term credit banks**, **trust banks** and *sogo* **banks**.

automated screen trading (AST) An electronic dealing system in which orders to buy or sell are entered, matched and executed by keystrokes on a computer system and at prices shown on video terminals. Such a system dispenses with **trading floors**, telephone dealing and paperwork and therefore with **back offices** and can operate worldwide on a 24-hour basis (see **24-hour trading**). At present automated screen trading in the major markets exists only in a limited way, e.g. under the **National Association of Securities Dealers Automated Quotation System** and in the **Stock Exchange Automatic Execution Facility**, but it is expected eventually to be available on all **stock exchanges**. The **Chicago Mercantile Exchange** introduced AST for out-of-hours trading in 1989 (see **post-market trading**). The first AST was in the New Zealand **futures** market in 1985 (see **automated trade system**), and the second was in the **Swiss Options and Financial Futures Exchange**, which commenced operations in 1988. See also **Toronto Stock Exchange**.

automated trade system (ATS) (NZ) An electronic system for trading on the **New Zealand Futures and Options Exchange**. The market in New Zealand is very small and geographically dispersed, which makes such a system important.

automatic teller machine (ATM) A computerized machine used for banking transactions, e.g. paying or withdrawing money, statement inquiries and transfers; operated by magnetic plastic cards and **personal identification numbers** (PINs).

aval A guarantee of payment of a **bill of exchange** under the commercial law of many European countries outside the UK, normally given by a third party, often a bank, for all or part of the nominal value of the bill. The existence of an *aval* is signified by the phrase 'pour aval' or 'bon pour aval' inscribed on the bill, followed by the signature of the party giving the *aval*.

avant-bourse (Swiss) See **Swiss stock exchanges**.

average 1. A single number calculated to summarize a group of numbers. An *arithmetic mean* is the sum of the values of the items in the group divided by the number of items. The *median* is the middle value in a group of items ranged in order of size. The *mode* is the most frequently occurring value in such a group. A *geometric mean* is the root of the *n*th product of a series of numbers multiplied together, where *n* is the number of values in the series. **2.** A term used, particularly in marine insurance, for the apportionment of a partial loss. *General average* describes a case where a part of a ship or its cargo is abandoned in order to save the ship and cargo as a whole; the owner of the abandoned portion is entitled to proportionate compensation from the other owners concerned. For this purpose the services of an *average adjuster*, somebody who is not necessarily an advocate but is well versed in the law of average, are used. Where a part of the ship or its cargo is lost not in order to preserve the remainder, then a situation of *particular average* is deemed to exist, and no claim on other owners is allowable.

average adjuster See **average**.

average rate option An **option** that is **settled** on the basis of the difference between the **striking price** and the average market value of the underlying security. Also known as an *Asian option*.

avoir fiscal (Fr.) A tax credit, equal to 50% of dividends paid, allowed to non-French holders of French **securities**. See also **tax credit**.

azione (It.) **Share**.

back See **backwardation**.

back office The department in a firm of **stockbrokers** that deals with **settlement** procedures, such as the forwarding of **share certificates** to clients and the maintenance of **accounts**. Sometimes referred to as 'the cage' in the USA, where a section dealing with cheques and certificates is protected by a metal grille.

back-to-back loan Borrowings in one currency that are matched by borrowings in another currency to overcome **exchange control** in aid of investment.

back-up credit A credit guarantee provided by a bank or **syndicate** of banks underpinning a **Euronote facility** or **note issuance facility**. The credit is operated where some or all of the notes fail to find a purchaser.

backward price (UK) See **crossed**.

backwardation (UK) 1. On the **stock exchange**, a sum of money paid by a **bear** to a **bull** for the right to delay delivery of **securities** sold forward at a fixed price. 2. The situation in a **commodity market** where **spot** prices are higher than prices quoted for future delivery. 3. See **crossed**.

badges of trade (UK) Criteria set out in 1954 by the Royal Commission on the Taxation of Profits and Income to define the distinction, in the **securities** and **commodity markets**, between trading and investment. Investment incurred the generally lower capital gains tax (see **capital gain**) upon realization of a gain; while trading is regarded as current business, the profits on which are subject to income tax or **corporation tax**. The definition is needed to establish a dividing line between frequent investment transactions and trade. Commodity market dealings are normally assessed as trade. Security market dealings can fall into either category.

baisse (Fr.) A fall, normally in the **stock market**.

balance In financial accounting, the balance is the amount required to be inserted in one of two columns of *debits* and *credits* to make the totals equal (see **double-entry bookkeeping**). A bank balance is the amount standing to the credit or debit (see **overdraft**) of a customer. See also **balance of payments**.

balance commerciale (Fr.) Visible, or merchandise, balance. See **balance of payments**.

balance of payments The total movement of goods, services and financial transactions between one country and the rest of the world; the term commonly used for the record of such movements. In money terms, therefore, the balance of payments is the total of all receipts from abroad, and of all payments to recipients abroad. All receipts and payments of whatever nature are included, whether they be payments and receipts for non-commercial purposes, such as legacies and for pensions; for goods sold or services rendered; for investment purposes; on behalf of government; or of private persons and agencies.

The balance of payments record or account is conventionally divided into the **current account**, or payments and receipts for immediate transactions, such as the sale of goods and rendering of services; and the *capital account*, or the money movements not immediately devoted to trade, such as investment. The current account is subdivided into the merchandise, or visible account (often also termed the trade account), comprising the movement of goods; and the invisible account, comprising the movement of services, transfers and investment income. Services comprise transport, travel, banking, insurance, broking and other activities; transfers comprise money movements for the transmission of legacies, pensions and other non-commercial items; investment income consists of the interest, profits and dividends deriving from capital placed abroad.

The capital account is normally divided into long-term and short-term capital, the former relating to capital employed for investment purposes, the latter to bank advances, trade credit and the like. Long-term capital is again subdivided into *direct investment* capital, or capital employed for the establishment of commercial premises and industrial plant; and *portfolio investment* capital, or capital employed for the purchase of bonds and shares.

A balance of payments account will normally resolve the various subordinate accounts into balances or net receipts and payments, summing these to an overall balance, subject to a balancing item (UK), net errors and omissions, or statistical discrepancy (US), against which the net outflow from or net inflow into the country's **reserves** is noted. The balance of payments account is also referred to as the *external account* of a nation.

balance sheet A statement of the wealth of a business or organization at a particular date, usually the end of the **financial year**, as distinct from a **profit and loss account**, which records changes over a period. The balance sheet is in two parts: **assets** on the left-hand side or at the top, and **liabilities** on the right-hand side or at the bottom. The assets of the company – **debtors**, cash investments and property – are equal to the claims or liabilities of the persons or organizations owning them: the **creditors**, lenders and **shareholders**. This is the principle of **double-entry bookkeeping**.

According to the basic accounting equation, assets equal liabilities plus equity; therefore, assets minus liabilities equal **equity**. Equity, shareholders' interest or *net worth* (which are all the same thing) may not reflect true market value, since assets are normally written into the balance sheet at historical cost (see **costs, historical**) without any adjustment for *appreciation* (see **appreciate, inflation accounting**). See also **Fourth Directive**.

balancing item See **balance of payments**.

balloon payment The final payment on a **loan** that is substantially larger than earlier payments. Designed to defer the burden of debt repayment.

ballot See **oversubscribed**.

Baltic Exchange Full title: Baltic, Mercantile and Shipping Exchange. A London market now primarily dealing in ship charters. It originated as the Baltic Coffee House, an 18th-century meeting place for merchants interested in trade in produce from the Baltic countries, then amalgamated with the London Shipping Exchange in 1899, and thereafter dealt primarily in shipbroking, although the London Grain Futures Market also trades on the exchange. Most shipbroking business is, however, now conducted by telephone, off the floor of the exchange. See also **Futures and Options Exchange**, **Grain and Feed Trade Association**.

bancassurance The merging of banking and assurance business within a banking business or a building society. Assurance services provided include life assurance and **pensions**. The emergence of bancassurance was due to the entry of banks into house loan business and the recognition both by such banks and by building societies that with their many outlets they were well placed to sell the life assurance policies used as collateral for mortgages. Ger. = *Allfinanz*.

band 1. The range of **maturities** in which the Bank of England conducts transactions daily with the **money market**, principally the **discount houses**, in **Treasury bills**, **eligible bank bills** and **local authority bills**, in order to influence **short-term** interest rates. There are four bands: Band 1, 1 to 14 days; Band 2, 15 to 33 days; Band 3, 34 to 63 days; Band 4, 64 to 91 days. 2. The range within which a **managed currency** was permitted to move under the **Bretton Woods** system. 3. The range within which member countries' currencies are permitted to move under the **European Monetary System** (EMS).

Bangkok Stock Exchange See **Securities Exchange of Thailand**.

bank See **banking**.

bank advance See **bank loan**.

bank bill A **bill of exchange** accepted by a bank.

bank charges Fees and other charges made by banks (see **banking**) for their services and debited (see **double-entry bookkeeping**) from customers' accounts, now commonly after the customer has received an itemized statement of charges.

bank credit proxy (US) A term used by the **Federal Reserve** to refer to the total deposits of member banks, accepted as a proxy for total credit extended.

bank deposit The amount of money standing to the **credit** of a customer of a bank. Bank deposits are simply IOUs written in the books of a bank and do not necessarily represent holdings of cash by the bank (see **banking**). A deposit may be on **current account** or **deposit account**. These two types of account are known as *demand deposits* and *time deposits* in the USA. See also **deposit**, **sight deposit**.

Bank for International Settlements (BIS) A **central bank** for central banks that accepts **deposits** and makes **loans**. The activities of the BIS include co-ordination and trusteeship (see **trustee**) for intergovernmental loans. The BIS was set up in 1930, originally to co-ordinate German war reparation payments, and is owned by a number of central and other banks. Although some of its functions have been taken over by the **International Monetary Fund**, the BIS continues to be an important forum for international monetary co-operation. See also **capital adequacy**.

bank loan A **loan** by a bank, normally for a fixed period and for a specific purpose. The term *bank loan* is also loosely used to include **overdrafts**, bank **mortgage** loans and **personal loans**, as well as **term loans**, though it is more common to use the generic term *bank advances*. Bank loans are normally secured (see **collateral security**) and repaid in regular instalments, with interest charged at rates that vary with the bank's **base rate**.

Bank of England The **central bank** of the UK. Founded in 1694 by a group of private bankers, chiefly to raise money for the Crown, it was chartered first to operate as a commercial *joint-stock bank* (see **commercial banks**). In succeeding centuries its royal charter favoured the circulation of its notes, and it became a leading banker to other banks. The Bank Charter Act of 1844 recognized it as the central note-issuing authority and the **lender of last resort**. By 1870 it was recognized as responsible for the general level of interest rates, which it regulated through the **bank rate**, and thus for the general state of **credit** in the country. By the early 20th century the Bank of England was recognized as the central organ for the execution of national financial and monetary policy, under the overall direction of the government. In 1946 the bank was nationalized, thus completing its identification with the state. The **Banking Act 1979** provided formal definitions under which the bank exercised its supervision of commercial banking practices.

Bank of France The **central bank** of France, established in 1800 and the oldest in the world after the Bank of Sweden and the **Bank of England**. In January 1994 the French authorities appointed a nine-member council of the bank, which with other measures is intended to give it a high degree of autonomy in the formulation of monetary policy in conformity with the **Maastricht Treaty**.

Bank of Japan (BOJ) Japan's **central bank**, which acts as **lender of last resort**, manages **monetary policy** and issues **currency**. It does not regulate the banking system, which is the role of the Banking Bureau.

bank rate The interest rate at which the **Bank of England** lent to the commercial banking system as **lender of last resort**. First recognized in 1702, it remained in existence for 270 years, until 1972 when it was replaced by the **minimum lending rate** (MLR). The bank's lending under bank rate took the form either of direct loans against collateral or of the discounting of **eligible bills**. For this reason it was frequently referred to as the *discount rate*.

banker's acceptance (US, Can.) A **bill of exchange** or *time draft* drawn on and accepted by a Canadian or US bank, usually as part of a **line of credit** under a **letter of credit** or **acceptance credit**. Synonymous with the UK term **acceptance**.

banking The business of taking **deposits** and making **loans**. As **financial intermediaries**, banks may also offer a whole range of other financial services, such as **insurance**, **credit cards** and **foreign exchange**, but their distinguishing characteristic is their role in the **money supply** though the creation of deposits. When a bank makes a loan it incurs a book debt to a customer in return for a promise to repay it. The ability of a bank to create money in this way is limited in most countries by government controls on lending (see **credit control**) as well as by its obligation to pay out **current account** deposits in cash on demand. Since the bank's customers meet most of their needs for money by writing **cheques** on their deposits, the cash holdings the banks need are only a small fraction of their total deposits (see **liquidity ratio**). The settlement of debts arising between banks through cheques drawn on one bank and deposited in another is made through a **clearing house**. Banks are supervised and regulated in most countries by the **central bank**, which acts as **lender of last resort**.

The traditional distinctions between banks and other financial intermediaries are breaking down; e.g. in the UK **building societies** now offer cheque accounts. In some countries banks are not allowed to hold **equity** stakes in their client companies or to act as **investment banks** (see **Glass–Steagall Act**), and some US states have *unit banking* laws that require each bank to be a single enterprise without branches. Germany, the Netherlands and Switzerland have *universal banking* systems that allow banks to act as investment banks and to provide a very wide range of other financial services. See also **Banking Act 1979**, **commercial banks**, **telephone banking**, **wholesale banking**.

Banking Act 1979 (UK) Legislation defining a bank (see **banking**) and a **licensed deposit-taker** for the purposes of supervision and **regulation** by the **Bank of England**. The Act defined a bank as a deposit-taking institution with either a wide range of banking services or a highly specialized banking service according to a number of specified criteria, and with net **assets** in excess of certain limits. The Act was made necessary by the **European Union**'s First Banking Co-ordination **directive**.

banknote A note issued by a bank promising to pay the bearer the **par value** of the note on demand. At one time banknotes were exchangeable for gold, but now the promise to pay simply means that they are legal tender.

bankruptcy A declaration by a court of law that an individual or company is insolvent, that is, cannot meet **debts** on the due dates. A bankruptcy petition may be filed either by the debtor or by their creditors requesting a receiving order. An inquiry into the debtor's affairs is then conducted by, in the UK, the official receiver; the business has then passed into receivership. If the receiver thinks fit, they may call a meeting of the debtor's creditors and, if the creditors wish it, declare the debtor bankrupt. The debtor's assets are then realized and distributed among the creditors either by the receiver or by a trustee appointed by the creditors. In the case of a company it goes into **liquidation**.

US procedures are similar to those of the UK, but under Chapter 11 of the Bankruptcy Reform Act 1978 a firm may apply to the court for protection from its creditors while it carries out a reorganization of its affairs so as to be able to pay off its debts. In a similar way companies in the UK may now be placed under administration rather than go into liquidation. The Insolvency Act 1985 and 1986 codified existing law and made the handling of the affairs of insolvent debtors the responsibility of a registered insolvency practitioner. The Acts introduced a wide range of sanctions against directors who act negligently, as did the Company Directors Disqualification Act 1986.

Bankruptcy Reform Act 1978 See **bankruptcy**.

banque d'affaires (Fr.) **Merchant bank**.

Banque de France See **Bank of France**.

BAPEPAM See **Jakarta Stock Exchange**.

Bar (Ger.) **Cash**.

Barber case See **equalization of pensions**.

Bardepot (Ger.) A regulation requiring West German borrowers on foreign markets to deposit part of the proceeds in a non-interest-bearing account at the **Bundesbank**; introduced to deter foreign inflows into West Germany, and thus to contain the West German balance of payments surplus. Withdrawn in the 1970s.

bargain (UK) A purchase or sale on the **London Stock Exchange**. Statistics on the number of bargains on that exchange do not record the number of transactions, since each transaction consists of two bargains, a purchase and a sale.

Bargeld (Ger.) See **cash**.

barratry A **peril** in marine insurance policy consisting in a deliberately wrongful act by the master or crew of a vessel involving a loss to the owner or charterer of the vessel.

barter See **countertrading**.

base period The reference date for which an **index number** of a time series is calculated.

base rate (UK) The rate of **interest** that forms the basis for the charges for **bank loans** and **overdrafts** and the deposit rates of the **commercial banks**. Actual rates are set at up to about five percentage points above base rate according to the creditworthiness of the borrower. In the USA the *prime rate* is the rate at which a bank will lend to its most creditworthy customer. Though to some extent now superseded by **cost of funds** rates, the prime rate is still an important indicator of **money-market** trends. See also **bank rate**.

base-weighted indices **Index numbers** in which the weights used are those of the reference or base year against which changes are to be measured. See **weighted average**.

basic balance The balance struck of the **current** and **long-term capital accounts** combined of the **balance of payments**.

basic rate of tax See **income tax**.

basis (US) The difference between the **futures** price and the **spot** price.

basis point 1/100th of 1%. A measure normally used in the statement of interest rates; e.g. a change from 5.75% to 5.81% is a change of six basis points. First used in the USA, now common elsewhere.

basis price 1. In the **commodity** markets, the price agreed between the seller and buyer at which an **option** can be exercised; generally the market price of the commodity at the time the option is sold; also known as the **striking price**. 2. The basis on which a **dealer** in the **over-the-counter market** attempts to match buyers and sellers of a **security**. Thus, their estimate of the market price.

Basle Agreement See **capital adequacy**.

Basle Concordat An understanding reached between the monetary authorities of the major countries in 1975 under which each authority is responsible for the supervision of foreign branches established by its domestic banks.

baud, baud rate The number of **bits** (units of information) per second that can be sent down a transmission line, such as a telephone line. Used in rating the capacity of equipment such as a **modem**.

bear A speculator who sells **securities** because they expect a fall in prices; the antonym of **bull**. A bear who sells securities that they do not possess is described as having *sold short* (see **position**). If they do possess the securities that they sell, they are described as a *covered* or *protected* bear. A *bear raid* is an attempt by a number of investors acting in collusion to drive down the price of a share by selling stock. This has been done to defeat a **take-over** by depressing the shares of the predator. A *bear market* is one in which prices are falling. See also **bear squeeze**.

bear market See **bear**.

bear position See **position**.

bear raid See **bear**.

bear squeeze The purchase of **securities**, **currency** or commodities in the markets by the authorities, thus raising prices and squeezing the **liquidity** of speculators who have been selling short (see **position**) in the expectation of falling prices.

bearer security A **share** or **bond** that is not registered in the name of the holder, who can sell it or claim **dividends** on simple presentation to a bank or **broker**. Common on certain continental European **stock exchanges**, bear securities have the attraction that the tax authorities cannot identify the owners. For this reason dividends and interest on bearer securities are usually subject to a **withholding tax**.

bed and breakfast (UK) The sale of a **security** on one day and its repurchase the following day in a previously agreed transaction for the purpose of establishing a **capital gain** or loss. A transaction of this kind does not establish a loss or gain for tax purposes in the USA but may do so in the UK.

Beige Book (US) A familiar term for the report on local economic and financial conditions prepared by the district banks of the **Federal Reserve System** and supplied to members of the **Federal Open Market Committee** before each meeting. It is one of three information documents so supplied. See also **Blue Book**, **Green Book**.

Bel-20 (Bel.) The Brussels Stock Exchange **share index**.

bénéfice (Fr.) **Profit**.

Berne Union The International Union of Credit and Investment Insurers, an international organization for both government and private export credit (see **Export Credit Guarantee Department**) and other trade insurance bodies.

BEST See **Stock Exchange Automatic Execution Facility**.

best price See **order**.

beta coefficient See **alpha coefficient**.

beta stocks See **alpha securities, stocks**.

BFE Baltic Futures Exchange. See **Futures and Options Exchange**.

bid price The price at which a **market maker** will buy **shares** or a **dealer** in a **commodity market** will buy commodities. **Unit trust** managers also quote a bid price at which they will repurchase units sold to the public. See **offer price**.

bid rate The **rate of interest** offered for a **deposit**. See **London interbank offered rate** (LIBOR).

Big Bang (UK) The term used to encapsulate the changes culminating on 27 October 1986 with the abandonment of the **commission** agreement between members of the **London Stock Exchange** and of strict segregation of **jobbers** and **brokers**. In July 1983 the government agreed to exempt the stock exchange from the provisions of the Restrictive Practices Act in return for lifting a number of restrictions. In 1982 the Stock Exchange Council had raised the limit placed on any one outside shareholder from 10% to 29.9% and in 1985 decided that this limit would also be abandoned. Many banks and other financial institutions have acquired interests in, or control of, stock exchange companies since March 1986. Other changes associated with the Big Bang have been in the closure of the trading floor of the stock exchange in favour of off-the-floor telephone dealing and a major expansion in dealings in international **securities**.

Big Board See **New York Stock Exchange**.

Big Four 1. The four dominating Japanese securities houses: Nomura, Daiwa, Nikko and Yamaichi. 2. Also used of the four biggest UK commercial banks: Barclays, Lloyds, Midland and National Westminster.

bilan (Fr.) 1. **Balance**. 2. **Balance sheet**. 3. **Accounts**.

Bilanz (Ger.) **Balance sheet**.

bill See **bill of exchange**, **commercial bill**, **Treasury bill**.

billet de trésorerie (Fr.) **Commercial paper**.

billion Originally a term meaning one million million, now conventionally used to mean one thousand million.

bill leak (UK) A device for evading the UK **supplementary special deposits** scheme ('the corset') whereby **bank bills** were negotiated and held outside the banking system; i.e. a bank *accepted* (see **acceptance**) a bill drawn by a commercial client, which was then sold to another non-bank holder, the acceptance remaining only as a contingent liability on the bank's balance sheet and not therefore included in its **interest-bearing eligible liabilities**.

bill of exchange An order in writing addressed by one person to another and signed by the person giving it, requiring the person to whom it is addressed to pay, on demand or at a fixed date, a specified sum of money. The bill is made out by the signatory (the *drawer*) always with the consent of the person to whom it is addressed, who signs or *accepts* it (see **acceptance**); and mainly in relation to the sale of goods or produce. Bills are **negotiable** in the **money market**, so enabling drawers to obtain their money at once. Bills of exchange are divided into the categories of **bank bills**, **trade bills**, **fine trade bills** and **finance bills**.

BIMBO Buy-in **management buy-out**.

binding authority Authority given to an agent by an insurance institution to accept business on behalf of that institution, within prescribed limits.

BIS See **Bank for International Settlements**.

bit Binary digit, i.e. 0 or 1.

Black Monday The **crash** of world stock market prices on Monday 19 October 1987.

Black Tuesday (US) The Wall Street (see **New York Stock Exchange**) stock market **crash** on Tuesday 29 October 1929.

Black Wednesday See **Maastricht Treaty**.

block (US) A large holding of **shares** or **stock** in one company. A block trade is usually considered to involve the sale or purchase of at least 10,000 shares.

block order exposure system (BLOX) (UK) Offers to buy or sell large **blocks** of **shares** carried on the **Teletext Output of Price Information by Computer** (TOPIC).

BLOX See **block order exposure system**.

Blue Book (UK, US) **1**. A familiar term for the review of **monetary control** options presented by the staff director for monetary policy reviews to members of the **Federal Open Market Committee** (FOMC) before each meeting (US) (see **Beige Book**, **Green Book**. **2**. A familiar term for the UK *National Accounts*, an annual collection of the main macroeconomic statistics compiled by the Central Statistical Office (CSO) and published by HMSO.

blue chips **Shares** in leading **quoted companies** that can be easily bought and sold without influencing their price (see **liquidity**) and are regarded as low-risk **investments**.

blue month (UK) The most actively traded month of a **derivative**, decided by the **London International Financial Futures Exchange** (LIFFE) in the light of trading activity. Designated in order to facilitate price quotation.

blue-sky laws (US) State laws in the USA that require a **security** to be registered with a state before it can be traded there. **National Market System** stocks traded on the **National Association of Securities Dealers Automated Quotation System** (NASDAQ) are now exempt from these laws.

Bobl An abbreviation used in English-speaking markets to denote a *Bundesobligation*, a German government five-year bond in which **derivatives** are also traded.

boiler room See **bucket shop**.

bolsa (Sp.) **Stock exchange**.

Bolsa de Comercio de Santiago See **Chilean Stock Exchange**.

Bolsa de Valores de São Paulo See **São Paulo Stock Exchange**.

Bolsa Mexicana de Valores See **Mexican Stock Exchange**.

Bombay Stock Exchange The largest **stock exchange** in India. There are also exchanges in Calcutta, Delhi and other cities. The exchanges are regulated by the Securities and Exchange Board of India (SEBI).

bon du trésor (Fr.) **Treasury bill** or **bond**.

bon marché (Fr.) Cheap.

bond A form of interest-bearing **security** issued by central or local governments, companies, banks and other institutions. Bonds are usually a form of long-term security; but they do not always carry fixed interest (see **variable rate security**), they may be irredeemable (see **redemption date**) and they may be secured or unsecured. In the USA the term *bond* includes **debentures** (see **bearer security**, **Eurobond**). See also **deferred coupon note**, **straight bond**.

bond washing See **dividend stripping**.

bonos Abbreviation used in English-speaking markets, derived from *bono*, a bond, to denote long-term Spanish government bonds.

bonus 1. A free share or *scrip* issue. See **bonus issue**. 2. A distribution of life assurance company investment profits. See **life assurance**.

BONUS (borrower's option for notes and underwritten standby) An arrangement by which a borrower receives a loan package comprising mixed **commercial paper** and **Euro-commercial paper** liabilities, e.g. an **uncommitted** (non-**underwritten**) **note issuance facility**, a US commercial paper programme and a **standby credit**.

bonus issue A term virtually synonymous with *scrip issue* and *capitalization issue* (US = *stock dividend* and *stock split*), describing **shares** given without charge to existing shareholders in proportion to the shares already held. A scrip issue does not add to the **capital employed** by the firm but is made where the capital employed has been increased by retaining profits and is therefore out of line with the **issued capital**. Consequently it is a pure bookkeeping transaction. For example, **dividends** will, after a scrip issue, be divided among a larger number of shares, so that the dividend per share will fall in proportion to the number of bonus shares issued. The motive for splitting shares in this way may be to capitalize retained profits or it may simply be to reduce the unit price of the shares (without altering the **yield**) and so improve their marketability. See also **heavy share**.

borrow Of **commodity markets**, to buy at current prices and simultaneously sell **forward**.

borrowed reserves (US) The total of **adjustment credit** and **seasonal borrowings** from the **Federal Reserve** held by US banks.

bors (Den.) See **drittmarkt**.

borsa (It.) **Stock exchange**.

Borsa Valori (It.) The main **stock exchange** in Milan. Unlisted shares are traded on the **mercato ristretto** and the *terzo mercato*.

Börse (Ger.) **Stock exchange**.

Börsenmakler (Ger.) See **freier Makler**.

Börsenumsatzsteuer (Ger.) An **ad valorem** tax on transactions on the **German stock exchanges**. Applies only to purchases and sales by residents.

Börsenvorstand (Ger.) The governing body of a German **stock exchange**.

bought deal (US) A commitment by an **investment bank** to purchase the whole of a **new issue** of share **capital** at a certain price, often made as the result of a competitive tender (see also **underwrite**). Bought deals of this kind are not common in the UK because of **pre-emptive rights**. The term is also used in **venture capital** where one institution provides finance to a company first and then sells part of that interest to others (see **syndicate**). This is done by the lead investor where speed or secrecy is important.

bourse (Fr.) French term for **stock exchange**, also used in Belgium, Switzerland and other European countries. See **Paris Bourse**.

boutique See **niche player**.

BOVESPA Bolsas de Valores de São Paulo. See **São Paulo Stock Exchange**.

box spread A combination of **options**, namely a **long-call** option held against a **short-***put* option with the same **exercise** price, coupled with a short-call option held against a long-put option, both with the same exercise price.

Brady Commission Report (US) Report of the commission of inquiry chaired by Nicholas Brady into the October 1987 stock market **crash**. See also **circuit-breaker mechanism**.

Brazilian stock exchanges See **São Paulo Stock Exchange**.

Bretton Woods A conference (official title: the United Nations Monetary and Financial Conference) held at Bretton Woods, New Hampshire, USA, in July 1944, called to consider the postwar organization of international monetary relations and resulting in the establishment of the **International Bank for Reconstruction and Development** (World Bank) and the **International Monetary Fund** (IMF).

bridge finance A short-term **loan** provided by a **venture capital** provider while a company is seeking alternative finance, e.g. by **flotation**.

bridging loan A short-term **loan** provided for an individual who has bought a new property before selling an existing one.

British Institute of Dealers in Securities (BIDS) (UK) A trade association of **dealers** in **over-the-counter securities**. Now defunct.

broker An intermediary between a buyer and a seller in a highly organized market, e.g. a **stockbroker**, a commodity broker or a market operator working on their own account, such as an **insurance** broker, **pawnbroker** or **bill** broker. On the **London Stock Exchange** a broker was an intermediary between the public and **market makers** or **jobbers**, but since the **Big Bang** many brokers have become **broker-dealers** (a firm of broker-dealers is known as a *brokerage house* in the USA), combining functions of the broker and the market maker. See also **commission broker**.

broker-dealer A person or organization buying and selling **securities**, **commodities** and **contracts**, both on their own account (i.e. as **principal**) and as an agent for clients. Prior to the **Big Bang** in the UK, **brokers** on the **London Stock Exchange** were not permitted to act in this dual capacity because of the possibility of conflicts of interest. See also **market maker**.

broker pool A grouping of **insurers** for the purpose of contracting **reinsurance** through one **broker**.

brokerage The **commission** charged by a **broker**.

brokerage account (US) The record of purchases and sales of **securities** on behalf of a client kept by a **stockbroker**.

brokerage house (US) See **broker**.

brutto (Ger.) Gross.

Buba Abbreviation of **Bundesbank**.

bucket shop A term of US origin meaning an unregistered and illegal firm of **stockbrokers**, but now used to refer to any low-price sales operation. A 'boiler room' is a **share**-pushing operation selling dubious **stock** by telephone.

Budapest Stock Exchange See **Eastern Europe**.

budget An estimate of income and expenditure for a future period, as opposed to an account, which records financial transactions after the event. In the UK the national budget sets out estimates of central government revenue and expenditure for the financial year and is presented to Parliament in the autumn by the Chancellor of the **Exchequer**. The fiscal year ends on 5 April in the UK. The US federal budget is prepared by the Office of Manpower and Budget (OMB) and reviewed and approved by the President for submission to Congress around January prior to the fiscal year, which runs from 1 July to 30 June.

Buenos Aires Stock Exchange The oldest **stock exchange** in Latin America, dating from 1872; called in Spanish El Mercado de Valores de Buenos Aires. There are four other exchanges in Argentina.

buffer stock A quantity of a **commodity**, normally established under an **international commodity agreement**, held by a desig-nated common agency for the purpose of release into the market, or of accumulation by drawing from the market, in order to influence the market price.

Building Societies Act 1986 See **building society**.

building society (UK) A UK financial institution engaged in the provision of **mortgages**, deriving its funds from **deposits** by the general public. Building societies are non-profit-making bodies.

Interest is paid on deposits at rates varying with amount and term of retention. By arrangement with the Inland Revenue a lump sum in respect of the income tax liability of depositors was until 1991 paid over by the building society and represented an advantageous settlement for the depositors. Interest payments are now subject to deduction of tax at the basic rate, with exemption for non-taxpayers. Interest on mortgages advanced attracts relief from the mortgagor's income tax liability on amounts paid on mortgages up to £30,000.

Under the UK Building Societies Act 1986 wider consumer services are permitted for building societies, including the provision of unsecured **personal loans**, the management of **unit trusts**, the operation of estate agencies, activity in insurance broking and the sale of **money purchase personal pensions**. These changes enabled the societies to compete on more equal terms with **commercial banks** and other **financial institutions**, competition from which reduced the societies' share of the new mortgage market from 75% in 1986 to 54% in 1987.

In 1994 further changes to the scope of operations of building societies were envisaged, including the provision of unsecured loans to small businesses, insurance services and higher limits on raising funds from **wholesale markets**. Building societies are also to be made more accountable to members.

See also **savings and loan associations**.

Bulis (Ger.) Contraction of *Bundesliquiditätsschatzwechsel*, German government one-year Treasury bills introduced in early 1993 with the purpose of absorbing excess liquidity in the non-banking sector.

bull A speculator who buys **securities** in the belief that prices will rise and that they will be able to sell them again later at a profit. The antonym of **bear**. The market is said to be 'bullish' when it is generally anticipated that prices will rise.

bull market A period of time during which **stock market** prices are rising. See also **bull**. Antonym of **bear market**.

bull position See **position**.

bulldog bond (UK) A sterling bond in the UK capital market issued by a non-resident. See **foreign bond**.

bullet (US) Repayment of the whole of the **principal** of a **loan** at **maturity**.

bulletin board See **company bulletin board**.

bullion Gold, silver or other precious metal in bulk, i.e. in the form of ingots or bars rather than in coin. Gold bullion is used in international monetary transactions between **central banks** and forms partial backing for many **currencies**.

Bund Abbreviation used in English-speaking markets to refer to a *Bundesanleihe*, a long-term German government bond, in which **derivatives** are also traded.

Bundesaufsichtsamt für das Kreditwesen (BAK) (Ger.) The Federal Supervisory Office for Credit. The institution is responsible for banking business and the regulation of investment activity by funds such as **unit trusts**.

Bundesbank The **central bank** of the Federal Republic of Germany (formerly West Germany), based in Frankfurt. Established in 1957 as a successor to the Bank Deutscher Länder, which was set up in 1948 after the Second World War, the Bundesbank (= 'federal bank') has an exceptional degree of independence from government in its role of safeguarding the **currency**. The Deutsche Bundesbank, to give it its full name, co-ordinates the 11 regional or *Länder* banks (*Landeizentralbanken*) in former West Germany and from 1990 has been responsible for monetary policy in former East Germany. Changes in **Lombard** and **discount rates** are usually announced after the fortnightly meetings of the Bundesbank Central Council, on which the presidents of the *Länder* banks are represented. See also **repurchase agreement**.

Bundesobligation (Ger.) A federal **bond**.

Business Expansion Scheme (BES) (UK) A scheme intended to encourage individuals to subscribe and hold on to **shares** in a small **unlisted company** raising funds to expand. Funds up to a specified limit invested in eligible BES companies were fully deductible for tax purposes (i.e. they could be deducted from taxable income at higher rates of **income tax**). There were a number of conditions, notably that subscribers could not be directors or employees; nor could they own more than 30% of the **equity**; nor could they dispose of the shares within five years without forfeiting tax relief. The BES was replaced by the **Enterprise Investment Scheme** at the beginning of 1994.

business finance The provision of money for commercial use; when relating specifically to companies it may also be referred to as corporate finance. The short-term **capital** of a business may come from **retained earnings** or from **factoring**, bank borrowings (see **banking**), other borrowings, **bills of exchange**, trade creditors (see **trade credit**) and expense creditors. These are all sources of short-term capital that in theory should be used only for investment in relatively liquid **assets** (see also **liquidity**), so that it is readily available to discharge the liability if necessary. Sources of long-term capital include **reserves** and **depreciation** provisions, **equity** share capital and long-term loans such as **debentures** and **term loans**.

Business Start-Up Scheme (BSS) (UK) A scheme intended to encourage individuals to subscribe to **shares** in an **unlisted company**. Up to a certain limit, such purchases were deductible for tax purposes from taxable income at higher rates of **income tax**. It was replaced in 1983 by the **Business Expansion Scheme**.

buy-out Purchase by the management of the shares of its company, so making it the owner; or purchase by a company of its shares held by the public, so making the company a private company. See **management buy-out**.

buying in shares See **incorporation**.

BV (Neth.) A private limited company. See **incorporation**.

bylaws See **memorandum of association**.

byte A set of **bits** or binary digits, eight in most computer systems, which is a unit of information representing a number or word or part of a word.

C-corporation See **sub-chapter S corporation**.

CAC 40 See **Paris Bourse**.

cage See **back office**.

caisses d'épargne (Fr.) A network of **savings banks**.

call 1. The act of a company in requiring the surrender of its bonds for repayment. 2. The repayment of a bond in the **Eurobond** market, possible under the terms of the issue at pre-set dates before **maturity**. 3. A requirement by the director of a company for payment for issued capital not yet **paid up**. 4. The period in a **commodity market** trading session in which business is conducted by the chair, as contrasted with **open outcry**. In this session **futures** prices are officially fixed for dissemination and use internationally. The session normally takes place several times a day. See also **call money**, **call–over**, **option** (*call option*).

call money A bank loan repayable on demand, i.e. at call. Most notably used in the UK as a means for the commercial banks to place short-term funds with the **discount houses**. This both provides a profitable outlet for the banks' liquid resources and furnishes the supply of funds with which the discount houses can conduct their transactions in **bills** with the Bank of England. Under the arrangements for **monetary control** brought in in 1981, the commercial banks guaranteed to keep aggregate call money with the discount houses at a level averaging 6% of their **eligible liabilities** and not falling below 4% on any one day. Call money is very short term, normally day to day, and is always, when taken on the above basis, **secured**. Until the abolition of the **reserve asset ratio** in 1981, call money was an important **reserve asset** of the commercial banks. Since then it has been recognized by the Bank of England, in its supervision of banks' *prudential* status (see **capital adequacy**), as a high-quality liquid asset.

call option See **option**.

call-or-put option See **as-you-like option**.

call-over The practice in **commodity markets** whereby the chair conducts the trading, as against trading by **open outcry**.

call-over price Price arrived at by **call-over** in a **commodity exchange**, then adopted and published as the official price for the session and used for **physical** trading generally.

call warrant A warrant giving the holder the right to buy the underlying asset at a predetermined date and price. Similar to a call **option**, but used chiefly for gold purchases.

cap A limit or ceiling, usually setting the maximum **interest** that may be charged on a **loan**. Where there is also a 'floor' or lower limit to protect the lender, the arrangement may be described as a 'collar' (see also **adjustable rate preferred stock**).

capacity Of insurance, the volume of insurance cover on offer at any particular time.

capital In general, the accumulated (i.e. unspent) wealth of a business or individual that is capable of generating income, but the term has no precise meaning out of context. Nominal share capital, for example, is the **par value** of funds subscribed by **shareholders** (see also **capital employed, paid-up capital, shareholders' equity**). Capital may be in the form of money or of physical **assets**.

capital, cost of The **rate of interest** paid on the **capital employed** in a business. Since capital will be drawn from a variety of sources, it will be an average cost derived from a **weighted average** of the costs of each source, including **equity**. The average cost of existing sources of capital may be higher or lower than the marginal cost, i.e. the cost of additional capital.

capital account See **balance of payments**.

capital adequacy Various regulatory bodies set minimum **capital** requirements for **financial institutions** such as **unit trust** managers. Until recently capital adequacy requirements were set only at a national level (see e.g. **Federal Reserve System**, **liquidity ratio**). The increasing globalization of the world financial system now requires international agreement on capital adequacy standards. In December 1987, 11 countries and the then European Community (see **European Union**) signed an international agreement for capital adequacy for **commercial banks** under the auspices of the **Bank for International Settlements** (the Basle Agreement). The agreement provided for common prudential ratios and a common definition of **risk-adjusted assets**. **Banks** operating in signatory countries now need to have capital (**equity** and long-term **debt**) equal to 8% of risk-adjusted assets (see also **liquidity ratio**). Under proposals made in 1993, the percentage adequacy requirement could vary with an individual bank's exposure to **foreign exchange** risks and **derivatives**. See also **Investment Services Directive**.

capital allowances (UK) Reductions in tax (see **taxation**) liability that are related to a firm's **capital expenditure**. In most countries expenditure on new capital assets is encouraged by various kinds of allowances (though more recently there has been a tendency for those to be phased out), and annual **depreciation** is recognized as an expense of the business in calculating tax liability. The tax authorities' methods of depreciating an **asset** are standardized in most countries and not necessarily the same as those used by the company in published **accounts**. Where a company may claim depreciation for tax purposes at will, e.g. to write off the whole of the cost of an asset against tax in a single year, or to spread it over 20 years as it chooses, this is known as *free depreciation* or *depreciation at choice*. In the UK from 1972 until 1983/4, a business could obtain a first-year allowance or **tax credit** of 100% of the cost of plant and machinery. This was known as *accelerated depreciation*, since the depreciation rate was faster than justified by the life of the asset. The business now qualifies instead for a *writing-down allowance* or *annual depreciation allowance* (see **depreciation**). See also **investment allowances**.

capital asset pricing model (CAPM) A model of the market in financial **assets** that assumes that, in equilibrium, asset prices will adjust to ensure that the return on an asset compensates investors for *systematic risk*, i.e. risk that cannot be eliminated by portfolio diversification. See also **portfolio theory**.

capital duty (UK) A tax (see **taxation**) levied on **companies** on the proceeds of a **new issue** of **shares**. Abolished in 1988. See also **stamp duty**.

capital employed 1. Shareholders' equity plus long-term **debt**. 2. Sometimes used as a synonym for **net assets**.

capital expenditure The purchase of fixed **assets** (e.g. plant and equipment), expenditure on **trade investments** or acquisitions of other businesses and expenditure on current assets (e.g. stocks).

capital formation See **investment**.

capital gain A realized increase in the value of a capital **asset**, as when a **share** is sold for more than the price at which it was purchased. A *capital loss* is the opposite: a reduction in the money value of an **asset**. The **taxation** of capital gains varies between countries and between individuals and companies. Traditionally, for individuals, capital gains are taxed at a lower rate than income, but the USA and the UK in principle now tax capital gains at the same rate as income. Some countries tax short-term and long-term gains at different rates, while a few do not tax capital gains at all. The rationale for this is, among other things, that some or all capital gains may be the result of **inflation**. See also **indexation**.

capital gains tax (CGT) (UK) See **capital gain**.

capital gearing (UK) Bank borrowings and other **debt** as a percentage of **net tangible assets**. See **gearing**.

capital loss See **capital gain**.

capital market(s) The market for longer-term loanable funds as distinct from the **money market**, which deals in short-term funds. There is no clear-cut distinction between the two markets, although in principle capital market loans are used by industry and commerce for fixed **investment** and acquisitions. The capital market is an increasingly international one and in each country consists of all those institutions that canalize the supply of and demand for capital, including the **banking** system, the **stock exchange, insurance** companies and other **financial intermediaries**.

capital shares See **investment trust**.

capital structure The make-up of the **capital employed** in a business or other organization. The most prominent characteristic of capital structure will be the relationship of **debt** to **equity** (see **gearing**).

capital transfer tax (CTT) (UK) A tax on the transmission of wealth by gift, both during a person's lifetime and on their death. Introduced in 1975 and replaced by **inheritance tax** with effect from 16 March 1986.

capitalization See **market capitalization**.

capitalization issue See **bonus issue**.

CAPM See **capital asset pricing model**.

capped floating rate note A floating rate note (FRN), the **coupon** of which is subject to a pre-agreed maximum.

captive A company providing **investment** or other services that is owned by an institution offering related services; e.g. an **insurance** company or **venture capital** company owned by a **bank** or a **hire-purchase** firm owned by a car manufacturer. See also **captive insurer**.

captive finance company See **finance house**.

captive insurer An **insurer** established and wholly owned by an industrial or commercial company, or a group of such companies, for the purpose of underwriting all the insurance **risks** of that company or those companies.

carried interest A share in, or **option** on **equity** or in the value of, a **venture capital** investment fund granted to the managers of that fund.

carry-over Of **commodity markets**, inventories held at the start of the marketing year.

carrying market A **commodity market** in which a commodity can be accepted on delivery in one month, then stored and redelivered in a later month. This is confined to commodities with durable life.

carte à mémoire (Fr.) See **smart card**.

cash 1. Money in tangible form, namely coins and banknotes, in contrast to bank cheques and deposits. 2. For purposes of **monetary control**, notes and coin, together with deposits at the central bank held by a **commercial bank**. 3. Of agricultural produce, those forms grown for sale, normally to other countries, rather than for local consumption: cash crops. 4. A **commodity** sold on a **commodity market** for immediate or very early delivery. See **actual price**, **physical price**, **spot price**.

cash and carry In **commodity markets**, the practice of buying **spot** with a view to selling later at a profit that, after meeting handling, storage and insurance charges, represents a higher rate of interest on dealers' money than they would obtain by investing in **fixed-interest securities**.

cash crops See **cash**.

cash flow The movement of money into (cash inflow) and out of (cash outflow) a business. It is generally defined as net **profit** plus **depreciation** (net cash flow) but may be used more loosely to include all cash movements. See **discounted cash flow**.

cash limits (UK) A method of government expenditure control introduced in 1976 to constrain the existing system whereby expenditure planning was in volume terms only, i.e. in terms of fixed prices relating to a previous period, with accordingly an unrestrained outturn in current price terms. Certain government expenditures were subjected to a limit in current price, or *cash* terms. In 1981 all planning reverted to cash terms, and cash limits became redundant.

cash price The price of a **commodity** immediately available for sale and delivery. Also known as *physical price* or *actual price*. See also **forward**, **futures**, **option**.

cash ratio 1. The ratio of **cash** to **deposits** in the banking system, frequently set by the **central bank** in the interests of **monetary policy**. A cash ratio has always been required by the **Federal Reserve** authorities of the USA and it has formed an important part of **monetary control** in that country. A cash ratio of 8% was informally required by the Bank of England up to 1971 (see also **credit control**). The banks themselves customarily maintained a ratio of 5% to 7% thereafter, until 1981, when a cash ratio of 8% of **eligible liabilities**, to be held at the Bank of England, was set for all banks. The Bank of England stressed, however, that the cash holdings were for the purpose of providing income resources to itself and played no part in monetary control. **2.** The ratio of **liquid assets** to the current **liabilities** of a business.

cash settlement The alternative in the **derivatives** market to **physical** delivery of the underlying instrument. The cash is the current market price of the security.

CATS See **Toronto Stock Exchange**.

caveat emptor 'Let the buyer beware.' An expression conveying purchasers' obligation to assure themselves that the object of their purchase satisfies their requirements. This does not, however, exonerate sellers from various forms of **liability** for their product.

CBOE See **Chicago Board Options Exchange**.

CBOT See **Chicago Board of Trade**.

CBS Index The Amsterdam **share index**.

CCIFP See **Chambre de Compensation des Instruments Financiers de Paris**.

CD See **certificate of deposit**.

cedant (ceding insurer) An **insurer** initiating **reinsurance**. See also **facultative reinsurance**, **reinsurance treaty**.

CEDEL See **Centrale de Livraison de Valeurs Mobilières**.

ceding insurer See **cedant**.

Census X-II (US) A computer program used by the **Federal Reserve** to apply seasonal adjustment to **money supply** totals.

central bank A bankers' bank at the centre of a country's monetary system (see **monetary control**). Central banks act as **lenders of last resort**, lead the interest rate structure, accept **deposits**, make **loans** to the **commercial banks** and in most countries supervise the **banking** system. The central bank also acts as the government's own bank, manages the **national debt** and controls the note issue (see **banknote**). Central banks deal with each other in conducting transfers of **currency** and **bullion** between countries and are heavily involved, with finance ministers, in international economic relations. See **Bank of England**, **Bank of Japan**, **Bundesbank**, **Federal Reserve System**. See also **Bank for International Settlements**.

Central Bank Advisory Board See **World Gold Council**.

central bank discount rate The interest rate at which a **central bank** will **discount eligible bills** (in the UK), **eligible paper** (in the USA) and **Treasury bills**.

Central Fund A reserve fund of **Lloyd's of London**, financed by the members, maintained as a **policy-holders'** protection fund, to be invoked should members fail to meet their **underwriting liabilities**.

central monetary institution See **central bank**.

central parity See **European Monetary System** (EMS).

Centrale de Livraison de Valeurs Mobilières (CEDEL) One of the two settlement systems for **Eurobond** trading, established in Luxembourg in 1970. CEDEL is both a clearing house and an agency for dividend collection. In collaboration with Citibank it provides capital to market dealers. It also collaborates with **SWIFT** in organizing settlements. Its owners are a number of international banks. See also **Euroclear**.

CentreWrite A wholly owned **subsidiary** of **Lloyd's of London**, established in 1991 to offer **reinsurance to close** to syndicates in **run-off**, where, after some years, this appears practicable; and also to **underwrite estate protection reinsurance**.

certain annuity See **terminable annuity**.

certificate 1. A document attesting ownership, usually one certifying a **debt**, thus used for most **securities**. Examples are **certificate of deposit**, **share certificate**, **tax deposit certificate**. 2. See **certificate of quality**.

certificate of deposit (CD) A **negotiable** claim issued by a bank in return for a term **deposit**. The document is normally a **bearer security**. The advantage of the CD to depositors is that the latter can place their money in a fixed-**term** or long-**maturity** deposit, so obtaining a higher rate of interest while knowing that they can sell the CD in the **secondary market** whenever they may need to recover the money. The advantage to purchasers in the secondary market is that they can invest in and divest the instrument at will. The advantage to the bank is that it can acquire deposits perhaps not otherwise forthcoming and can hold them. CDs can be sold and resold at a **discount**, so varying the **yield**.

CDs were first issued in the USA in 1961 and gained immediate favour. After the partial suspension in 1970, and final suspension in 1973, of the application to CDs of **Regulation Q**, the market grew rapidly. CDs were issued in **Eurodollar** form in London in 1966. Sterling CDs were issued in 1968. The market in CDs is made up by the **discount houses** and the **interbank market** in London and by the banks in the USA. **Special drawing right** CDs have been issued in London, and a substantial yen CD market has developed in Japan, after introduction in 1979. In 1983 the US Tax Act required all dollar CDs to be registered (i.e. not in bearer form). **Futures** contracts in CDs are traded in the USA and on the **London International Financial Futures Exchange** (LIFFE). See also **parallel money markets**.

certificate of quality (UK) A document attesting that a **commodity** has passed the test of **grading**, valid in the case of most **soft commodities** for six months.

certificate of tax deposit See **tax deposit certificate**.

CFTC See **Commodity Futures Trading Commission**.

chain-base indices See **chain-linked index**.

chain-linked index An **index number** in which each change in a number is measured against the value of the number in the immediately preceding period instead of against a fixed base (see **base-weighted indices**). Chain-linked indices are used where the composition of the different components alters frequently over time.

chakuchi (Jap.) **Forward** trade in **bonds** in the *gensaki* market.

Chambre de Compensation des Instruments Financiers de Paris (CCIFP) (Fr.) The clearing house for the **Marché à Terme des Instruments Financiers** (MATIF), the French financial **futures** exchange.

Chambre Syndicale des Agents de Change (Fr.) The governing body of the **Compagnie des Agents de Change**. Members are elected for one year by the *compagnie*; the *chambre* is responsible for the application of the *compagnie*'s rules. The chairperson of the *chambre* has the title of *syndic*, and the members are known as *gouverneurs*.

CHAPS Clearing House Automated Payments System. See **clearing house**.

Chapter 11 See **bankruptcy**.

charge 1. To **debit** to, or impose a price for a good or service, as in bank charges. 2. To take a pledge, **assignment mortgage** or **collateral** against a **loan**.

charge account See **revolving credit**.

charge card See **credit card**.

charter(ed) 1. (UK) An organization or member of an organization authorized to trade by royal charter, such as a company, e.g. the East India Company, or a member of a chartered governing body of a profession, e.g. a chartered accountant who is a member of the Institute of Chartered Accountants in England and Wales. 2. (US) A charter, which consists of the articles of incorporation (see **memorandum of association**) and a certificate of incorporation or registration issued by a state or federal regulatory body, thus a **chartered bank**. The term *charter* is also used in the general sense of

1., i.e. a contract between the government and a private body that confers privileges.

chartered bank (US and Can.) US and Canadian banks are authorized by charter. In the USA the charter may be granted either by the authorities of a state or by those of the federal government, in the latter case the Comptroller of the Currency. The banks are known alternatively as state-chartered or nationally chartered banks. The practice of chartering derives from that previously in existence in the UK where companies and banks were authorized by royal charters, a system replaced by authorization under the Companies and Banking Acts.

chartist A stock market analyst who predicts **share** price movements solely from the study of graphs of share prices and sometimes trading volumes. See also **technical analysis**.

checkable (US) Of bank deposit accounts, one on which cheques (US = *checks*) may be drawn.

checking account (US) See **current account**.

cheque (UK) An order written by the drawer to a **commercial bank** or **central bank** to pay on demand a specified sum to a bearer or a named person or **company** (US = *check*). A cheque may be open or crossed. Crossed, the cheque is payable only into the bank account of the payee. A cheque becomes **negotiable** when endorsed by the payee.

cheque card (UK) A plastic card issued by a bank (see **banking**) to its customers to guarantee, up to a specified limit, usually £50, cheques drawn on the customer's account. The recipient of the cheque notes the cheque card number on the back of the cheque, payment of which is then guaranteed by the bank.

Chicago Board of Trade (CBOT) A **commodity** market, first established in 1848 as a trading centre for grain. The CBOT quickly became a centre for **futures** dealing, instituting the first contract in 1851. The market deals also in **options**. Trade is in maize, crude soya bean oil, soya beans, soya bean meal, oats, silver and gold. After the Second World War the CBOT became an important market for **financial futures**, trading in contracts in GNMAs (see **Government National Mortgage Association**), the major market index, US Treasury bonds and US Treasury notes. Total volume of sales in September 1993 was 13.8m contracts.

Chicago Board of Trade Clearing Corporation An independent organization guaranteeing trades by the **Chicago Board of Trade**, so maintaining the latter's top credit rating. This function may be extended to the **Chicago Mercantile Exchange** should a projected merger of the two exchanges take place.

Chicago Board Options Exchange (CBOE) Established in 1973 as an **options** exchange; one of the major world markets in this instrument.

Chicago Mercantile Exchange (CME) Instituted in 1919 as a **commodity futures** market, the CME developed in 1972 the **international monetary market** in which **currency futures** were initiated. These were the first **financial futures** to be traded. The market deals in futures contracts in livestock (live cattle, feeder cattle, live hogs, pork bellies), in which it was a pioneer. The financial futures division is now the more active and comprises contracts in Swiss francs, Mexican pesos, D-marks, Canadian dollars, pounds sterling, yen, French francs, domestic **certificates of deposit** (CDs), Eurodollars, time deposits and 90-day US Treasury bills. The index and **options** division of the market also trades in futures and options in **Standard and Poor's** stock index and in options in D-marks, live cattle and random-length lumber. The CME accounts for some 30% of all US futures trade; and with a nominal value of underlying assets at $85,000bn in 1993 it was the world's largest exchange, comparing with the **London International Financial Futures Exchange** (LIFFE) at $27,000bn, the **Chicago Board of Trade** at $13,000bn, and the $2,000bn nominal value of stock traded on the **New York Stock Exchange**.

Chicago School See **Friedman, Milton**.

Chicago Stock Exchange See **Midwest Stock Exchange**.

Chilean Stock Exchange The Bolsa de Comercio de Santiago is the only **stock exchange** in Chile. The exchange at Valparaiso closed in 1982.

China The Shanghai Securities Exchange reopened in 1990. There is a screen-based quotation system linking traders in Shanghai with various cities including Shenzhen in the Special Economic Zone adjacent to Hong Kong. The **price indices** are the Jingan Index for Shanghai and the Shenyen Stock Price Index.

China International Trust and Investment Corporation (CITIC) (China) A Chinese-government-owned entity issuing bonds to finance joint ventures in China. The main bond in circulation is the CITIC 10-year bond.

Chinese Gold and Silver Exchange Society A gold and silver market in Hong Kong set up in 1910.

Chinese wall A communications barrier between members or departments of a financial institution intended to prevent the transfer of price-sensitive information. Chinese walls are imaginary but are taken seriously in an attempt to minimize conflicts of interest, e.g. between clients of a broking department of a **merchant bank** advised to buy **shares** that an investment department might wish to dispose of.

CHIPS Clearing House Interbank Payments System. See **clearing house**.

chooser option See **as-you-like option**.

churning Buying and selling **shares** by a **broker** on a **discretionary account**, primarily for the purpose of generating **commission**.

chusho shoken (Jap.) All **securities houses** except the **Big Four**.

CIBOR See **Copenhagen interbank offered rate**.

circuit-breaker mechanism (US) Price change limits and trading halts intended to control excessive fluctuations in market prices recommended by the **Brady Commission**. Following **Black Monday** there were many calls for new restrictions of these kinds including the limitation of **programme trading**.

CISCO See **City Group for Smaller Companies**.

CITIC See **China International Trust and Investment Corporation**.

City (UK) A popular term for the financial institutions located in the financial district to the east of St Paul's Cathedral in London. Also referred to as the Square Mile. The term is often used to refer to all financial institutions, wherever located.

city bank (Jap.) Each of the thirteen major **commercial banks** based in the cities of Kobe, Nagoya, Osaka, Sapporo, Tokyo and Urawa, but with national branch networks (Japanese = *toshi guiko*). See also **regional bank**. Not to be confused with Citibank, the US bank.

City Group for Smaller Companies (CISCO) A lobby group formed in December 1992 with wide membership among **venture capital** companies, **institutional investors**, **stockbrokers** and others to further reform of the UK **equity** markets following the announced closure of the **unlisted securities market**.

claim 1. An entitlement to a financial **asset**, frequently applied to the document evidencing such a claim. 2. In the **money market** and **banking**, the **assets** of a financial institution, namely outstanding loans and holdings of **Treasury bills** and **commercial bills**, as against the institution's **liabilities**. 3. In insurance, an application by a policy-holder for payment of a loss under the terms of the policy.

claims-made policy An insurance policy under which the **insurer** is obliged to pay only those claims made during the policy period, regardless of the date of the loss.

claims outstanding reserve A fund set aside by an insurance company to meet **claims** under its insurance policies that are still in the course of settlement.

clausing An entry on a **bill of exchange** of details of the parties to, and the nature of, the transaction underlying the bill.

clearing The offsetting of **liabilities** or purchases and sales between two parties. See **clearing house**.

clearing banks (UK) Members of the London Bankers' Clearing

House (see **clearing house**). Now used synonymously with **commercial banks**.

clearing fee The fee charged on market transactions by the **clearing house** of a **commodity exchange**.

clearing house Any institution that settles mutual indebtedness between a number of organizations. The London Bankers' Clearing House was set up to net-out interbank indebtedness by offsetting **cheques** drawn on each other's accounts and presented by each **clearing bank** on a daily basis. There are separate arrangements for **City** banks and Scottish banks, and a Clearing House Automated Payments System (CHAPS) that will supplant the City or town clearing system. Similar institutions exist in other countries, e.g. the Clearing House Interbank Payments System (CHIPS) in New York. There are similar arrangements on the **commodity exchanges** (see **International Commodities Clearing House**), the **stock exchanges** (see **Transfer Accounting, Lodgement for Investors, Stock Management for Jobbers**, TALISMAN), the **futures** markets and for payments in the **Euromarkets** (see **Centrale de Livraison de Valeurs Mobilières, Euroclear**). The clearing house is normally financed by membership subscriptions and other dues of the market.

Clearing House Automated Payments System (CHAPS) See **clearing house**.

Clearing House Interbank Payments System (CHIPS) See **clearing house**.

CLOB International Central Limit Order Book. See **Singapore Stock Exchange**.

close company (UK) A **company** effectively controlled by not more than five shareholders.

close out An offsetting transaction in two or more **instruments** leaving the investor in a net zero position, i.e. neither in credit nor in debt.

closed-end fund An investment company with a fixed capitalization. See **investment trust**.

closing prices Prices as they stand at the end of each day's trading session in the **securities** and **commodity markets**.

CME See **Chicago Mercantile Exchange**.

CMO See **collateralized mortgage obligation**.

CNMV See **Madrid Stock Exchange**.

COB (Fr.) See **Commission des Opérations de Bourse**.

Cocoa Association of London A company limited by guarantee, the Cocoa Association of London was founded in 1929, with the mandate to 'promote, protect and regulate the cocoa trade' and to 'protect the status and interests of all persons engaged therein'. In pursuit of these aims the association has formulated the rules and regulations for the conduct of trade by the **London Cocoa Terminal Market Association**, and provides arbitration and appeal facilities. The Cocoa Association has some 100 voting members, and some 30 non-voting and non-trading members, drawn from all parts of the world and representing the world's cocoa producers, the chocolate and cocoa butter industry, trading houses, shipping and insurance companies, superintendence companies and related international trade associations.

Code of Liberalization See **Organization for European Economic Co-operation** (OEEC).

COFACE See **Compagnie Française pour l'Assurance du Commerce Extérieur**.

Coffee, Sugar and Cocoa Exchange Inc. of New York A **commodity** market first established to deal in coffee in 1882, to which were added sugar in 1916 and cocoa in 1925; name changed to present style in 1971. It trades in **futures** contracts in these commodities as well as in **options** in sugar. Together with London, a main world market in cocoa.

Coffee Terminal Market Association of London Ltd A major world **commodity** market founded as the Coffee Trade Association in 1888 and reopened under its present name in 1958. The market is principally a **futures** market, trading chiefly in contracts for African coffee of the Robusta variety. An attempt was made in 1973 to install a contract for South American coffee of the Arabica variety, but this proved unsuccessful, and the contract was withdrawn in 1974. The market is a member of the **International Commodities Clearing House**.

collar An **instrument**, on which interest is contained within a maximum and minimum bracket. See also **cap**.

collateral Originally the US term for **security**, now used more widely. The official US definition (under the US Commercial Code) includes goods, intangibles, paper (**negotiable instruments** and documents of titles) and proceeds.

collateral security A second **security** (in addition to the personal security of the borrower) for a **loan**.

collateralized mortgage obligation (CMO) (US) A **bond**, the **security** of which is a **portfolio** of **mortgages** issued by the Federal Home Loan Mortgage Corporation (see **Federal Home Loan Bank Board**) offering certainty of redemption date.

collateralized mortgage security (US) A **bond**, the **security** of which is a **portfolio** of **mortgages**. The **yield** and **redemption** of the bond are paid out of the interest and capital repayments of the mortgagors, such payments being made through **pass-through** arrangements.

Coloroll case See **equalization of pensions**.

COMEX See **Commodity Exchange of New York**. The name Comex is also often used to refer to the price of copper as fixed in New York.

Comisión Nacional del Mercado de Valores (Sp.) See **Madrid Stock Exchange**.

Comit Index (It.) The **share index** for the **Milan Stock Exchange**, published by the Banca Commerciale Italiana.

Comitato Direttivo degli Agenti di Cambio (It.) The association of **stockbrokers** on the **stock exchange** in Milan, having the task of supervising the conduct of business. Its rules have legal force, and it is subject to the **Commissione Nazionale per le Società e la Borsa**.

commercial banks Privately owned banks (see **banking**); otherwise referred to as **clearing banks** (UK), national banks and state banks (US), joint-stock banks and, in Western Europe, credit banks, to distinguish them from **investment banks**.

commercial bill Any bill other than a **Treasury bill**. Commercial bills are **bank bills** or **trade bills**. See also **bill of exchange**.

commercial credit company See **finance house**.

commercial loan selling The sale by one bank to another of a loan to a commercial company. The sale is normally from an originating bank, having access to a reputable borrower but not wishing for overhead cost reasons to keep the loan on its books, to another bank without access to the borrower but with the capacity to absorb the loan. As a result of the transaction, the originating bank makes a turn on the sale, the client borrows on more favourable terms, and the purchasing bank obtains a good asset not otherwise available. The practice began in the USA in 1986 and developed rapidly.

commercial paper (CP) An **unsecured note** issued by companies for short-term borrowing purposes. It differs from a **bill of exchange** in that it is *one-name* paper; a bill of exchange contains the names of the drawer and the drawee, both of whom are liable, whereas commercial paper has only the name of the issuer. Commercial paper has been in use in the USA for many years but was for long frowned on in the UK. In April 1986 sterling commercial paper was authorized by the **Bank of England**, subject to a number of conditions, in particular that maturities should be not less than seven days and not more than a year and that the right to issue should be restricted to companies having net assets of not less than £50m and that are listed on the **stock exchange**. Issues began in May 1986. CP is frequently sold by the issuer direct to the investor, the latter normally being institutions, namely **money-market** funds, **insurance** companies, corporations, bank trust departments and **pension** funds. CP is also placed by intermediary banks or securities dealers. Unlike **acceptances**, CP is not tied to a particular trade transaction.

CP has been introduced in recent years not only into the UK but also into Australia, Spain, Hong Kong, Sweden, Singapore, Norway, France and the Netherlands. In 1987 $359bn of CP was outstanding in all countries, but $323bn of this was accounted for by the USA. There were also £356bn of **Euronote** and **Euro-commercial paper** issues. In 1981 only $170bn of CP was outstanding and issued only in the USA, Canada and Australia.

Commercial paper issues in the USA are sometimes backed by a bank's *irrevocable* **letter of credit**. Most issues are **rated** by a **rating agency**, and to secure a good rating borrowers must maintain a committed credit facility equal to the value of the paper involved. In Canada issues are normally backed by a pledge of assets (e.g. **receivables**) and rated. In France issues may be made only by French-based companies, and issues are increasingly rated. There are legal requirements for disclosure of financial details, and all issues up to two years' **maturity** must be backed by a credit line equal to 75% of their value. CP in France is known as *billets de trésorerie*. There is a commercial paper clearing house in Australia, Austraclear, established in 1984, and many issues are rated and underwritten; letters of credit are used as backing for lesser-known borrowers. In Norway commercial paper, known as loan certificates, is one of the four classes of short-term negotiable paper authorized by the Ministry of Finance in December 1984; issues are restricted to Norwegian borrowers. The third largest CP market, after the USA and Canada, is Sweden, where back-up credit is not legally required; rating is not undertaken. See also **note** (*promissory note*).

Commissão de Valores Mobiliaros See **São Paulo Stock Exchange**.

commission Payment made to a salesperson or intermediary, e.g. a **broker**, in return for their services in promoting a transaction, usually a sale, usually determined as a percentage of the value of the transaction.

commission broker (US) A **dealer** on the **stock exchange** who executes orders to buy or sell securities for the public in return for a **commission** or fee.

Commission des Opérations de Bourse (COB) (Fr.) The

official body for the supervision of the **stock exchanges** in France, established by legislation of 1967. Its specific tasks are to approve, on the advice of the **Chambre Syndicale des Agents de Change**, securities for official listing; to ensure full disclosure, under the law, of listed companies' affairs; to prevent **insider dealing**; and to transmit complaints on, and initiate new rules for, the conduct of business. There is a similar body with the same name in Belgium.

Commissione Nazionale per le Società e la Borsa (CONSOB) (It.) The official body for the supervision of the **stock exchange** in Italy, instituted in 1974; responsible for the approval of new *listings* (see **listed security**), fixing of brokers' commissions, invigilation of company finances, notification of abuses and the overview of company ownership.

commitment Of a **note issuance facility** (NIF), undertaking by a bank or **syndicate** of banks to **underwrite** or provide **back-up credit**.

commitment fee A fee charged by a bank in respect of an unused balance of a **line of credit**, designed to offset the bank's cost of keeping the funds available.

committed Of **Euronote** or **Euro-commercial paper** issue, guaranteed by a bank **syndicate** that either **underwrites** the issue or provides **back-up credit**.

committee of subscribers (UK) The elected body of **London Metal Exchange** members responsible for the administration of the exchange.

commodity 1. In economic theory, all subjects of production and exchange, i.e. all goods and services. 2. Raw materials, or primary products, used in manufacturing and industrial processing, consumed in their natural form. 3. Those commodities traded in **commodity markets**.

Commodity Exchange of New York (COMEX) A major **commodity** market in metals, established in 1870, dealing principally in **futures** contracts and sharing with the **London Metal Exchange** a dominant role in world metal trading. Trades are in copper, silver, gold and aluminium futures and in gold options. The term *Comex* is commonly used in the commodities market to mean the New York copper price. In 1993 an offer for the exchange was made by the **New York Mercantile Exchange**, the effect of which would be to merge two of the world's largest markets in energy and in precious metals.

Commodity Futures Trading Commission (CFTC) (US) A regulatory body with authority over all US **commodity** futures exchanges, established by the Commodity Futures Trading Act 1974. It consists of five members (commissioners) appointed by the US President. Originally set up to supervise trade in agricultural products, its remit has been continuously extended. In the early 1990s it was given powers to regulate dealings in **derivatives**. Under new powers granted on its 1992 reauthorization, the commission exempted off-exchange swap, hybrid and energy contracts from its purview.

commodity market A market, or exchange, in which **commodities** are bought and sold. Such commodities are those required to satisfy production, food and ornamentation needs, e.g. cotton, grain and precious metals. Commodities are traded in the light of their basic distinguishing characteristics: (a) physical properties, (b) time of availability and (c) place of availability. Characteristic (a) determines the initial desirability of the commodity; (b) and (c) influence the price. Commodity markets are no longer chiefly physical markets, where deals are made out of warehouses, but are places for the sale and purchase by contract of commodities available anywhere in the world and at any point in time. Contracts for the latter are known as **forward contracts** and **futures**; those for immediate delivery are known as **cash, physical** or **actual** transactions. Major world commodity markets are in London, Chicago, Amsterdam, New York, Sydney and Singapore. Individual markets, with brief details of their history and characteristics, are to be found under the separate names.

Commodity Research Bureau (US) A research institution specializing in **commodity** price trends, whose index of commodity prices is deemed an important indicator of future consumer price movements.

Common Market See **European Union**.

common stocks (US) Shares in the **equity** capital of a business. See **ordinary shares**.

community charge See **local taxation**.

Compagnie des Agents de Change (CAC) (Fr.) The association of French **stockbrokers**. All stockbrokers active on all French **stock exchanges** are required to be members, and the CAC has official recognition and support from the government. The rules of the CAC, known as the Règlement Général de la Compagnie des Agents de Change, regulate the conduct of business on all stock exchanges and have the backing of the ministry. The CAC maintains close relations with the official **Commission des Opérations de Bourse** (COB). The governing body of the CAC is the **Chambre Syndicale des Agents de Change**. See also **Paris Bourse**.

Compagnie Française pour l'Assurance du Commerce Extérieur (COFACE) (Fr.) The French export credit guarantee system, providing **insurance** against political as well as commercial risks and also insuring foreign exchange risks where these cannot be **covered forward**. COFACE's capital is supplied from public resources.

Companies Acts See **incorporation**.

company 1. An incorporated business. See **incorporation**. 2. More loosely, any business organization, which may be a **sole proprietorship**, a **partnership** or another form.

Company Bulletin Board A screen-based system for trading least liquid stocks (see **liquidity**), introduced on the **London Stock Exchange** in April 1992 and replaced by the **Stock Exchange Alternative Trading Service** in November of the same year.

Company Directors Disqualification Act See **bankruptcy**.

company limited by guarantee A company (see **incorporation**) in which the **liability** of the **shareholders** is limited to the amount they guarantee to pay in the event of **liquidation** rather than by the amount of the **equity**.

competition and credit control (UK) See **credit control**.

compliance department, officer All official **stock exchanges**

and many large **financial institutions** have people responsible for ensuring that laws and **regulations** governing **share** dealing and **investment** are complied with. Compliance officers may be required to investigate transactions carried out by their colleagues. See also **Chinese wall**.

composite company An insurance company transacting both **general insurance** and **long-term** business.

compound option An **option** to buy an option at a prescribed price and date.

comptant (Fr.) **Cash**, **spot**.

Comptroller of the Currency See **national bank**.

Confederation of Coffee Producing Countries A grouping of South and Central American producers brought together in 1993 with the aim to limit exports in an effort to counteract the steep fall in world prices. The members were reckoned to produce more than two-thirds of world supplies. See **International Coffee Organization**.

conflict of interest A situation where a financial institution is acting for the parties on both sides of a transaction, or where the institution itself has a financial interest in the outcome of the transaction; e.g. a **merchant bank** both placing **shares** on the **stock exchange** on behalf of a client company and recommending the purchase of those shares to an investor client whose **portfolio** it manages; or a **securities house** offering to an investor shares with which it is itself oversupplied and that it is under pressure to sell. See also **Chinese wall**.

conglomerate (US) A business organization generally consisting of a **holding company** and a group of **subsidiaries** engaged in dissimilar activities. See *konzern*, **trust**, *zaibatsu*.

conseil d'administration (Fr.) Board of directors.

consideration Something given in exchange for something else, i.e. the total amount of cash, goods or other property, or rights to cash or property, transferred from buyer to seller in settlement of a transaction. In **securities** trading, the amount paid for securities before **commission** and **taxation**. In the UK a transaction may not be legally binding until the consideration is paid.

CONSOB See **Commissione Nazionale per le Società e la Borsa**.

consolidated accounts Financial statements that bring together the **balance sheets** and **profit and loss accounts** of parent and subsidiary companies so that the financial affairs of the group can be treated as a whole. Where the parent controls (i.e. owns more than 50% of the equity of) a subsidiary, the balance sheet may include the **assets** of the subsidiary at market value, with any premium paid for **goodwill** included in the parent's balance sheet and written off against earnings. This is called *acquisition accounting* (US = *purchase acquisition*) or *full consolidation*. Adjustments are made to eliminate the double counting of purchases and sales, borrowing and lending between subsidiaries. Where subsidiaries are not wholly owned, the profits and assets attributable to the minority shareholders (minority interests) have to be shown separately. Under merger accounting (US = *pooling of interests*), assets of acquired subsidiaries are put in at historic cost (see **costs, historical**); i.e. the balance sheets of parents and subsidiaries are added together line by line. Merger accounting gives a more favourable view, and this may be particularly desirable where the subsidiary has been acquired by an exchange of shares.

The term *subsidiary* is usually reserved for companies controlled by the parent. Companies in which the parent has between about 20% and 50% of the equity are *associate companies*, which it has influence over but does not control. The accounts of these associates may be partially consolidated by valuing them in the balance sheet at their investment cost plus the proportion of undistributed profits attributable to the parent. Companies in which the company has less than about 20% of the equity are referred to as *trade investments*.

The techniques of financial consolidation are complex, and practices differ between countries. Generally, consolidation of earnings is less usual in Japan and continental Europe than in the UK and the USA, and this may affect comparisons of **yields**.

The European Union's Seventh Directive harmonizes the requirements for the consolidated accounts of companies.

Consolidated Fund (UK) The UK government's main expenditure and income account, kept with the Bank of England.

consols (UK) Abbreviation for *consolidated stock*: irredeemable government stock, first issued in the 18th century and bearing a **nominal interest rate** of $2\frac{1}{2}$%.

Consorzio per investimenti (It.) **Investment trust**.

constant-dollar plan See **pound-cost averaging**.

consumer credit Short-term **loans** to the public for the purchase of specific goods. Consumer **credit** takes the form of credit by shopkeepers and other suppliers, **credit accounts**, **personal loans** and **hire purchase**.

Consumer Credit Act 1974 (UK) Legislation introducing a licensing system for all agencies involved in **consumer credit**. The Act provides protection for the borrower in consumer credit business. The Act applies to bank and **hire-purchase credit**, to **credit sales**, **credit cards**, private loans and **mortgages**, and also to debt collectors. The Act principally provides for full disclosure of cost information, including the **annual percentage rate** (APR), for a **cooling-off period** and for a written agreement, except in the case of **overdrafts**.

consumer instalment loan (US) See **hire purchase**.

consumer price index See **retail price index**.

contango A situation in a **commodity market** in which prices for future delivery are higher than those for immediate or very early delivery. Also known as *forwardation*.

contemporaneous reserve requirements (CRR) (US) The constitution by banks of reserves against deposits made simultaneously with the calculation of the level of deposits for the period in question.

contingent liability See **provisions**.

contract 1. Any agreement under law, including an agreement to buy or sell a **security** (see **contract note**). **2**. Traded **options** and **futures** are agreements to buy or sell a security or **commodity** at a specified price and date and thus are referred to as contracts.

contract note (UK) A document sent by a **broker** soon after a transaction, showing the price at which a **security** was bought or sold, a note of any benefits attached or excluded (e.g. **ex-dividend**), the broker's **commission**, tax charge, the **consideration** and the terms of payment.

contracting out (UK) The act of an occupational **pensions** scheme in withdrawing from the State Earnings-Related Pension Scheme (SERPS), subject to a guarantee of equivalent benefit, and attracting a reduction in contributions to the state.

contractual savings See **savings**.

contratto a premi (It.) An **option** contract.

conversion 1. Transfer of one type of **security** into another, e.g. convertible loan stock or convertible bond, a fixed-interest security that on **maturity** or at a specified date or dates may be exchanged for **equity** at a fixed price. There may be an option to receive cash for those who do not wish to exercise their conversion rights. Convertibles usually carry a lower interest rate than similar fixed-interest securities, since the investor may make a **capital gain** if the price of the underlying equity rises above the conversion price. See also **conversion premium**, **warrant**. **2**. Change in legal form, e.g. conversion of a **building society** to a public limited company (plc; see **incorporation**) under the Building Societies Act 1986.

conversion discount See **conversion premium**.

conversion premium The difference between the current market price of a **share** and the price at which a convertible security (see **conversion**) or **warrant** can be exchanged for the share. Expressed as a percentage of the market price of the convertible security, this is the conversion premium or, if the difference is negative, the conversion discount.

convertible 1. A currency is said to be convertible when it can be

63

bought or sold without restriction in exchange for other currencies. See **exchange control**. **2**. A **security** is convertible when it carries the right for the holder to exchange it at a fixed price for another form of security. See **conversion**. See also **adjustable rate preferred stock**.

convertible adjustable rate preferred stock See **adjustable rate preferred stock**.

convertible bond A **bond** that can be converted at a fixed price into the **shares** of a company, usually within a given time period. See also **conversion**.

convertible debenture See **debentures**.

convertible loan stock See **conversion**.

convertible revolving credit A **revolving credit** convertible at the end of the **term**, or earlier, into a fixed-term loan.

cooling-off period (UK) A period, provided under the UK Insurance Companies Act and the Consumer Credit Act 1974, during which a person having entered into a long-term **life assurance** policy or a **hire-purchase** agreement has the right to withdraw from the commitment. The period is of 10 days of effecting the life assurance policy and payment of the first premium; and five days of receipt of confirmation of the hire-purchase agreement. See also **Truth in Lending Act** (US).

Copenhagen interbank offer rate (CIBOR) (Den.) The Danish equivalent of the **London interbank offered rate** (LIBOR). The rate is available to banks and savings banks depositing three-month uncollateralized kroner with a prime bank.

core price index The retail price index from which items deemed unrepresentative of the true movement of prices have been removed. In the USA these items are those relating to food and energy; in the UK the item usually removed is mortgage interest payments; food and seasonal foods can also be removed.

CORES Computer-Assisted Order Routing and Execution System. See **Tokyo Stock Exchange**.

corporate finance See **business finance**.

corporate raider (US) An individual organization that makes hostile **take-over** bids for **quoted companies**. These bids may be financed by **junk bonds** and involve *greenmail* in which the target company may avert the take-over by buying in at a premium the **share** stake built up by the raider or a risk arbitrageur (see **arbitrage**). The latter buys stakes in companies that are expected to be the subject of a contested bid (see **merger**), selling the **stock** of the acquiring company. In a take-over bid, the shares of the acquiring company usually fall on announcement of the bid, while those of the victim rise. The term *greenmail* derives from the colour of dollar bills and the implication of blackmail in some threatened take-over bids. See also **poison pill**, **white knight**.

corporation See **incorporation**.

corporation tax A tax (see **taxation**) levied on the assessable **profits** of companies. In the UK under the imputation system, the company pays tax on its profits at the corporation tax rate before any distribution, while shareholders are given a **tax credit** against their **income tax** liabilities in respect of the part of the corporation tax paid on distributed profits. The total amount of the tax imputed to shareholders is remitted to the Inland Revenue as *advance corporation tax* (ACT) and is deductible from liability for mainstream corporation tax. Some companies may not have sufficient tax liabilities against which to offset ACT; this is known as *unrelieved corporation tax* or *surplus ACT* and may arise where a high proportion of profits are earned overseas. From 1 July 1994 a company may opt to classify a **dividend** as a *foreign income dividend* (FID). FIDs do not carry tax credits but are treated as having borne income tax at the lower rate. The shareholders receive their dividend without tax deductions and with a credit for the amount of tax imputed to them. If they pay tax at the lower rate (see **income tax**) they are considered to have prepaid their income tax on the dividend. The purpose of this complex arrangement is to ensure that shareholders are not taxed twice on their dividends, once by corporation tax and once by income tax.

Germany, France, Italy, Japan and other countries operate the imputation system. The Netherlands, Switzerland, the USA and others use the classical system of corporation tax that treats the company as having a fiscal as well as a legal identity distinct from its shareholders; these countries tax company profits and also dividends in the hands of shareholders. Several countries, including the USA and the UK, have a lower rate of tax for smaller companies. For 1994/5 the UK corporation tax rate was 33%, with a rate of 25% for companies whose profits do not exceed £300,000. In the UK, as in many other countries, companies are also liable to tax on **capital gains**. **Unincorporated businesses** are subject to business **income tax**. See also **sub-chapter S corporations**.

correspondent bank A **bank** in one country that acts as an **agent** for a bank in another country, e.g. in the transmission of funds.

corset See **supplementary special deposit**.

cost of capital See **capital, cost of**.

cost of funds (US) A term used to describe banks' setting of lending rates in relation to the rates paid by themselves for funds raised in the **wholesale** market. See **base rate**.

cost of sales (UK) The cost of producing what is sold before making an allowance for contribution to general **overheads**, i.e. material costs, manufacturing wage costs and production overheads.

costanti (It.) A sale for **cash**.

costs, historical Actual costs at the time incurred. An **asset** in the **balance sheet** at historical cost is shown at the price paid for it, even though it may be worth more or cost more to replace (see **inflation accounting**).

cotation (Fr.) A **stock exchange listing**.

cote (Fr.) The official price of a **security** on the **stock exchange**.

cote officielle (Fr.) The full term for *cote*, also used to denote the **stock market** itself. The word *officielle* derives from the fact that the market was until 1962 divided into a market at official prices and the *coulisse* or market at unofficial prices.

coulisse (Fr.) The unofficial securities market in the **Paris Bourse**, the *coulisse* closed in 1962. See *cote officielle*.

council tax See **local taxation**.

countertrading Another term for barter, i.e. the exchange of goods or services without any monetary consideration.

coupon A counterfoil or tag that, when detached from a **bond**, serves as evidence of entitlement to interest. It is invariably used to refer to the rate of interest itself; and by extension is also used to refer to the rate of interest on most financial **instruments**, particularly **notes**.

coupon issue (US) See **coupon security**.

coupon pass (US) The purchase outright of a **security**.

coupon security (US) US government **securities** that pay a rate of interest, or **coupon**, as compared with those bought at a **discount**. Coupon securities are **Treasury bonds** and certain **Treasury notes** or **bills**.

coupure (Fr.) The total number of shares in an issue.

cours (Fr.) **1. Rate. 2. Market price** (of **securities** or **commodities**), i.e. in the sense of the going market price, as against *prix*, the price paid in a particular transaction.

Court of Auditors A panel of expert **auditors** with the task of examining all revenues and expenditures of the **European Union** and having the right to comment on these and, where requested, to offer advice on them. The Court of Auditors was set up in 1975 and is composed of 12 members, one from each member country, appointed each for a term of six years by the Council of Ministers, in consultation with the European Parliament.

courte échéance (Fr.) **Short term**.

courtier (Fr.) A **broker** on the French unofficial stock market or *coulisse*, which closed in 1962.

cover 1. To **hedge. 2.** To obtain the **currency**, **security** or **commodity** needed to honour a contracted sale. **3.** To insure. **4.** Of **dividends**, the amount by which the *pay-out* is covered by the company's earnings (see **dividend cover**).

cover note A temporary confirmation that an **insurance risk** has been covered, issued pending the completion of a full insurance contract.

covered interest arbitrage Taking advantage of differences in **interest** rates between two countries by borrowing in one **currency** and investing the proceeds to earn the higher rate while covering the **exchange rate** risk in the **forward** market.

CP See **commercial paper**.

CPI Consumer price index. See **retail price index**.

crash A precipitate one-day fall in stock market prices.

crawling peg Revaluation or devaluation of an **exchange rate** in small amounts spread over time and linked to a **moving average** of past rates or a country's gold **reserves**.

créance (Fr.) A **claim**.

credit Granting the use or possession of goods and services without immediate payment. See **bank credit**, **consumer credit**, **double-entry bookkeeping**, **trade credit**.

credit availability theory (US) The theory that a modest increase in interest rates could lead to capital losses in banks' portfolios of **Treasury securities**, so inducing the banks to restrict the availability of business loans for investment.

credit card A plastic, personal, magnetized card issued by an agency, bank or other institution against which purchases, up to a prescribed ceiling (*credit limit*), may be credited on signature of a voucher franked by the card. The vendor recovers the cash from the issuer of the card (less a percentage **commission**), and the purchaser pays the issuer on receipt of a monthly statement. If desired, the purchaser has the option of paying a minimum amount and settling the account in instalments plus interest. Credit cards are sometimes available free to creditworthy users; other cards, known as *charge cards*, are paid for by an annual fee and do not offer the option of a loan. A *debit card* works in the same way as the credit card but debits the purchaser's bank account immediately. Credit cards may be used to withdraw cash from an **automatic teller**

machine, and the card may be magnetically inspected for authenticity. Credit cards are popularly referred to as 'plastic money'. See also **cheque card**, **smart card**.

credit control (UK) The **regulation** of bank and other forms of **credit** in the interests of **monetary policy**. Specifically the term applies to the arrangements for the control of bank credit announced in September 1971, to replace credit ceilings, entitled competition and credit control, which led to the introduction of the **minimum lending rate** and were intended to stimulate competition in the **banking** system. See also **monetary control**.

credit guarantee A type of **insurance** against default, provided by a credit guarantee association, government body or other institution, to a lending institution, to allow small firms that lack **collateral security**, or are unable to obtain loans for other reasons, to obtain credit from banks. A government loan guarantee scheme of this type was introduced in the UK in 1980. Not to be confused with **deposit insurance**.

credit line (US) See **overdraft**.

crédit mixte (Fr.) A combined package of bank **credit** and official aid funds for financing an export transaction.

credit rating An assessment of the likelihood of an individual or business being able to meet its financial obligations. Credit ratings are provided by credit agencies or **rating agencies** for sellers who wish to verify the financial strength of buyers, for lenders and for investors (ratings for specific **securities**). Banks also provide confidential trade references.

credit sale A sale agreement under which payment is made in instalments, but with ownership of the object of the sale passing immediately to the purchaser.

credit union A non-profit organization accepting **deposits** and making **loans**, operated as a cooperative; a **mutual** organization that is in effect a **savings bank**. Similar credit associations exist in many countries, e.g. the *shinyo kinku* and the smaller *shinyo kumiai* credit co-operatives in Japan, which act as banks for small firms.

creditor One to whom money is due.

CREST See **Transfer and Automated Registration of Uncertified Stock** (TAURUS).

cross See **crossing**.

cross-border listing Shares and other **securities** may be traded on official **stock exchanges** only where they are listed on an exchange. Residents in other countries may purchase or sell securities through their own **broker**, who will get a broker in the country of listing to trade the securities. The practice known as cross–border listing means securities being listed on exchanges in more than one country.

cross-currency interest rate swap An **interest rate swap** in which two different streams of interest, in two different currencies, are exchanged.

crossed (US) A situation where one **market maker** has a lower **offer price** than another's **bid price**. This is referred to as a locked or crossed market and in the UK sometimes as **backwardation** or backward price. On the **London Stock Exchange**, market makers are supposed not to take advantage of the opportunity presented to buy from one **dealer** and sell to another at a profit (**arbitrage**), but should draw the dealers' attention to the discrepancy and allow them to change their **quotation**.

crossing The purchase and sale of a quantity of **securities** by the same **broker**. **Stock exchange** rules normally require such transactions to cross the market so as to ensure that the buyer or seller has the opportunity to get a better price if it is available. Where the two orders are for the same individual, or by another acting in collusion with them, a crossed sale is known in the USA as a **wash sale**.

crowding in The theory that a national budget deficit in periods of economic depression, involving higher public expenditure and monetary growth and offsetting increased government borrowing, can lead to higher economic activity and so to an increase in private investment.

crowding out The theory that excessive central government borrowing on **capital markets** will consume funds otherwise available for private **investment**.

CRS Computer-readable systems.

cum-dividend With-**dividend**; the purchaser of a security quoted cum-dividend is entitled to receive the next dividend when due. The term *cum* is used in a similar sense in relation to **bonus issues**, **rights issues** or **interest** attached to **securities**, etc.

cumulative preference shares (UK) See **preference shares**.

Curb Exchange See **American Stock Exchange**.

currency 1. Notes and coin that are the *current* medium of exchange in a country. A *soft* currency is one whose **exchange rate** is tending to fall because demand for it is weak. This may be the result of changes in capital movements, patterns of trade or speculation. A *hard* currency is one that is tending to rise against other currencies. 2. In US and UK banking, all foreign currencies. 3. In US **money supply** terminology, currency refers to **cash**.

currency future A form of **financial future** in which the contract is in respect of the exchange rate of a currency.

currency interest rate swap An **interest rate swap** consisting of the exchange of two streams of the same interest rate but in different currencies. These are sometimes termed *fixed-rate currency swaps*. In the case of trade in currency interest rate swaps, the **principal** may also change hands.

currency option See **option**.

currency overlay manager (US) An investment manager concerned with devising programmes to **hedge** or enhance investment portfolios of foreign **stocks** (and more rarely **bonds**) against **currency** risks or opportunities. These managers have come into prominence as **equities** denominated in foreign currencies have become more important in the portfolios of **institutional investors**. Investors may wish their equity returns to offset the **interest** or **capital gain** returns irrespective of currency changes, or they may actually wish to enhance their exposure to foreign currencies.

currency swap See **currency interest rate swap**, **swap**.

currency translation exposure The effect of currency movements on a company's accounts when foreign sales are recorded in the domestic currency.

current account 1. The most common type of **bank** account, on which **deposits** do not necessarily earn **interest** but can be withdrawn by **cheque** at any time (US = demand deposit, checking account). See also **bank charges**. **2**. That part of the **balance of payments** recording current, i.e. non-capital, transactions.

current account deposit See **sight deposit**.

current assets See **assets**.

current cost accounting See **inflation accounting**.

current liabilities See **liabilities**.

current prices Prices adjusted for changes in the purchasing power of money.

current ratio See **working capital**.

current yield See **yield**.

cursor A marker on a computer screen showing where the next text entered on the keyboard will be displayed. In most programs it can be moved around the screen by arrows on the keyboard.

customer repurchase agreement (US) A **repurchase agreement** arranged by the **Federal Reserve** for foreign central bank customers.

customer RP See **customer repurchase agreement**.

customized option An **option**, generally offered in **over-the-counter** trade, allowing the holder various departures from the fixed terms, strike prices, and exercise and settlement dates required for instruments traded on options exchanges. See also **flex stock option**.

Customs and Excise, HM See **Inland Revenue**.

CVM Commissão de Valores Mobiliaros. See **São Paulo Stock Exchange**.

cylinder option An **option** with a specially reduced **premium**.

DA See **discretionary account**.

DAC Development Assistance Committee. See **Organization for Economic Co-operation and Development** (OECD).

Dachgesellschaft (Ger.) **Holding company**.

daimyo bond (Jap.) A **bearer security** issued by the **International Bank for Reconstruction and Development** on the Japanese **capital market** and also in the **Eurobond** market. **Market makers** are permitted to take **short** positions in these bonds, unlike the provisions for **samurai bonds**.

Danish Futures and Options Market A market opened in 1988, supported by the **Guarantee Fund for Futures and Options**. In 1993 the first money-market future, based on the three-month **Copenhagen interbank offer rate** (CIBOR), was launched with a contract size of DKr5m. This complemented the existing range of futures instruments for government bonds, long-term mortgage bonds, and the KFX index of most traded shares. There were plans for options on CIBOR futures and possibly on other money-market securities.

Darlehen (Ger.) A **loan**.

date d'échéance (Fr.) **Redemption date**.

dated securities **Bonds**, **bills of exchange** or other **securities** that have a stated date for redemption (repayment) of their nominal value. Short-dated securities are those for which the **redemption date** is near; long-dated securities are those for which it is a long time ahead.

dawn raid (UK) The acquisition of a large **block** of **shares** on the **stock exchange**, sometimes as a prelude to a **take-over** bid.

Usually purchases are carried out simultaneously by a number of **brokers** first thing in the morning.

DAX See **Deutsche Aktienindex**.

day order An order placed in a **commodity market** for execution in the same trading session, or in the same day, following which the order lapses.

day-to-day money See **overnight money**.

DCF See **discounted cash flow**.

de minimis See *de minimis non curat lex*.

de minimis non curat lex 'The law is not concerned with trifles.' An expression meaning that a law or proceeding consecrating a general principle should not be overturned by a contrary detail. In taxation, refers to amounts too small to be worth inclusion in legislation. Generally quoted simply as 'de minimis'.

dealer Someone who buys and sells on their own account. See **broker-dealer**.

dealerboard A fast telecommunications package enabling almost instant contact between dealers at the touch of a button, e.g. a **touch screen**.

debentures, debenture stocks (UK) Fixed-interest **securities** issued by limited companies (see **incorporation**) in return for long-term **loans**. The former term is sometimes also used to refer to any title on a secured interest-bearing loan. Debentures are dated for redemption between 10 and 40 years ahead (see **redemption date**). Debentures are usually secured against specific **assets** of the company (*mortgage debentures*) or by a *floating charge* on the assets. Debenture interest must be paid whether the company makes a **profit** or not. In the event of non-payment, debenture holders can force **liquidation**, and they rank ahead of all **shareholders** in their claims on the company's assets. Convertible debentures carry an option at a fixed date to convert the **stock** into **ordinary shares** at a fixed price (see **conversion**).

debit See **double-entry bookkeeping**.

debit card See **credit card**.

debt A sum of money or other property owed by one person or organization to another. Debt comes into being through the granting of **credit** or through raising **loan capital**. Debt servicing consists of paying interest on a debt. The term *debt* is, by extension, used to refer to the total loan exposure of an enterprise or public authority, or to the choice of **bonds** rather than **equity** in raising funds – 'to issue debt'.

debt–equity swap See **debt swap**.

debt instrument A medium for raising a **loan**, usually a short-term loan. See **instrument**.

debt ratio See **capital gearing**.

debt rescheduling See **moratorium**.

debt swap A term used to describe the practice begun by banks in the late 1980s of disposing of their outstanding loans to Third World borrowers, chiefly governments, at large discounts to other banks. The swaps take three forms: debt–debt exchanges, where a bank more willing to extend credit takes over a loan from another bank; debt–equity swaps, where a country's debt is converted into the bank's holding of **equity** in a domestic company; and debt–peso swaps, where nationals of the debtor country buy the debt and convert it into local currency. Debt may also be exchanged for equity in **venture capital** packages and in **privatizations**.

debtor One who owes money to another.

declaration The act of exercising rights in an **option**. Buyers indicate, through their and the seller's broker, that they are implementing the option. This must be done by a specified time before the **prompt date**, failing which the option is deemed to have been abandoned.

deductible The portion of a loss that must be borne by the **insured**. The deductible has the effect, unlike the case of an **excess**, of reducing the total sum insured. Thus a deductible of £10m in a contract of £100m leaves the insurer under an obligation to pay a claim, if made, of £90m, whereas with an excess and contract value of the same amounts, the insured pays the first £10m, and the insurer pays the next £100m; in the latter case, the insurer gains if the loss is £10m or below.

default Usually a failure to make payments or repayments of **interest** or **principal** on the due date. A country may be declared in default if it ceases to service a **loan** from another government or an international agency such as the World Bank (see **International Bank for Reconstruction and Development**).

deferred annuity An **annuity** whose commencement occurs on a specified date after purchase.

deferred coupon note A **bond** upon which **interest** is paid only after a specified date. US = *deferred interest bond, extended bond.*

deferred interest bond See **deferred coupon note**.

deferred start option See **deferred strike option**.

deferred strike option An **option** permitting the holder to postpone setting the **striking price** either indefinitely or to an agreed date. Also known as a deferred or forward start option.

defined benefits scheme Occupational **pensions** schemes promising a definite pension, with the employers binding themselves to make up, for this purpose, any shortfall in the proceeds of contributions.

defined contributions scheme An occupational **pensions** scheme in which the level of contributions is fixed, with no promise of a specific level of pension. In effect, a **money purchase** scheme.

del credere The risk of non-payment; an amount added to a charge to cover this risk.

del credere **agent** An agent taking on themselves, in return for a higher **commission**, the risk of non-payment of bills by the customer they introduce.

delivery month The month that is the subject of a **futures** contract and in which physical delivery must be made; a specific date within the month is prescribed for this purpose in the contract. Also known as the terminal month.

delivery versus payment A concept in the **settlement** of multi-currency deals, under which the transfer of one currency does not proceed unless the transfer of the other currency is simultaneously taking place. The concept is intended to avoid **Herstatt risk**.

delta A measure in the **options** market of the propensity of the option's price to follow that of the underlying instrument.

delta stocks See **alpha securities, stocks**.

demand deposit See **current account, sight deposit**.

demurrage Damages due to a shipowner where the contracted completion of loading or unloading is delayed.

denomination 1. The value, as printed on its face, of a **security** and the sum payable on **redemption**. See **face value**. 2. The specification in the **foreign exchange** market, the international **money market** and the **securities** market of the **currency** to be used; often employed to refer to the currency itself.

Department of Trade and Industry (DTI) UK government department responsible for promoting trade with other countries and overseeing UK business and finance, including **regulation** of **financial intermediaries**.

déport (Fr.) **Backwardation**.

deposit 1. A sum of money lodged with a **bank, discount house** or other financial institution. 2. A sum of money proportionate to the total size of the transaction, lodged to secure a **forward**, **futures** or **option** contract. Also termed a premium or a margin.

deposit account A bank account in which **deposits** earn interest, and withdrawals from which require notice (US = *time deposit*). In France and other European countries deposit accounts are called savings accounts.

deposit insurance A form of **insurance** providing compensation to lenders with **deposits** with **financial institutions** in the event of failure of the **bank** or other institution. The Deposit Protection Scheme was set up in the UK under the Banking Act 1979; under this scheme the Deposit Protection Fund guarantees up to 75% of the first £100,000 of a sterling deposit. In the USA the Federal Deposit Insurance Corporation (FDIC) provides protection for depositors with members of the **Federal Reserve System** and other banks that choose to join.

Deposit Protection Fund, Scheme See **deposit insurance**.

deposit-taking institution A bank (see **banking**) or another **financial intermediary** that accepts **deposits**.

Depository Institutions Deregulation and Monetary Decontrol Act 1980 (DIDMCA) (US) An Act that removed interest-rate ceilings from passbook savings accounts, thus allowing these **deposit** rates and borrowing costs to rise to market levels. Part of a continuing process of *deregulation* (see **regulation**) of the US **banking** system, it led to difficulties for many **savings and loan associations**.

Depository Trust Company (DTC) (US) The central depository for stock exchange **securities** in the USA.

depreciation 1. The reduction in the value of an **asset** through wear and tear. An allowance for the depreciation on a company's assets is always made before the calculation of **profit**, on the grounds that the consumption of **capital** assets is one of the costs of earning the revenues of the business and is allowed as such according to special rules by the tax authorities. Annual depreciation provisions are normally calculated either by the *straight-line method*, where the estimated residual value of the asset (e.g. scrap) is deducted from its original cost and the balance divided by the number of years of estimated life to arrive at an annual depreciation expense; or by the *reducing balance method*, in which case the actual depreciation expense is set at a constant proportion of the cost of the asset, i.e. a diminishing annual absolute amount. In periods of rising prices, the replacement cost of an asset may be very much greater than its original cost. This problem may be dealt with by revaluing assets at intervals and adjusting depreciation charges accordingly. This is called *replacement-cost* as opposed to *historic-cost* depreciation (see **inflation accounting**). **2**. A reduction in the value of a **currency** in terms of gold or other currencies in a free market. Also used to refer to a reduction in the purchasing power of any form of currency.

depreciation at choice See **capital allowances**.

deregulation See **regulation**.

derivative A generic term for **futures**, **options** and **swaps**, i.e. instruments derived from conventional direct dealings in securities, currencies and commodities. Trade in derivatives increased substantially in the 1990s, given their usefulness to company treasurers and fund managers as a **hedge** against security price changes and currency fluctuations, particularly in the disturbed currency markets of the period. Between 1992 and 1993, for example, turnover on the **London International Financial Futures Exchange** (LIFFE) and the **Marché à Terme des Instruments Financiers** (MATIF) increased by 20% and 30% respectively. In the 10 years to 1993, 18 derivatives exchanges were created in Europe, trading 98 different contracts. The market, which had come to be dominated by trade in swaps and to be handled chiefly by a relatively small number of banks, was estimated to have reached a total value of some $4bn by 1992. This figure was questioned by some commentators, who held that the true measure was not the total value of the instruments traded but the level of risk involved, a figure around a tenth of the total value. Moreover, many, including the **Group of 30** in a report published in July 1993, pointed out that the derivatives market was small in comparison with total bond, equity or foreign exchange transactions ($900bn).

In the same report the Group of 30, while suggesting guidelines for the proper conduct of business, concluded that further regulation was unnecessary. However, central banks in particular remained unconvinced, noting that most business was **over the counter**, that the instruments were complex and not universally understood, and that the potential for undercapitalization, faulty systems, inadequate supervision and human error was greater than in other markets.

dernier cours (Fr.) See **closing prices**.

designated investment exchange (DIE) (UK) An overseas investment exchange recognized by the Securities and Investment Board as having equivalent operating procedures to its own recognized investment exchanges (see **Financial Services Act**).

designated market maker (UK) A **market maker** receiving fee and publicity concessions from the **London International Financial Futures Exchange** (LIFFE) in return for an undertaking to maintain two-way and up-to-date prices and to be physically present in the *pit* (see **pit trader**) throughout trading.

designated order turnaround (DOT) (US) An electronic order-processing system on the **New York Stock Exchange** that allows members to place, e.g., a limit **order** for **stock** that will be executed automatically.

desk (US) A familiar term for the **open market desk**.

Deutsche Aktienindex (DAX) (Ger.) A share price index (see **share indices**) for 30 leading **equity** shares quoted on the Frankfurt **stock exchange** (see **German stock exchanges**). The DAX is recalculated minute by minute from the Frankfurt market share information system known as Kurs Information Service System (KISS).

Deutsche Börse AG See **German stock exchanges**.

Deutsche Bundesbank See **Bundesbank**.

Deutsche Kassenverein (DKV) The clearing and settlement agency for German **stock market securities**, based in Frankfurt.

Deutsche Terminborse (DTB) The German **futures** and **options** exchange, opened in Frankfurt in 1990 after various problems relating to German gambling law had been resolved.

deuxième marché See **Swiss stock exchanges**.

Development Assistance Committee (DAC) Se~~~
**tion for Economic Co-operation and Developmen~~~

development capital Finance provided, usually b~

institution, in the form of **equity** and **loans** to an established business. It is distinct from, though often used synonymously with, **venture capital**

Devisen (Ger.) **Foreign exchange**.

devises (Fr.) See **Foreign exchange**.

dilution An increase in the number of **shares** in a company, for example by the **exercise** of **warrants**, which reduces **earnings per share**.

direct business Of **insurance**: **1**. A **policy** concluded between the **insurer** and the insured, without the intervention of an **intermediary**. **2**. Business between the insurer and the policy-holding public, as against **reinsurance**. Also known as primary business.

direct investment **Investment** in the foreign operations of a company, e.g. by a **multinational company**. Direct investment implies control, and managerial and perhaps technical input, and is generally preferred by the host country to **portfolio** investment. See also **balance of payments**.

direct placement The sale of **shares** directly to **financial institutions** without recourse to **underwriters** or a public subscription (see **offer for sale**) in the **stock market**. See also **placing**.

direct quotation In **foreign exchange**, the quotation of a rate of exchange in terms of one unit of the domestic currency, i.e. £1 = $1.50, in the UK, rather than $1 = £0.67.

direct tax See **taxation**.

directive **1**. Written instructions from the **Federal Open Market Committee** to the Federal Reserve Bank of New York, regarding the conduct of open market operations. **2**. A decision of the **European Union**, binding as to the result but optional as to the form and method of achieving the result.

directives of the EU See **Fourth Directive**.

disclosure Enforced or voluntary publication of information. Under company law and other aspects of **regulation**, businesses are required to reveal information that they might otherwise wish to keep confidential; e.g. in the implementation of the **Financial Services Act**, brokers are required to reveal rates of **commission** on certain insurance policies. See also **Form 10K**, **Fourth Directive**.

discount 1. Reduction in the **face value** of a financial **claim**, such as a **bill of exchange** or **Treasury bill**, by the amount of money represented by the interest due on the claim during the remainder of its **maturity**. The reduction involved is the discount. It also denotes the action of selling a claim at a discount, i.e. to discount. **2**. The term is used to refer specifically to the purchase of bills at a discount by the central bank, although **rediscount** is more accurate. It is also used to denote direct lending to the commercial banks by the central bank, although more exactly an interest rate is charged rather than a discount deducted. **3**. The amount by which the future value of a **currency** is less than its **spot** value; opposite of **premium**. **4**. The amount by which a **security**'s price in the **secondary market** is less than the **issue** prices. **5**. The amount by which an **option** trades below its **intrinsic value**. **6**. See **discounting**. **7**. The amount (usually expressed as a percentage) by which the price of a share in an **investment trust** is less than **net asset value**.

discount factor See **discounted cash flow**.

discount house A financial institution in the City of London founded originally (early 19th century) to act as **broker** for the **acceptance** by banks of **bills of exchange**, Discount houses now broke in a variety of **debt instruments** and act as principals for the purchase of **market instruments** and of **Treasury bills**, financed chiefly by borrowing from the banks, with the support of the Bank of England as lender of last resort. By convention of some 50 years' standing the discount houses guarantee to take up the whole of the Treasury bills offered by the Bank of England at the weekly **Treasury bill tender**. Discount houses are so called because they became the principal purchasers of **bills of exchange** sold by the merchant banks, always at a **discount**. In the UK discount houses are members of the London Discount Market Association. In more recent years, and particularly since 1981, the discount market has traded heavily in **commercial bills**, particularly **bank bills**, in consequence of the Bank of England's increased resort to use of this **instrument** for purposes of **monetary control**.

discount market The market operated by the **discount houses**, particularly in respect of **commercial bills**, **interbank** money, **certificates of deposit**, **local authority stock** and **short-term government stocks**. Also known as the money market.

discount market deposit A deposit, normally repayable at call (see **call money**) or very **short term**, made with a London **discount house**, usually by a clearing bank. Discount market deposits are a principal source of funds to discount houses. When functioning as **reserve assets**, discount market deposits were always **secured** and referred to as *money at call* or call money. Other discount market deposits are placed for reasons of liquidity. See also **discount market**.

discount market deposit rate The interest rate paid on **discount market deposits**.

discount rate The interest rate used in determining the **discount** on the **sale** of a financial **instrument**. The term is frequently used in relation to **central banks**. The discount rate of the **Bank of England** is the rate at which it will discount **eligible bills**. In the USA the term has a more special meaning; the discount rate of the **Federal Reserve** is the interest rate at which it will lend, as **lender of last resort**, to the commercial banks. It is thus the US equivalent of **bank rate**. See also **discount window**.

discount window The supply of **short-term** funds by a **central bank** to the banking system, subject to commencement (*opening*) or termination (*closing*) at any time. The supply will be either by purchase of **Treasury bills** or by lending, against security, usually by discounting in the USA and by charging an interest rate in the UK; the term *discount* in the latter context is therefore a slight anomaly. In Germany the term refers to the suspension of normal **Lombard rate** and the substitution of **special Lombard rate** lending. In all cases the discount window is used to assist **monetary policy**. See also **bank rate**, **minimum lending rate**, **window**.

discounted cash flow (DCF) A sophisticated set of methods for

investment appraisal that take the time value of money fully into account. For example, £100 today is worth more than £100 in a year's time, risk apart, because if received today it could be invested for one year; so that, at an annual **rate of interest** or discount factor of 10%, we should receive £110 a year from now. For an investment to have a *present value* (PV) of £100 now, therefore, we should need to expect a return of £10 in a year's time from that investment, i.e. the *net present value* (NPV) of the investment – the total return minus the cost of the investment.

This principle can be used to calculate the NPVs of the **cash flows** arising from more complex industrial and commercial investment projects where cash inflows and outflows are lumpy and spread over long periods of time. For two such projects, the one with the highest NPV will add most to the wealth of the business. An alternative method is to calculate the rate of interest that will equate the PV of the net cash flows and the cost of the investment. This is the *internal rate of return* (IRR), which will be the discount factor at which the NPV is zero and can be compared with the firm's borrowing costs (see **capital, cost of**). If the IRR is higher than the cost of capital, then the project is worth undertaking. There are circumstances where the IRR method and the NPV method do not give the same result; in these circumstances the NPV method is generally to be preferred. Investment appraisal is not straightforward, since cash inflows and even cash outflows will be subject to uncertainty. An allowance for this can be made by choosing a higher discount factor for risky projects. DCF techniques will not necessarily rank investment projects in the same order of attractiveness as conventional accounting methods, such as **payback** or **return on investment**, which do not allow for the timing of receipts and payments.

discounting 1. The application of a **discount** or **rate of interest** to a **capital** sum. Calculations of present value (see **discounted cash flow**) or the price of a bill before **maturity** are made by discounting at the current appropriate rate of interest. **2.** The future effects of an anticipated event, e.g. a decline in **profit**, are said to be discounted if selling leads to an adjustment of present prices in line with expected future changes in these prices.

discretionary account (DA) Funds for investment placed with a

stockbroker, **commodity** broker or other authorized investment
manager, with either no, or only general, instructions as to how
they should be invested. The broker decides upon the distribution
of the investments and keeps the client informed of purchases, sales
and the value of the **portfolio**. An account in which a **broker** or
manager may trade without the prior assent of the **principal**.

discretionary funds See **discretionary account**.

disintermediation Flows of funds between borrowers and lenders
avoiding the direct use of **financial intermediaries** whose normal
role is to carry out the intermediation between the users of funds
and the suppliers of funds. Disintermediation occurs, e.g., when
companies withdraw funds from the banks and lend them directly
to each other or issue bills guaranteed (accepted) by the banks but
sold to non-banks. Disintermediation may make it more difficult to
measure and control the **money supply** and indeed is often moti-
vated by a desire to avoid **credit controls**.

dispersion, measures of The variation of the values of any
variable from the **average** or between the extremes. See **standard
deviation**.

disponibilités monétaires (Fr.) The French term for the monetary
aggregate *M1*. See **money supply**.

disponibilités quasi-monétaires (Fr.) The French term for the
monetary aggregate *M3*. See **money supply**.

distributed earnings Profits paid to **shareholders** in the form of
dividends, as distinct from **retained earnings**.

divergence indicator See **European Monetary System** (EMS).

dividend The amount of a company's **profit** distributed to ordinary
shareholders; usually expressed either as a percentage of the *nominal
value* (see **par value**) of the **ordinary share** capital, or as an
absolute amount per **share**. A dividend is the same as a **yield** only
where the shares stand at their nominal value. The amount of the
dividend is decided by the board of directors depending upon
profitability and the need for **retained earnings**. Where profitability is poor, if the outlook is good, then the dividend may be

maintained at the previous year's level or even increased out of **reserves**. The profits after tax from which dividends are paid are those after payments to holders of **preference shares** and **debentures** have been allowed for, the balance being split between dividends and reserves.

Dividends are paid to shareholders after deduction of **income tax** at the lower rate, **corporation tax** where applicable having already been paid out by the company. The larger **quoted companies** pay dividends quarterly or biannually (*interim dividends*). In these instances the last dividend declared in the **financial year** is known as the final dividend. See also **cum-dividend**, **ex-dividend**.

dividend check See **dividend warrant**.

dividend cover (UK) The number of times the net **profits** available for distribution exceed the **dividend** actually paid or declared. In US terminology the *pay-out ratio* is the dividend as a percentage of the profit available.

dividend stripping Buying **fixed-interest securities** when they have gone **ex-dividend** and selling them before the next **dividend** is paid, so as to avoid receiving dividends that in some countries are taxed at a higher rate than **capital gains**. Also called *bond washing*.

dividend warrant The **cheque** by which companies pay **dividends** to **shareholders**. US = *dividend check*.

dividend yield See **yield**.

Divisia monetary aggregates A theory of money measurement that assigns index numbers to money forms, based on rates of return, indicating the weighting to be used in adding them together. Named after the French economist.

DKV See **Deutsche Kassenverein**.

DM (Ger.) The German mark, unit of German currency; an abbreviation of 'die deutsche Mark'. The two initials are generally used, or the form D-mark or Deutschmark; otherwise problems with the inflection of the adjective *deutsche* would arise.

documentary credit Credit advanced by a bank to a buyer of goods, under which the bank pays the seller immediately and receives payment from the buyer at the end of a specified period, subject to receiving a specified set of shipping documents.

dollar pool (UK) The pool of foreign currency (chiefly in dollars) available under UK **exchange control** for the purchase by UK residents of foreign **securities** and residential property. The pool was fed only by sales of existing securities and property, no currency being furnished by the **Bank of England** for new acquisitions. Accordingly such currency became available only at a premium, which varied according to the level of demand. At one time the pool actually shrank in consequence of a ruling that 25% of the foreign currency value of such overseas property was to be surrendered, on sale, to the Bank of England. The system was disbanded on the abolition of exchange control in 1979. The dollar pool was also variously known as the *premium pool* and the *investment currency pool*.

domestic open market desk (US) See **open market desk**.

DOT See **designated order turnaround**.

double auction An auction in which both bids (see **bid price**) and offers (see **offer price**) are made competitively; the normal form of **open outcry** trading in **commodity markets**.

double-entry bookkeeping The accounting system in which every business transaction, whether a receipt or payment of money, sale or purchase of goods or services, gives rise to two entries, a debit and a corresponding credit, traditionally on opposite pages of a ledger. Since every debit entry has an equal and corresponding credit entry, it follows that the book will (or should) balance.

double option An **option** conveying the right either to buy or to sell the underlying asset, equivalent to a combined *put* and **call option**. Only one of the alternatives may be exercised. The **deposit** is double that of a put or a call option.

double taxation The situation in which the same tax base, e.g. personal income, is taxed more than once. Double-taxation agreements are designed to avoid, e.g., incomes of non-residents being taxed both in the country where they live and in their country of origin. See also **tax credit**.

Dow-Jones Composite See **Dow-Jones indexes**.

Dow-Jones indexes (US) Dow-Jones & Co. compiles daily indices of the closing prices of **securities** quoted on the **New York Stock Exchange**. The Dow-Jones Industrial Average (DJIA) measures changes in the unweighted arithmetic average of 30 leading industrial shares (using a variable divisor to clean out the effect of **stock splits**). There are similar indices for 15 public utility stocks (DJ Utility Average), 20 transportation stocks (DJ Transportation Average) and an average for all 65 stocks called the Dow-Jones Composite or 65 Stock Average. There is also a Dow-Jones 40 Bond Average, a municipal bond index and a commodity future index.

Dow-Jones Industrial Average See **Dow-Jones indexes**.

down-and-in call/put option An **option** that is not valid until the price of the underlying security falls below a specified price.

down-and-out call/put option An **option** that becomes valueless when the underlying security falls below a specified price.

downstream (US) To take action anticipating a later stage in a chain of financial operations, e.g. the issue of **commercial paper** at market rates by a bank holding company for on-lending to the subsidiary bank, thus enabling the latter to accumulate **liabilities** in the face of official limits on the level of interest rates that may be offered to depositors.

dragon bond A **foreign bond** issued in the markets of Far Eastern countries. Most purchasers have been found in Hong Kong, with some also in Singapore and South Korea. See also **dragons**.

dragons Second wave of *newly industrialized countries* (NICs) in Asia – Indonesia, Malaysia, the Philippines and Thailand – following the **tigers**.

drawdown The drawing of the funds available under a bank

credit, usually a **Eurocredit**, the term normally being used where drawdown is in stages, e.g. *flexible drawdown*.

drawing rights The mechanism by which member countries of the **International Monetary Fund** (IMF) receive financial assistance from that body when in balance of payments difficulties. The drawing right is the right to borrow needed foreign currency from the IMF. The amount available is fixed in relation to the member's own contribution to the IMF's central funds, its **quota**. 25% of the quota is available automatically on demand; a further 25% may be obtained without great difficulty. Succeeding portions, or **tranches**, may be obtained only subject to conditions, chiefly in regard to economic policy, of increasing rigour. In 1970 a drawing right denominated in a group of currencies and intended as a new form of *international liquidity* (see **liquidity**) was created, known as **special drawing rights** (SDRs).

drittmarkt (Den.) The second-tier **unlisted securities market** at the Copenhagen **stock exchange**. Also called Bors III because the stock exchange formerly had two upper segments, Bors I and Bors II, which differentiated listed companies according to their **market capitalization**.

droit de timbre (Fr.) **Stamp duty**.

drop-lock A **bond** that earns a floating return but automatically switches to a fixed return if **rates of interest** fall below a predetermined level.

DTB See **Deutsche Terminborse**.

DTC See **Depository Trust Company**.

dual capacity The situation where a **market maker** can buy or sell shares to and from members of the public or other members of the **stock exchange** without the need for a **broker**. The market maker acts as both **jobber** and broker.

due diligence The analysis and appraisal of a business in preparation for a **flotation** or **venture capital** investment. Investors have a right to expect that these investigations are carried out thoroughly.

durée (Fr.) Maturity.

DVP See **delivery versus payment**.

dynamic risk Of insurance, a **risk** arising out of change caused by people, e.g. changes in economic policy, in technology, in competition.

EAGGF See **European Agricultural Guidance and Guarantee Fund**.

early stage investments Investment by **venture capital** institutions in the provision of *seed capital* (funds to finance research and development before a business is operating) and start-up finance for new companies.

earmarking The assignment of moneys in the **central fund** of **Lloyd's of London** to cover a deficiency arising where a member's assets (see **funds at Lloyd's** and **premium trust fund**) do not equal their liabilities.

earn-out Tying the purchase price paid for a company to future earnings. If the company performs less well than expected, for example, a final instalment on the purchase price many not fall due. A *ratchet* is a similar arrangement sometimes used by **venture capital** institutions to motivate the management of the companies they finance by giving them a large share in **equity** if performance is better than expected.

earned income Income from wages, salaries and certain **pensions** and social security benefits that are treated as earned income for tax purposes. In the UK in the past, and in many countries still, earned income was taxed on a more favourable basis than *unearned income*, which includes dividends, interest and other investment income.

earnings per share (EPS) The total **profits** of a company after **taxation** and **interest**, divided by the number of **shares** at issue. Earnings per share will usually be higher than the **dividend** per share, because some earnings will be retained in the company and not distributed as dividends.

earnings yield See **yield**.

East African Tea Trade Association A **commodity** market set up in Nairobi in 1958, trading in black tea.

Eastern Europe Capital markets, including **banking** systems, **stock exchanges** and **commodity markets**, are developing rapidly in the Eastern European countries, which are in transition from centrally planned to market economies. The former Yugoslavia was the most advanced, but civil war has halted activity. The Budapest Stock Exchange opened in mid-1990, and the Warsaw Stock Exchange, for which the share index is the Wig Index, opened in April 1991. There are commodity markets in Sofia, Budapest, Moscow and elsewhere. See also **Moscow Central Stock Exchange**.

EBRD See **European Bank for Reconstruction and Development**.

EBS See **Electronic Broking Service**.

EC See **European Union**.

écart (Fr.) **Spread**.

ECGD (UK) **Export Credit Guarantee Department**.

échéance (Fr.) **Maturity**.

ECHO See **Exchange Clearing House**.

Economic and Monetary Union (EMU) See **European Union** (EU), **Maastricht Treaty**.

economic structural adjustment programme See **International Bank for Reconstruction and Development**.

ECP See **Euro-commercial paper**, **Euro-Commercial Paper Programme**.

ECSC European Coal and Steel Community. See **European Union**.

ECU European Currency Unit. See **European Monetary System**.

ECU deposit A **deposit** made in European Currency Units (see **European Monetary System**).

EDF See **European Development Fund**.

Edgar (US) Electronic **disclosure** system for the receipt, storage, retrieval and dissemination of public documents filed with the **Securities and Exchange Commission**.

Edge Act 1919 (US) Legislation that first permitted US banks to set up subsidiaries to engage in banking activities overseas.

EDI See **electronic data interchange**.

EDSP (UK) See **exchange delivery settlement price**.

EEC European Economic Community. See **European Union**.

EEIG See **European Economic Interest Grouping**.

EFAS European Financial Analysts' Society.

Effekten (Ger.) See **securities**.

effets privés (Fr.) Generic term for **private-sector money-market instruments**.

efficient market hypothesis (EMH) The theory that all available information affecting the price of a **security** will be immediately reflected in that price.

EFL See **external financial limit**.

EFMA European Financial Marketing Association.

EFP See **exchange for physical**.

EFT See **electronic funds transfer**.

EFTA See **European Free Trade Association**.

EFTPOS See **electronic funds transfer at point of sale**.

EIB See **European Investment Bank**.

eigyo tokkin **funds** (Jap.) Funds illegally placed by companies with **securities** houses against a guaranteed rate of return (guarantees of rates are illegal).

Einheitskurs (Ger.) A method of trading on the **stock exchange**, under which each **security** is traded at a single price only once each day.

elastic currency (US) The doctrine that a domestic **currency** should meet the needs of trade, through a stable relationship between the expansion of business activity and the expansion of **credit**. Also known as the *real bills doctrine*.

electronic banking The automated facility to call up bank account details, give instructions for payments and make use of other services by means of a computer, **modem** and telephone line or **viewdata** system. Used by businesses; retail customers appear to prefer **telephone banking**.

Electronic Broking Service (EBS) An automated **broking** system for **currency** dealing, developed by a consortium of major exchange trading banks in conjunction with Quotron, a specialist informatics company, and introduced in 1993. The EBS is in competition with two similar systems: Reuters 2000-2, launched in 1992; and Minex, created by a consortium of Japanese banks, together with the Japanese telecom company KDD and Dow-Jones Telerate, and introduced in 1993.

electronic data interchange (EDI) Means by which organizations may send and receive data, e.g. on orders, insurance contracts for processing and invoices and payments.

electronic funds transfer at point of sale (EFTPOS) (UK) A system that allows the automatic transfer of money from a buyer to a seller of goods or services at the time of sale. In the UK, EFTPOS is not yet widespread, with only Barclays' Connect card being promoted for the purpose.

electronic funds transfer (EFT) system A system for the automatic transfer of funds from one account to another by electronic means, e.g. **electronic funds transfer at point of sale**.

electronic mail or e-mail A system for sending messages automatically between computers via mailbox numbers using telephone or private circuits. Also refers to the message itself.

Electronic Price Information Computer (EPIC) (UK) The

original **London Stock Exchange** system for recording and transmitting price via TOPIC (see **Stock Exchange Automated Quotation System**).

eligible bill 1. A **bank bill** issued by a bank on the **eligible list**, which may be **rediscounted** at the Bank of England. 2. **Eligible paper** (US).

eligible liabilities (ELs) (UK) A measure of the **deposits** of the UK commercial banks used in the exercise of **monetary policy** by the **Bank of England**. With a view to limiting the degree to which banks could lend out their deposit holdings, the Bank of England required them to place a certain proportion of their eligible liabilities with it, as **special deposits** and **supplementary special deposits**. Eligible liabilities were defined as: sterling deposits, up to two years' **maturity**, of UK residents; all net sterling deposits of banks; all net holdings of **certificates of deposit**; and net liabilities in non-sterling **currencies**. See also **interest-bearing eligible liabilities**, **liquidity ratio**.

eligible list (UK) A list of banks entitled to discount acceptances at the Bank of England.

eligible paper (US) US **bankers' acceptances** that may be **rediscounted** at the **Federal Reserve**. They broadly comprise acceptances in respect of foreign trade or documented home deliveries of less than six months' **maturity**, and in respect of staple goods in receipted storage.

eligible reserves (US) Forms (**vault cash** plus balances at **Federal Reserve banks**) in which banks' **required reserves** must be held.

EMA See **European Monetary Agreement**.

EMCOF European Monetary Co-operation Fund. See **European Monetary System**.

emerging markets Security **markets** in **newly industrialized countries**, in **Eastern Europe** and in other countries with **capital markets** at an early stage of development.

Some emerging equity markets
31 December 1992

	Equity market value £m
Hong Kong	113,595
Delhi	108,469
Mexico	91,641
South Korea	71,110
Taiwan	66,155
Kuala Lumpur	60,418
Quito	48,707
Thailand	37,532
Singapore	31,321
Rio de Janeiro	29,998

Source: *Stock Exchange Quarterly*, April–June 1993. Reproduced with permission.

émission (Fr.) **Issue**.

Employee Retirement Income Security Act 1974 (ERISA) (US) Law regulating private **pensions** plans. Provisions included the setting up of the Pension Benefit Guarantee Corporation (PBGC), which protects beneficiaries in corporate pension schemes from loss in the event of insolvency or premature termination of a pension scheme.

employees' buy-out The purchase of all the **shares** of a **company** by its employees. An example of such a buy-out was that of the National Freight Corporation on **privatization**. See also **management buy-out**.

employees stock ownership plan (ESOP) A scheme to allow employees to acquire shares in the company in which they work. In the UK, ESOPs are employee share ownership plans that differ from Inland Revenue-approved profit-sharing schemes in that employees are liable to income tax when the shares are transferred at less than their market value. However, the costs of ESOPs borne by employers are deductible for **corporation tax** purposes.

emprunt (Fr.) **Loan**, loan **stock**.

EMS See **European Monetary System**.

EMU See **Economic and Monetary Union**.

endaka (Jap.) Literally 'high yen'. A term describing the yen's appreciation (see **appreciate**) after the **Plaza Agreement** of September 1985.

endowment life assurance See **life assurance**.

Enterprise Investment Scheme (EIS) (UK) A scheme providing 20% up-front **income tax** relief on investments by private individuals in the shares of qualifying unquoted companies (see **unlisted company**) and on **capital gains** and tax relief on losses. Capital gains are tax free. Investors are allowed to become paid directors. This replaced the **Business Expansion Scheme** in January 1994.

E&O, E&OE See **errors and omissions**.

EOE See **European Options Exchange**.

EPC See **European political co-operation**.

EPP Estate protection policy.

EPS See **earnings per share**.

equalization of pensions Equal entitlement to **pensions** for men and women. Three cases submitted to the European Court of Justice in 1990 – the Barber case, the Ten Oever case and the Coloroll case – questioned the unequal pension rights of men and women. These cases were based on Article 119 of the **Treaty of Rome**, which requires equal pay for equal work. By 1993 the Court had ruled that pensions deriving from contributions made on or after 17 May 1990 should be equalized. However, problems remain, arising from the actuarial implications of women's greater longevity and from the fact that state pensions still have to be equalized.

equity The residual value of a company's **assets** after all **liabilities** (other than those to holders of **ordinary shares**) have been allowed for. The equity of a company is the property of the ordinary shareholders, hence these shares are popularly called equities (UK). In a **mortgage** or **hire-purchase contract**, equity is the amount left for the borrower if the asset concerned is sold and the lender repaid.

equity gearing (UK) The ratio of borrowings to **equity** or risk capital. See also **capital gearing**, **gearing**.

equity kicker See **mezzanine**.

ERDF See **European Regional Development Fund**.

ERISA See **Employee Retirement Income Security Act**.

ERM See **Exchange Rate Mechanism**.

Eröffnungskurs (Ger.) **Opening price**.

errors and omissions (E&O) 1. 'Errors and omissions excepted' ('E&OE') used to be included on invoices in an attempt to protect the issuer against clerical mistakes. It had no legal validity, and the term *errors and omissions* (E&O) is now little used except in the sense of: 2. A cause of faulty accounts or records, against which insurance is frequently taken out. In **Lloyd's of London**, the E&O insurance of managing and members' agents, normally placed within the market, stands as the first source of finance for agents requiring to meet compensation claims from **action groups**.

ESAP Economic structural adjustment programme. See **International Bank for Reconstruction and Development**.

escompte (Fr.) **Discount**.

escrow, escrow account An escrow is a document of agreement held by a third party until one or both of the other two parties have fulfilled certain conditions. Thus funds on an escrow account will be released by a bank when agreed conditions are met.

estate protection reinsurance Cover, in the event of death, for all outstanding **underwriting liabilities** of a member of **Lloyd's of London**.

estoppel The doctrine that forbids a person from denying a truth already admitted by them. In **insurance**, the doctrine prohibits an insurer, having begun to deal with a claim known by them to be faulty, from refusing to continue.

étalon-or (Fr.) **Gold standard**.

EU See **European Union**.

Euratom European Atomic Energy Community. See **European Union**.

Euro-commercial paper (ECP) Commercial paper (CP) issued in a Eurocurrency (see **Eurodollar**). The Euro-commercial market can be said to have been established in 1985. There is no underwriting commitment by banks; the paper is normally issued direct or through dealers. The market is chiefly centred on London. Some linkage both with the US domestic commercial paper market, often through **swing lines**, and with other domestic CP markets has recently come about. Daily publication of interest rates by the Bank of England began in August 1987. In 1992 total issues outstanding were reckoned at $8.2bn, after some years of decline, attributed to overcapacity. In 1993 the French authorities decreed that *sociétés d'investissement à capital variable* (**unit trusts**) should not hold more than 10% of their assets in Euro-paper or other unregulated investments. See also **BONUS** (borrower's option for notes and underwritten standby), **non-underwritten**, **underwritten**.

Euro-commercial paper programme (ECP) See **non-underwritten**.

Eurobond A **bond** issued in a **currency** other than that of the country or market in which it is issued; i.e. a bond composed of claims in a particular currency but held outside the country of that currency. Eurobonds are identical in principle to **Eurodollars** or **Eurocurrencies** and arose out of the Eurodollar and Eurocurrency market. Most Eurobonds are **bearer securities**, and interest is paid without deduction of tax. Eurobonds are normally sold by international **syndicates** of banks, are **medium term** and **long term** in nature, are usually issued by governments, international organizations and large public bodies and are bought for the main part by wealthy individuals and families. Eurobonds can be **convertible** or **straight**. There are two main settlement clearing houses, **Euroclear** and **Centrale de Livraison de Valeurs Mobilières** (CEDEL). See also **Euroequity**, **Eurosterling bond**.

Euroclear One of the two settlement systems for **Eurobonds**, formed by a number of banks and securities houses under the leadership of Morgan Guaranty and set up in Brussels in 1968. It provides clearing house, accounting and dividend collection services, as well as providing working capital to dealers through Morgan Guaranty. See also **Centrale de Livraison de Valeurs Mobilières** (CEDEL).

Eurocredit A loan, generally at **medium term**, made by a bank in a **Eurocurrency**. The loan is always large, not less than $500,000, and is usually raised by **syndication**. See also **Euronote facility**.

Eurocurrency A **currency** used in the **Euromarket**. See **Eurodollar**.

Eurocurrency market See **Eurodollar**.

Eurodeposit See **Eurodollar**.

Eurodollar A deposit in dollars in a US bank held outside the USA, e.g. a credit account with a bank in New York held by a French bank in Paris. The characteristic of Eurodollars is that they are on-lent by the holders to other banks or individuals outside the USA. The practice was begun in the 1950s by Eastern European bank branches in the main Western European banking centres, specifically, it is said, by the Moscow Narodny Bank in London, which held unspent balances in the USA that they feared might be frozen. Accordingly they lent them to other Western European parties. Other banks then followed suit, the practice being nourished by the continuance over decades of US **balance of payments** deficits, which produced a flood of credit balances surplus to the requirements of their holders outside the USA.

The advantage to the holders of Eurodollar accounts, which at first had been that of the avoidance of exchange transactions and of a possible profit on interest rate **arbitrage**, quickly became that of participation in a large international money market, into and out of which parties could move easily. The market was further advantaged by the fact that interest on the US deposit was free of withholding tax and also of **Regulation Q**, and so was further enhanced by the movement into it of US companies and bank branches based abroad, anxious to share in these advantages. It was also enhanced by the US banks' willingness to create Eurodeposits, given their freedom in the setting of interest rates.

The Eurodollar market has been thought to bring about the continuous creation of **credit** in accordance with the usual bank **multiplier**, in that it produces a succession of bank deposits from which new advances can be generated. In the light of this, the absence of any control by national banking authorities causes some concern. There has, however, been much argument as to whether the total volume of credit has been enlarged, given that the inherent movement has been the onlending of the same deposit between banks outside the US banking system. The use of the deposit by non-banks for payment, thus leading to the creation of further deposits in the US banking system, does not in principle cause a multiplication of credits greater than would have occurred by the use of the same deposit by domestic US transactors. In short, it has been argued that the Eurodollar market has increased the **velocity**, but not the **volume**, of the US **money supply**.

With the advent of **certificates of deposit** the market was further enlarged. A further development was the emergence of the **Eurobond** market, for longer-term loans. The Eurodollar technique was quickly adopted for other currencies, the market in these for some time being erroneously referred to as the Eurodollar market. These are now known under their respective names, the whole complex being referred to as the Eurocurrency market.

Termed *Euro*dollar because the first participants were in Europe, the market quickly ceased to bear out that title, with dealing taking place in Japan and in most other parts of the world.

Euroequity An international equity issue made on **stock exchanges** outside the country in which the company whose **stock** is being issued is based and denominated in a foreign currency. Since **exchange rates** fluctuate, the issue of equity in multiple currencies by established companies may create problems.

Euromarket The generic term for all transactions in **Eurocurrencies**, namely bank lending in Eurocurrencies, **Eurobonds**, **Euronotes**, **Euro–commercial paper**, **Euroequity**.

Euronote A **note** used in a **Euronote facility** issued in **bearer** form and **negotiable**. Euronotes are invariably **short term**. They have been issued chiefly in US dollars, but other currencies have been used, including ECUs (European Currency Units; see **European Union**) and Singapore dollars. **Non-banks** have been increasing purchasers since 1983, with the result that the **spread** has come to be related more to the *London interbank bid rate* (LIBID) than to the **London interbank offered rate** (LIBOR).

Euronote facility A form of **note issuance facility** (NIF) for the issue of **Euronotes** managed by a group of banks, or **syndicate**, and guaranteed by the latter. A **front-end fee** and a **commitment fee** are charged by the syndicate to the issuer. Euronote facilities were first introduced in 1981. Where banks provide the underlying credit by buying the notes, this is done by inviting a tender panel of banks to subscribe. Otherwise the notes are sold by *placement* organized by a sole placing agent. In either event, the syndicate **underwrites** the issue by undertaking to buy any notes not taken up, or supplies **back-up credit**. The term *Euronote facility* is sometimes used, more loosely, to refer to **Euro-commercial paper** issues.

European Agricultural Guidance and Guarantee Fund (EAGGF) A fund, set up under the common agricultural policy of the **European Union**, whose function is to purchase all agricultural products, when offered to it, at a fixed minimum price and, in theory, to sell produce stocks when prices are high; also to finance the modernization of, and reduction of costs in, Union agriculture. The EAGGF has been heavily criticized for its substantial expenditure, which has amounted over most of the existence of the Union (and previously the European Community) to between 65% and 80% of the total budget.

European Atomic Energy Community (Euratom) See **European Union** (EU).

European Bank for Reconstruction and Development (EBRD) An intergovernmental financial institution founded in 1990 to finance industrial and economic development in the countries of Eastern Europe by means of loans, guarantees, equity investment and underwriting. The EBRD has a membership of 43 countries, comprising all member states of the **European Union** and of the **Organization for Economic Co-operation and Development** (OECD), virtually all Eastern European countries – including the separate states of the former Soviet Union – Mexico, a number of African and Middle Eastern countries, the European Commission and the European Investment Bank. The EBRD had initial capital of ECUs 10bn ($12.2bn), of which 51% was subscribed by the EC and its member countries, 10% by the USA and $8\frac{1}{2}$% by Japan, with the remainder coming from other non-EC and non-OECD members and the countries of Eastern Europe itself. There was a board of 23 directors. Some disquiet was occasioned by the disclosure at the end of 1992 that the EBRD had spent some $300m on fitting out its headquarters, as against only $150m disbursed in financial aid; this led to the resignation of the bank's first president, Jacques Attali, and the institution of various reforms.

European Coal and Steel Community (ECSC) See **European Union** (EU).

European Community (EC) See **European Union** (EU).

European Currency Unit (ECU) See **European Monetary System** (EMS).

European Development Fund (EDF) A fund set up by the European Community (see **European Union**) in 1976 for the provision of aid finance to developing countries associated with the then EC (now EU) through the Lomé Convention; to certain non-associated states; and to a number of developing countries in the Mediterranean Basin. The funds are dispensed under five-year programmes in the form of grants and loans on advantageous terms. Sixty-six countries benefit under the Lomé Convention, and a further 14 under the Mediterranean programme. The fund's capital is supplied by the member states and it is administered by the European Commission. Annual outlays are about £2bn.

European Economic Area See **European Free Trade Association** (EFTA).

European Economic Community (EEC) See **European Union** (EU).

European economic interest grouping (EEIG) A recognized form of grouping that allows companies incorporated in the **European Union** (EU) to establish joint ventures employing up to 500 people throughout the EC without **capitalization** and with the simplification of **fiscal transparency**.

European Free Trade Association (EFTA) A group of countries that have removed import duties (see **tariffs**) on imports from each other. EFTA was formed in 1959 by Austria, Denmark, Norway, Portugal, Sweden, Switzerland and the UK. Finland effectively joined in 1961 and Iceland in 1970. Denmark and the UK left in 1973 and Portugal in 1986 on joining the European Community (EC) (see **European Union**). After negotiations that began in 1984, EFTA and the EC reached agreement in 1992 for a European Economic Area that would include the member countries of both institutions.

European Investment Bank (EIB) An international bank formed in 1958 by the then European Community (see **European Union**) to provide loan finance for member countries and associated countries, for the purposes of regional development, projects of common interest to the EC and projects for modernization and conversion. The bank finances itself through its capital, contributed by member countries, and by loans at fine rates raised on the international **capital market**.

European Monetary Agreement (EMA) see **Organization for European Economic Co-operation** (OEEC).

European Monetary Co-operation Fund (EMCOF) see **European Monetary System** (EMS).

European Monetary System (EMS) Instituted by the then European Community (see **European Union**, EU) in 1979 with two main purposes: (i) to stabilize the currencies of member states; and (ii) to create a joint reserve fund and ultimately a common monetary system, including a common currency.

(i) An Exchange Rate Mechanism (ERM) was set up. A European monetary unit known as the European Currency Unit (ECU) was created as a composite of the member countries' currencies weighted in accordance with country shares in EC (now EU) output; so 1 ECU = DM0.719 + FFr1.310 + L140 + FL0.256 + FrB3.71 + FrLux0.14 + £stg0.0378 + £Ire0.00871 + DKr0.217 + Dr1.15. The ECU fluctuates as a whole in relation to non-EU currencies. Member countries maintain their national currencies in a strict relationship (a central parity) to the ECU, being allowed to depart from this parity only by a margin determined for each currency (a divergence indicator). The ERM was an integral part of the EMS, requiring close alignment of EC currencies. Under this mechanism, EC currencies were permitted to diverge from each other only by a fixed percentage, ± 2.25% (Italy ± 6%). This was a resumption of an earlier version of the same mechanism, known as the Snake, which had operated fitfully in the 1970s. The UK entered the ERM only in 1990. In September 1992 severe turbulence in the foreign exchange market brought about the withdrawal of the UK and Italy from the mechanism, and forced general adjustments in the relative parities of the remaining members. In July/August 1993 renewed turbulence led to the widening of the permitted divergence to ± 30%, and the future of the ERM remained uncertain. The ECU is used for the internal accounting of the European Union institutions. It has also been used in private syndicated loans, for bond issues and for money market deposits.

(ii) A European Monetary Co-operation Fund (EMCOF) has been established by crediting ECUs to member countries in exchange for their depositing 20% of their gold and foreign exchange **reserves**. The UK has participated in this arrangement. The fund serves as a clearing house for the **central bank** operations in maintaining national currency alignment in accordance with the EMS. In due course the fund is intended to be replaced by a European Monetary Fund, which would act as a central bank for a fully integrated Union monetary and currency system, i.e. with a single currency after European Monetary Union (see **Maastricht Treaty**). See also **intervention mechanism**, **medium term financial assistance** (MTFA), **short-term monetary support** (STMS).

European Monetary Union (EMU) See **Maastricht Treaty**.

European Options Exchange (EOE) A market for *traded options* (see **option**) founded in Amsterdam in 1978. The market operates within the Amsterdam Stock Exchange. Trade is in options in gold and silver and in certain **currencies** and **securities.**

European Payments Union (EPU) See **Organization for European Economic Co-operation** (OEEC).

European Political Co-operation See **European Union** (EU).

European Recovery Programme See **Organization for European Economic Co-operation** (OEEC).

European Regional Development Fund (ERDF) Established in 1975 by the European Community (see **European Union**), the ERDF makes grants, normally to the governments of member states, for the purpose of improving the infrastructure in regions showing particular need, e.g. the assisted areas of the UK and the Mezzogiorno of Italy. The grants can be made only in relation to investment programmes presented by member-state governments and are intended to supplement, rather than replace, money spent by the latter. Grants are usually made up to a quota established for each Union member.

European style An **option** that can be **exercised** only at expiry.

European Union (EU) The European Union, until 1992 known as the European Community (EC), comprises three component communities: the European Coal and Steel Community (ECSC), founded in 1952 under the Treaty of Paris of 1951; the European Economic Community (EEC), founded in 1958 under the Treaty of Rome of 1957; and the European Atomic Energy Community (Euratom), also founded in 1958 under a separate Treaty of Rome of 1957. At the outset each Community had a separate Council, in which member-country ministers made policy decisions; a separate central administration, the High Authority in the case of the ESCS and the Commission in the case of the EEC and Euratom; separate provision for the industries for which they were responsible (coal and steel in the case of ECSC, atomic energy in that of Euratom and all others in that of the EEC); a separate court of justice; and separate financial resources, levied on member states.

Under the Treaty of Brussels of 1965 the institutions were

amalgamated into a single Council, Commission, Court of Justice and Parliament, and common revenues were set up. However, policy and administrative decisions continued to be taken in line with the provisions of the individual treaties. In 1978 specific member-state contributions for the financing of the then Community were replaced by a system of own resources under which the Community claimed an automatic proportion of the import duty and value added tax (VAT) revenues arising in the member states.

The original membership of the European Community comprised Belgium, France, West Germany, Italy, Luxembourg and the Netherlands. In 1973 these were joined by the UK, Ireland and Denmark, in 1981 by Greece and in 1986 by Spain and Portugal.

The purposes of the Community were at the outset to achieve far-reaching integration of the member countries' economies and, less well defined, a single Western European economy and a cohesive, if not federal, political framework. These purposes were to be attained primarily through the principle of supranationality, i.e. through the paramountcy of Community legislation over national laws, and by majority rather than unanimous voting on policy decisions. These principles were to be translated into common policies for the free movement of goods, services, labour and capital throughout the Community.

Total elimination of national tariffs was achieved by 1961, as was the establishment of a common external commercial policy and a common agricultural policy. The planned introduction of majority voting met with French opposition in 1965 and was indefinitely postponed. Other policy objectives, such as common transport and energy policies, proved difficult to attain. Some progress in financial policies was achieved through the establishment in 1978 of the **European Monetary System** (EMS) and the extensive alignment of Community exchange rates. In 1979 direct elections to the European Parliament were instituted, and further powers accrued to this body. By the 1980s a measure of consultation and common action on foreign affairs had been attained.

A major advance in EC integration was denoted by the Single European Act (SEA), signed in February 1986, and ratified in the following year. The SEA was in itself a document amending and expanding the three original treaties of the European Community so as to bring about its desired objectives. In signing, the member states stated their intention to be 'to transform relations . . . among their States into a European Union'. Two basic changes in procedure were: (i) abolition of the right of veto, i.e. the substitution of majority voting for unanimous voting on proposed legislation, on all subjects except taxation, free movement of people and the 'rights and interests of employed persons' (essentially wages); and (ii) greater involvement of the European Parliament in the legislative process.

A major element of the Single Act was a commitment to complete the unification of the internal market: 'an area without internal frontiers in which the free movement of goods, persons, services and capital is ensured'. To this end, a programme of some 300 measures, to be incorporated in Community/Union law by 31 December 1992, was agreed. By the due date 95% of the programme had indeed been adopted, although it was estimated that only half of this had been 'transposed' – enacted into national law – by the member states. A number of articles built on the EMS to fore-shadow an Economic and Monetary Union (EMU), and on this basis a project for a European central bank and an eventual common currency was elaborated. Some further articles were used as the basis for a 'social charter' enunciating the rights of workers, signed in 1989 by all member states except the UK. Other articles called for greater alignment of economic conditions in the regions of the Community; for various efforts in the fields of research and develop-ment and the environment; and for the further development of European Political Co-operation (EPC), particularly in foreign policy. The European Community was renamed the European Union following agreement of the **Maastricht Treaty** in 1992.

Eurosterling bond A **Eurobond** denominated in British pounds.

ex-coupon See **ex-dividend**.

ex-dividend (xd) Without **dividend**. The purchaser of a **security** quoted ex-dividend does not have the right to the next dividend when due; this belongs to the seller. The prefix *ex-*, meaning 'excluding', is also used in a similar sense in several other ways, e.g. *ex-coupon* excludes the next interest payment on a fixed-interest

security; *ex-rights* means that there is no entitlement to a **rights issue**; *ex-warrant* excludes rights to a forthcoming warrant issue; *ex-all* (US) excludes all impending benefits (see **bonus issue**).

ex gratia Action taken, or payment made, in order to reach a settlement while denying formal liability.

ex-parte The action by one party to a matter where other parties are absent.

ex-rights See **ex-dividend**.

excess 1. Of **shares**, the quantity remaining unsold and available for other buyers after a **rights issue**. 2. Of bank reserves (US), a level of cash higher than that required by law or convention. As this impeded the **Federal Reserve**'s power to influence the bank's operations, authority to regulate cash levels was given to the Federal Reserve. 3. Of insurance, the amount of the **risk** to be borne by the **policy**-holder or, in the case of **reinsurance treaties**, by the *ceding insurer* (see **cedant**). See also **excess of loss treaty**.

excess of loss See **excess**.

excess of loss reinsurance Excess of loss cover as for normal insurance, but with an upper limit on the cover. See **excess.**

excess of loss treaty A **non-proportional reinsurance treaty** under which a reinsurer refunds to the insurer the amount of all claims paid by the latter over and above a predetermined limit.

excess reserves (US) Reserves held by banks and other financial institutions over and above **required reserves**.

exchange 1. A market, e.g. a **commodity** exchange or **commodity market**. 2. Foreign currencies or **foreign exchange**. 3. Any form of trade.

Exchange Clearing House (ECHO) A **clearing house** for **foreign exchange derivatives** contracts, established by Barclays Bank, Commerzbank, Rabobank and Banque Nationale de Paris.

exchange control A method by which governments seek to control the **exchange rate** of their national **currency** and to preserve the national **reserves**, consisting in the imposition of limitations or prohibitions on the movement of currency across national frontiers. Exchange control normally operates on payments to foreigners, since these place an immediate demand on foreign-currency holdings; receipts of foreign currency and of domestic currency originating from abroad are also frequently controlled. Exchange control is in the main operated on the capital account of the **balance of payments**, too great a restriction on the current account being likely to endanger the country's essential trade. Restrictions on the capital account may take the form of an outright ban on the use of foreign currency for portfolio investment, and restrictions on the type and conditions of direct investment that may be tolerated. Foreign currency for private travel is nearly always strictly constrained.

All industrialized countries have, over time, enforced exchange control, some forms still being maintained, e.g. by France and Italy. The UK operated comprehensive exchange control from the Second World War until 1979, when it was abolished. In the USA the **interest equalization tax**, and in Germany the *Bardepot*, had exchange control purposes. Many developing countries now maintain exchange control. The **International Monetary Fund**, the **Organization for Economic Co-operation and Development** and the **European Union** have all striven for its elimination.

exchange delivery settlement price (UK) The price for delivery or **cash settlement** of the instrument underlying a **derivative** traded in the **London International Financial Futures Exchange** (LIFFE).

exchange for physical A **swap** of a **futures** position in a currency for one in the **spot** market, undertaken when delivery of a currency in a futures contract is desired before the expiry of that contract.

exchange rate The rate at which one **currency** may be exchanged against another, i.e. the number of units of the currency deemed to be equal to one unit of another; e.g. 1.60 units of US$ have been at various times deemed equal to £1 sterling. Terms with a similar meaning are **parity** and **par value**. Exchange rates may be set by supply and demand for the currency (**floating rate**) or may be fixed, i.e. tied or linked to gold (see **gold standard**) or to other currencies. See also **crawling peg**.

Exchange Rate Mechanism (ERM) See **European Union** (EU), **Maastricht Treaty**.

Exchequer (UK) Historically, the financial accounts of the government. More exactly at present, the account kept at the **Bank of England**, through which all government receipts and payments pass.

excise duty Taxes levied upon goods (e.g. alcoholic drinks and tobacco) produced for home consumption as distinct from customs duties or tariffs.

execution 1. Effecting a trade, as when a **broker** buys or sells **securities** in the execution of an **order**. 2. A legal term meaning that a **contract** has been signed, witnessed if necessary and delivered to the respective parties.

execution only The provision of **security** dealing services without advice, research or other services.

executive share options See **profit-sharing scheme**.

exercice (Fr.) **Financial year**.

exercise 1. A **financial year**. 2. To implement a **contract**. 3. To put an **option** into effect, i.e. to buy or sell the **security** that is the subject of the option.

exercise date The date on which an **option** can be **exercised**; usually after three, six or nine months.

exercise notice A formal intimation that an **option** will be **exercised**.

exercise price The price at which the **security**, the subject of an **option**, is agreed to be bought or sold. Also known as the **striking price** or **strike price**.

Eximbank (US, Jap.) See **Export-Import Bank**.

exit The realization of an **investment**, usually in the context of

venture capital, where an **equity** investment in an **unlisted company** may be realized by a trade sale (sold to a larger company or another venture capital company), by a **management buy-out** or by **flotation**.

Export Credit Guarantee Department (ECGD) (UK) Established in 1919, a government department for the provision of insurance cover against risks of default on export credit, and of cover against the risk of expropriation of assets invested abroad. Since the ECGD also covers against official payment and licensing restrictions for the foreign purchase of UK goods and services, it may be said to be the only significant insurer of long-term **sovereign risk**. The ECGD's short-term credit insurance operations were **privatized** in 1991.

Export-Import Bank (Eximbank) (US) Founded in 1934 by the US government, Eximbank provides loans direct to foreign importers of US goods and services, and guarantees and **refinances** export credit granted by US banks. Through the associated **Foreign Credit Insurance Association**, it offers insurance of foreign credits. Operating independently as a Washington, DC, registered bank, Eximbank's task is to operate at a profit. Lending limits are, however, fixed by Congress, and the five members of its board are appointed by the President and confirmed by the Senate.

Export-Import Bank of Japan (Jap.) An institution for the financing of export credit, established in 1950, based on capital supplied by the government, by borrowings from the Trust Fund Bureau and by foreign exchange borrowings from commercial banks.

extended credit (US) Borrowing from the **Federal Reserve** by financial institutions in prolonged reserve shortage; the loans being charged at an interest rate normally above **discount rate**. Since such institutions will not normally deal in the **Federal funds** market, such loans are counted as **non-borrowed reserves**.

external account See **balance of payments**.

external bond A **bond** issued in one country but denominated in the **currency** of another.

external financial limit (EFL) **Cash limits** imposed by the UK government on the borrowing of nationalized industries.

external member A member of **Lloyd's of London** providing capital to the market but not engaged in the actual performance of underwriting. As such members finance the operation, they are properly said also to be underwriting.

FAC See **Food Aid Committee**.

face value See **par value**.

facility A generic term denoting a bank loan in various forms, e.g. **acceptance**, **Eurocredit**, **overdraft**.

factor See **factoring**.

factoring A business activity in which a company takes over responsibility for collecting the **debts** of another. Typically, the client debits all its sales to the factor and receives immediate payment from it less a charge of about 2% to 3% and **interest** for the period of **trade credit** given to the customer. There are a number of different types of factoring; the simplest is invoice discounting. In its most elaborate form the factor maintains the company's sales ledger and other accounting functions, and does not seek recourse to its client if unable to obtain payment from that client's customers (*non-recourse factoring*). The customer need not know that a factor is being used.

facultative reinsurance A **reinsurance** arrangement under which the reinsurer can opt to accept or not to accept any risk offered; contrast treaty reinsurance (see **reinsurance treaty**).

fair value The price of a **derivative** that is equivalent, after transaction costs, to that of the underlying instrument.

FAL See **funds at Lloyd's**.

fallen angel (US) A **bond**, initially of US investment grade quality, subsequently declining below that standard, then sold at high **yield**.

Fälligheit (Ger.) **Maturity**.

Fannie Mae (US) See **Federal Home Loan Bank Board**.

FCIA (US) See **Foreign Credit Insurance Association**.

FDI See **foreign direct investment**.

FDIC See **deposit insurance**.

FECDBA See **Foreign Exchange and Currency Deposit Brokers' Association**.

Fed (US) See **Federal Reserve System**.

Fed funds (US) **Deposits** made by **commercial banks** in their local **Federal Reserve bank**. Fed funds include cash balances in excess of the reserve requirement, which may be loaned to other banks overnight to enable them to meet their reserve requirement. See also **Federal funds rate**, **Federal Reserve System**.

Federal Deposit Insurance Corporation See **deposit insurance**.

Federal funds (US) See **Fed funds**.

Federal funds rate (US) Rate of interest charged on **Fed funds** loaned by and to **commercial banks**. Owing to the large scale of Federal funds borrowing, the rate is regarded by the **Federal Reserve System** regulatory authorities as an important determinant of bank **liquidity**.

Federal funds rate band (US) The target range within which the **Federal Open Market Committee** (FOMC) expects the **Federal funds rate** to vary as specified in the FOMC minutes.

Federal home loan bank (US) Member of a system of 12 US banks established by the Federal Home Loan Act 1932 for the purpose of extending loan credit to institutions engaged in housing credit, such as **savings and loan associations**, building and loan associations, savings banks and insurance companies. The bank's advances are secured by mortgages or by US government bonds. See also **Federal Home Loan Bank Board**.

Federal Home Loan Bank Act See **Federal Home Loan Bank Board**.

Federal Home Loan Bank Board (FHLBB) (US) Regulatory body for the **savings and loan associations** (S&Ls) set up in the 1930s. The Federal Home Loan Bank System provides credit reserves for **mortgage** lending institutions through 12 regional Federal Home Loan banks and was established by the Federal Home Loan Bank Act 1932. In the following year the Home Owners Loan Act established the FHLBB, which now **charters** federal S&Ls. The Federal Home Loan Bank System also holds the **stock** of the Federal Home Loan Mortgage Corporation (FHLMC) on behalf of the S&Ls. The FHLMC, established in 1970 and referred to as Freddie Mac, purchases home mortgages from S&Ls and other **thrifts** and securities under guarantees for sale in the secondary market. An older and government-sponsored, though publicly **quoted**, organization, the Federal National Mortgage Association (FNMA or Fannie Mae), performs a similar function, especially for mortgages guaranteed by the Federal Housing Administration. The FNMA is the largest source of housing finance in the USA. See also **collateralized mortgage obligation**.

Federal Home Loan Bank System See **Federal Home Loan Bank Board**.

Federal Home Loan Mortgage Corporation See **Federal Home Loan Bank Board**.

Federal National Mortgage Association See **Federal Home Loan Bank Board**.

Federal Open Market Committee (FOMC) The monetary policy body of the **Federal Reserve System**. Composed of seven members of the board of governors and the 12 presidents of the regional Reserve Banks, it meets each month in Washington, DC, to review the economic situation and to decide on the policy to follow in the succeeding month with regard to the Federal Reserve's **open market operations**. The policy decision is communicated as a guideline to the Reserve Bank of New York, the member bank of the system that handles open market operations on its behalf. In deciding policy, one vote is allotted to each of the seven members of the board and to the president of the Reserve Bank of New York. The presidents of the remaining Reserve banks share four votes between them in rotation. The deliberations of the FOMC are published after an interval of about a month.

Federal Reserve bank (US) See **Federal Reserve System**.

Federal Reserve bond (US) See **Federal Reserve System**.

Federal Reserve float (US) The effect of **float** on the US banking system as a whole, i.e. where the overall timing of credits to and claims from banks, arising out of the **Federal Reserve**'s cheque-clearing function, leaves the system either liquid or illiquid (see **liquidity**).

Federal Reserve System (Fed) (US) The central banking system of the USA, established by the Federal Reserve Act 1913 and organized on a regional basis, given the large area involved and the multiplicity of small and medium-sized banks. The system is composed of 12 regional *Reserve banks*, 25 branches and 11 offices under the control of a board of governors located in Washington, DC (the Federal Reserve Board). The board of governors consists of seven governors appointed by Congress on the nomination of the President, each serving for 14 years, with one reappointment falling due every two years. The regional Reserve banks are controlled by boards of nine directors, of whom three are commercial bankers, three represent local labour and commerce, and three are appointed by the board of governors; the president and vice-president of each Reserve bank are drawn from the last three. The chairman of the board of governors is the head of the Federal Reserve System, appointed for a term of four years.

The regional Reserve banks supervise banking practice and management, act as **lenders of last resort**, provide common services in cheque clearing, statistics and research, and apply monetary policy at the instance of the board of governors. Monetary control is exercised chiefly through open market operations and is determined by the board of governors' **Federal Open Market Committee**, day-to-day transactions in pursuance of this being handled by the Reserve Bank of New York. The board of governors' constitutional independence is guaranteed by the long-term appointment of the governors and by the fact that the system generates a surplus (mostly paid as a dividend to the Treasury), relieving it of financial dependence on Congress. The chairman, members and staff of the board frequently explain Federal Reserve policy to congressional committees and maintain close contact with the US administration, but retain final responsibility for their policy.

Since the Monetary Control Act 1980, all US banks are members of the Federal Reserve System. The system was modified by the Banking Act 1935. See also **Fed funds**, **Federal funds rate**, **Federal Deposit Insurance Corporation**.

Fédération Internationale des Bourses de Valeurs Private international organization formed in 1961 for the exchange of views and information on **stock markets**.

Fedwire (US) An electronic system used by the **Federal Reserve** for large interbank **clearing**.

FEOGA See **Fond Européen d'Orientation et de Garantie Agriculturale**.

Festverzinslich (Ger.) **Fixed interest**.

FETCL (Jap.) See **Foreign Exchange and Trade Central Law**.

FHLBB See **Federal Home Loan Bank Board**.

FHLMC Federal Home Loan Mortgage Corporation. See **Federal Home Loan Bank Board**.

FIBOR The Frankfurt interbank offered rate; the German equivalent of **London interbank offered rate** (LIBOR).

FID See **corporation tax**.

FII Foreign **institutional investors**.

FIL (Jap.) See **Foreign Investment Law**.

file server See **local area network**.

filiale (Fr.) Subsidiary company.

FIMBRA Financial Intermediaries', Managers' and Brokers' Regulatory Association. See **Financial Services Act**.

final dividend See **dividend**.

final salary scheme An alternative term for an occupational pension scheme (see **pensions**).

finance The provision of money when and where required. Finance may be short term (usually up to one year), medium term (one to seven years) or long term. Finance may be provided in the form of loan finance, i.e. **debt**, or **equity**, or as a grant. Finance may be required for consumption or for **investment**. When provided for the latter, it becomes **capital**. See also **business finance**, **consumer credit**, **public finance**.

finance bill, finance paper A **bill of exchange** relating to the **receivables** of a **finance house**.

finance house (UK) A financial institution engaged in the provision of **hire purchase** and other forms of instalment credit for customers and business, sometimes known as *industrial banks*. (US = *small loan company* for **consumer credit**, and *commercial credit company* for business credit.) Some suppliers, e.g. motor manufacturers, have their own finance houses, known in the USA as *captive finance companies*.

finance house base rate (UK) The rate of interest charged by UK **finance houses** to their borrowers. Calculated (1986) by averaging the three-weekly average of three-month **London inter-bank offered rate** (LIBOR) and rounding to the nearest one-half % above, it was first published in 1970 and since published monthly.

finance house deposit (UK) A deposit placed by a bank or other large lender with a **finance house**; a method of recruiting funds much used by finance houses in the face of their lack of a branch network through which retail funds (see **retail deposit**) could be collected.

financial asset See **asset**.

financial future A **future** in a financial **asset**, i.e. a contract for the purchase of a specific standard quantity of a financial asset at a specific price on a specific future date. Dealing is through markets or exchanges, namely the **Chicago Board of Trade** and the **London International Financial Futures Exchange** (LIFFE). It differs from a **forward** contract in that futures contracts are in standard amounts intended to be traded, whereas forward contracts are once-only transactions. **Currency futures** were the earliest financial futures and were traded on the US **International Commercial Exchange** in 1970. **Interest rate futures** were first traded on the **Chicago Board of Trade** in 1975. Since then a number of other forms of financial futures have been devised (LIFFE). The advantage of financial futures contracts to a commercial company in comparison with borrowing, or **spot**, as against **forward** transactions, is that no **assets** or **liabilities** are created and thus they do not enter into the company's **balance sheet**; nor are the **spreads** of the forward exchange market incurred.

financial institutions The group of major commercial and public organizations engaged in exchanging, lending, borrowing and investing money. The term is often used as an alternative for **financial intermediaries**.

financial instrument See **instrument**.

financial intermediaries Institutions that hold money balances of, or borrow from, individuals and other institutions, in order to make loans or other **investments**. Hence they serve the purpose of channelling funds from lenders to borrowers. **Banks**, **building societies**, **hire-purchase** companies, **insurance** companies, **savings banks** and **investment trusts** are financial intermediaries; but it is usual to distinguish between bank and non-bank financial intermediaries because of the role of the former in determining the **money supply**. In the **Financial Services Act** the term has a narrower meaning (see **intermediary**).

Financial Intermediaries', Managers' and Brokers' Regulatory Association (FIMBRA) See **Financial Services Act**.

financial mechanism An arrangement made by the European Community (see **European Union**) in 1976 under which the UK's net contribution to the then EC's budget was reduced; it was amended in 1980 to permit a further reduction.

financial ratios 1. Measures of creditworthiness such as the current ratio (see **working capital**), **gearing**, **dividend cover**, **interest cover** and the ratio of long-term **debt** to **net tangible assets**. 2. Calculations based on company accounts and other sources to indicate the profitability or other financial aspects of a business. See **price–earnings ratio**, **return on investment**.

Financial Reporting Review Panel (UK) A body set up to ensure compliance with accounting standards set by the UK Accounting Standards Board.

Financial Services Act (FSA) (UK) Legislation enacted in November 1986 but coming into force on 29 April 1988 ('A' day) to regulate the investment business in the UK. The Act followed a report on investor protection commissioned in 1981 from Professor Jim Gower and completed in 1984. The Gower Report recommended that the new regulatory system should cover **life assurance**, **unit trusts** and other forms of investment business in addition to **stock exchange** investments. The Act set up a Securities and Investment Board (SIB), run and paid for by investment professionals, but with statutory powers and reporting to the Department of Trade and Industry. Investment businesses must be registered with the SIB directly or with one of four *self-regulating organizations* (SROs). The original SROs were: the Financial Intermediaries', Managers' and Brokers' Regulatory Association (FIMBRA), which covers independent intermediaries such as **insurance brokers**; the Securities Association (TSA), for **securities** dealing such as by **market makers**; the Association of Futures Brokers and Dealers (AFBD), for dealing in **futures** and **options** (these last two bodies were merged to form the Securities and Futures Authority Ltd (SFA) in 1991); the Investment Managers' Regulatory Organization (IMRO), for investment management such as pension funds; and the Life Assurance and Unit Trust Regulatory Organization (LAUTRO). FIMBRA and LAUTRO were replaced by the Personal Investment Authority in 1994.

The SIB maintains a central register of firms authorized by itself or the SROs. Certain investment markets also have to be approved by the SIB or via the appropriate SRO; these markets are *recognized investment exchanges* (RIEs), e.g. the *International Stock Exchange* (see **London Stock Exchange**) and the **Baltic Exchange** (see also **designated investment exchange**). Lawyers and accountants for whom the provision of investment advice is only a minor part of their business are self-regulated by their own professional bodies.

Recognized professional bodies (RPBs) have been approved by the SIB, including the Institute of Chartered Accountants of England and Wales.

Financial Statement and Budget Report (FSBR) (UK) A document published by the Chancellor of the Exchequer on Budget day, and supplementing the Chancellor's statement that day to the House of Commons, summarizing the objectives and main provisions of the Budget, the situation of public-sector finances and the general state of the economy. Familiarly known as the Red Book.

Financial Times share indices *FTO* (*Financial Times (Industrial) Ordinary*) or *FT 30 Share Index*, an unweighted (see **weighted average**) *geometric* **average** of 30 leading **blue chips** quoted on the **London Stock Exchange**, was introduced in 1935 and calculated hourly. The FT 30 has been superseded by the *FT/SE 100* ['*Footsie 100*'] *Index*, a **market capitalization** weighted average calculated minute by minute (real time). The **base period** for the FT 100 is 3 January 1984 = 1,000, and its constituents are the 100 largest quoted industrial and commercial companies by capitalization, reviewed quarterly (**investment trusts** are excluded). The *FT/SE Mid-250 Index*, also calculated minute by minute, covers the next 250 companies, ranked by market value; and the *FT/SE/Actuaries 350 Index* includes all the constituents of the 100 and 250 indices. The 350 Index covers about 92% of total market value and the 100 Index about 72%. The *FT/Actuaries All-Share Index* has been published daily since 10 April 1962; it now covers some 800 shares and fixed interest **stocks** and covers some 98% of total market value, and has indices for industry *baskets* and subsections. The *FT/SE Small Cap Index*, introduced in 1993 and calculated daily, covers those shares within the FT/A All-Share Index but not within the 350. In 1987 the *FT/Actuaries World Share Index* was introduced, based on a weighted sample of 2,400 share prices, initially from 24 countries. *The FT/Actuaries Fixed Interest Indices* measure the prices and **yields** of UK **gilts**, index-linked (see **indexation**), **debentures** and **loans**. Total return figures are calculated for all the UK indices and published daily. These figures, which are gross of tax, take account of both price performance and income received from **dividends**. See also **index number**.

financial year A 12-month period in respect of which financial accounts are kept. Years of account for financial purposes often do not coincide with calendar years and hence are referred to as financial years. A financial year 1993/4, for example, might run from 31 August 1993 to 1 September 1994. Government financial years are called fiscal years. See also **budget**.

fine trade bill A **trade bill**, the drawer and drawee (see **bill of exchange**) of which are reputable parties, or good **names**, and that commands a fine rate of **discount** in the **money market**.

firm order An order to buy or sell a **security** within a specified time limit that can be executed without further confirmation.

first notice day The first day on which notice can be given that physical delivery is intended, or expected, on a **futures** contract.

fiscal agent 1. A function of the **Federal Reserve** *vis-à-vis* the US Treasury: the Federal Reserve processes all payments to and from the government. **2.** An agent for the issuer of a **Eurobond**, who delivers the interest and capital payments on the bond to the **paying agent** and assists the borrower in other ways, such as by aiding in the receipt of the bond certificates on redemption.

fiscal transparency A **partnership**, a **European economic interest grouping** and a **sub-chapter S corporation** are said to be fiscally transparent because in these business–legal forms (see **incorporation**) the **liabilities** for **taxation** fall not upon the business as such but on the people who own it.

fiscal year See **financial year**.

Fitch Investors Service See **Standard and Poor's Ratings**.

fix To settle a price by trading, normally in the **commodity markets**, including the gold market.

fixed assets See **asset**.

fixed charge See **mortgage**.

fixed exchange rate See **exchange rate**.

fixed interest Generally, refers to **securities** such as **bonds** on which the holder receives a predetermined and unchanging rate of interest on the *nominal value* (see **par value**); as opposed to the non-guaranteed, variable return on **equities**. Specifically, refers to **debt instruments** having a fixed rate of interest, such as **gilts**, as against those with a variable rate, e.g. **floating rate notes**.

fixed price offer for sale See **offer for sale**.

fixed rate currency swap See **currency interest rate swap**.

flat yield See **yield**.

flex stock option An **option** introduced by the **Chicago Board of Trade** in the early 1990s, allowing clients the choice of terms, **striking prices** and expiry dates.

flexible drawdown See **drawdown**.

flip-flop See **floating rate note**.

float 1. (US) A situation where the cheque-clearing function of the **Federal Reserve** may have a timing gap between the posting of matching **credits** and **debits** to pairs of banks, thus artificially draining or bolstering those banks' reserves. See **Federal Reserve float**. **2.** See **floating rate, variable rate security**. **3.** Cash in hand at a bank, or funds in course of transfer between banks.

floater See **variable rate security**.

floating capital Capital invested not in fixed **assets**, such as buildings, but in work in progress, wages paid, etc. See **working capital**.

floating charge An assignment of the total **assets** of a company or individual as **collateral security** for a **debt**; as opposed to particular assets, when such an assignment is known as a fixed charge or **mortgage**.

floating policy A policy for the **insurance** of ships' cargoes covering a number of anticipated movements, each of which must be declared separately to the **insurer**. The policy is fixed in duration.

floating rate 1. A rate of interest that varies with the market, more particularly with an agreed reference standard, e.g. the **London interbank offered rate** (LIBOR) (see **variable rate security**). **2.** A **rate of exchange** that is not fixed by the national authorities but varies according to supply and demand for the currency.

floating rate certificate of deposit (FRCD) A **certificate of deposit** (CD) on which the issuing bank pays a variable **coupon**, or interest rate. FRCDs were first issued in the USA in 1975. Normally of one-year **maturity**, the FRCD carried a coupon adjusted every 90 days in line with that paid on 90-day CDs. The advantage to the depositor is that of partial protection against interest rate changes in the market. The advantage to the bank is that of attracting long-term funds. FRCDs were thereafter introduced on the London market, generally in **Eurodollar** form, the coupon being linked to the London interbank rate, usually by a **spread** over **London interbank offered rate** (LIBOR).

Recent innovations have included: perpetual FRNs, on which there is no **redemption**; flip-flop FRNs, or perpetual FRNs convertible at one or two years' notice into lower-yielding four-year FRNs, which can themselves be converted back into perpetual FRNs; mismatch FRNs, where the coupon is paid monthly at a longer-term rate; and capped FRNs, where the coupon is subject to a predetermined ceiling. In 1986, owing to falling interest rates and some increase in credit risk in the loan portfolios of hitherto active US banks, there were indications of a decrease in the rate of FRN issues. By then the total market, including international fixed-rate bonds, amounted to $750bn. See also **variable rate security**.

floating rate note (FRN) A **note** issued in the **Euromarket**, the **coupon** of which fluctuates according to interest rate changes. Floating rate notes are bonds, having a maturity of seven to 15 years, and came into being in face of the difficulties encountered in the 1970s in issuing fixed-interest bonds in conditions of high interest rates and high inflation. The first FRN was issued by the Italian concern ENEL in 1970, following a period of rapidly rising interest rates and at a time when bond buyers virtually refused any **denomination** higher than $25m. The floating rate transferred the risk from the lender to the borrower. The FRN does not have the option for flexible **drawdown** or interest payment timing offered under **syndicated credits**. However, as time went on, the advantages to borrowers – particularly those of lesser credit rating, and most of all as a means for banks themselves of acquiring liquid funds – became apparent. Thus FRN issues rose from under $5bn in 1980 to $55bn in 1985; banks were reckoned to have accounted for half of these. Banks frequently also found FRNs preferable to **certificates of deposit** (CDs) owing to their longer maturities. Where **subordinated** to **deposits**, FRNs issued by banks have been recognized as bank capital in most major countries, except Germany, Japan and France. Most borrowing has taken place in the USA and the UK, and most issues have been denominated in US dollars, although issues have been made in Euro-sterling, Euro-Dmarks, Euro-yen, Euro-Dutch-guilders and other currencies. FRNs have also been used as **asset-backed securities**.

FRNs are normally issued as **negotiable bearer notes** in denominations of at least $1,000, with a **coupon** related to three- or six-month **London interbank offered rate** (LIBOR), above which there is a **spread**. Since they are **bonds**, their issue must be accompanied by a **prospectus**.

floor broker (US) **1**. A member (or employee of a member firm) of the **stock exchange** who buys or sells **securities** on the **trading floor** on behalf of clients; as distinct from floor traders, who do so on their own account. **2**. The representative of a member of a **commodity market**, authorized to deal on the trading floor of the market. A full member of the market and thus also called a floor member.

floor member (US) See **floor broker**.

floor official (US) An employee of the **stock exchange** who settles disputes arising on the **trading floor**.

floor trader (US) See **floor broker**.

floppy disk A magnetic data-storage device that can be inserted into and read by a computer. Floppy because it is made of thin plastic sheet; the standard sizes are $3\frac{1}{2}$ and $5\frac{1}{4}$ inches.

flotation The issue of shares in a company on a **stock exchange**

or **unlisted securities market** for the first time. The method may be an **introduction**, an **intermediate offer**, a **placing** or an **offer for sale**. When a private company (see **incorporation**) becomes a public company and has its **shares** listed in this way, the process is known as *going public*.

flow of funds See **sources and uses of funds**.

flow of funds account (US) Statistics kept by the **Federal Reserve** of the total demand and supply of credit funds in the US market, broken down by type of borrower and lender and by type of borrowing instrument.

FOMC See **Federal Open Market Committee**, **FOMC minutes**.

FOMC minutes (US) The official, summary record of the deliberations of the **Federal Open Market Committee**, together with the text of the **directive**, published about a month after the FOMC meeting.

Fond Européen d'Orientation et de Garantie Agriculturale The **European Union**'s farm fund. See under English title, **European Agricultural Guidance and Guarantee Fund**.

fonds (Fr.) **1. Funds**. **2. Capital**.

Fonds (Ger.) **1. Funds**. **2. Capital**. **3**. Estate.

fonds d'état (Fr.) Government **stocks**.

fonds publics (Fr.) Government **stocks**, **public bonds**.

Food Aid Committee (FAC) A body established in the 1950s but since 1986 administering the Food Aid Convention forming part of the **International Wheat Agreement** (IWA). The task of the Food Aid Committee is to ensure the annual supply to developing countries of at least 7.5m tonnes of grain or grain products promised by each of the member governments of the Food Aid Convention. There are 23 member governments, all of them, with the exception of Argentina, industrialized countries. The actual target is 10m tonnes, and this has normally been exceeded.

Food Aid Convention See **Food Aid Committee**, **International Wheat Agreement**.

Footsie See **Financial Times share indices**.

foreign bond A **bond** held in one country, issued in another country and denominated in the currency of that country. In the UK known as a **bulldog bond**, in the US as a **yankee bond**.

Foreign Credit Insurance Association (FCIA) (US) Established in 1962 by some four dozen insurance companies to **underwrite** the risk of default on export credit, particularly that **refinanced** by the **Export-Import Bank**, with which it is closely associated.

Foreign Desk (US) The section of the *Reserve Bank* of New York (see **Federal Reserve System**) that carries out **exchange** market operations at the direction of the US **Treasury**.

foreign direct investment (FDI) **Investment** in the foreign operations of a business. See **balance of payments**.

foreign exchange 1. All foreign **currencies.** 2. The activity of exchanging currencies through purchase and sale; hence *foreign exchange market.*

Foreign Exchange and Currency Deposit Brokers' Association (FECDBA) (UK) The professional body for **brokers** dealing in **foreign exchange** and foreign **currency** deposits.

Foreign Exchange and Trade Central Law (Jap.) Legislation, introduced in 1949, setting a standard form of settlement of import invoices. The settlement must conform to the Japanese national interest, and if this requirement is satisfied an import licence is issued. In other cases a special permit must be obtained from the Ministry of International Trade and Industry (MITI). Modifications were made in the law following Japan's entry to the **Organization for Economic Co-operation and Development** (OECD) and acceptance of that body's code of liberalization.

Foreign Investment Law (Jap.) A law regulating foreign investment in Japan between 1950 and 1979.

forex A contraction of '**foreign exchange**'.

forfaiting A form of export finance in which the forfaiter accepts, at a discount from the exporter, a **bill of exchange** or *promissory note* (see **note**) from the exporter's customer; the forfaiter in due course collects payment of the debt. The notes are normally guaranteed by the customer's bank. **Maturities** are normally up to three years.

Form 10 K (US) A return made to the **Securities and Exchange Commission** by companies listed on one of the national stock exchanges, giving financial and other information. A public document available on **Edgar**.

forward A prospective amount of a **currency** or a **commodity** obtained by a contract between a buyer and a seller. Under this, the seller undertakes to provide the client with a fixed amount of the currency or commodity on a fixed future date at a fixed rate of exchange, or price. This differs from a **futures** contract in that each forward contract is a once-only deal between the two parties, while futures contracts are in standard amounts traded on exchanges.

forward-forward 1. A transaction for the purchase, at a future date, of an **instrument** maturing at a further future date. 2. Purchase **forward** of a currency for one term (e.g. three months) against sale forward of the same currency at another term (e.g. six months).

forward price See **forward market**.

forward rate agreement (FRA) An agreement whereby a currency is bought and sold at a future date at an agreed **exchange rate**. See **forward**.

forward start option See **deferred strike option**.

forwardation See **contango**.

401 K (US) A savings scheme under which employees may have up to 10% of their salary deducted before **taxation** for investment in **securities**.

Fourth Directive The most prominent of a series of **European Union directives** leading to the harmonization of company law in member states. The Fourth Directive introduced detailed schedules for the form and content of company accounts and was implemented in the UK in the 1981 Companies Act (see **incorporation**). Directives are prepared by the Commission of the European Communities but are not mandatory until approved by the Council of Ministers. See also **consolidated accounts**.

FOX See **Futures and Options Exchange**.

FRA See **forward rate agreement**.

frais de cotation (Fr.) An annual **listing** fee.

franc fort (Fr.) A term ('strong franc') applied to the French government's policy throughout the 1980s of maintaining the foreign exchange value of the French franc, particularly against the German mark; the policy was seen to be in some doubt after the currency turbulence of August/September 1993. See **European Monetary System** (EMS).

Frankfurt Stock Exchange See **German stock exchanges**.

Freddie Mac See **Federal Home Loan Bank Board**.

free asset ratio The ratio of the market value of an **insurance** company's **assets** to the value of its **liabilities**.

free capital (UK) That proportion of the **equity** of a **company** available for trading by the public on a stock market. (US = *free float*). It excludes equities held by controlling shareholders.

free depreciation See **capital allowances**.

free float (US) See **free capital**.

free reserves 1. Those **reserves** of a bank that exceed the level prescribed by the monetary authorities (see **monetary control, monetary policy**). In the USA **excess reserves** less **borrowed reserves**, i.e. those reserves accumulated by the banks by reason of their own business that exceed the reserves that they are required by the **Federal Reserve** to maintain, less the amounts they have borrowed from the Federal Reserve. **2**. Those reserves of an insurance company that exceed the level prescribed by the relevant supervisory authorities.

free resources The excess of an insurance company's **assets** over **liabilities**. In the case of a **proprietary** company equivalent to **paid-up capital** plus **free reserves**.

free stocks Of **commodity markets**, inventories held in commercial hands, as against those still held by producers.

Free Trade Agreement (FTA) An agreement signed between the USA and Canada in 1988 and ratified in 1989, abolishing all tariffs between the two countries. See also **North American Free Trade Agreement** (NAFTA).

Freier Makler (Ger.) An independent dealer on the German **stock exchange** authorized by the *Börsenvorstand*, dealing chiefly in the unofficial market. Also known as a *Börsenmakler*.

Freiverkehr (Ger.) The unofficial or **unlisted securities market** on **German stock exchanges**.

Friedman, Milton (US) Professor of Economics at the University of Chicago, and most celebrated for his monetary theory, popularly known as monetarism, based on the quantum theory of money. The theory propounds, in brief, that variations in **money supply** cause variations in the general price level and that therefore the growth in the stock of money should be maintained within stable dimensions consonant with the real growth of the economy. The theory had great influence on the financial policies of the major industrial countries during the 1970s and early 1980s, but difficulties encountered in the measurement and control of the money supply, and in demonstrating the link between this and the level of prices, led thereafter to a weakening of this influence.

FRN See **floating rate note**.

front-end fee A fee charged by a bank or **syndicate** of banks at the outset of a loan, e.g. management fee, **participation** fee, **underwriting** fee. Most commonly occurring in the **Euro-market** and in the US securities market.

front-end loading Of insurance premiums, unit trust prices and loan interest, the incorporation of administration expenses into the first payment by the customer or borrower. See **loading**.

front month The first month available for trading in a **derivative**. Also known as the *nearby month*.

FSA See **Financial Services Act**.

FSBR See **financial statement and budget report**.

FT/Actuaries World Share Index See **Financial Times share indices**.

FTA See **Free Trade Agreement**.

FTO See **Financial Times share indices**.

FT/SE futures contract (UK) A standardized **futures** contract based upon the **Financial Times share indices** and traded on the **London International Financial Futures Exchange** (LIFFE).

FT/SE Index See **Financial Times share indices**.

full consolidation See **consolidated accounts**.

full listing (UK) The inclusion of a **company** in the **official list** of the **London Stock Exchange**.

fund A sum of money, as in an amount of savings, handed to a **stockbroker** for investment and management (see **discretionary account**), or subscribed to a savings scheme or invested by a **life assurance** company to meet the claims of policy-holders. Fund management consists in carrying out administration such as the receipt of **dividends** and **interest**, subscribing to **rights issues** and adjusting the **portfolio** by purchases and sales with the objective of maximizing capital growth or income. The term is frequently used to denote the institution managing the fund, e.g. a pension fund (see **pensions**).

fund management See **fund**.

fund of funds See **managed unit trust**.

fundamental analysis See **technical analysis**.

funded debt Generally, short-term **debt** that has been converted into long-term debt. See **funding**.

funded pension scheme See **pensions**.

funding The process of converting short-term to long-term **debt** by the sale of long-term **securities** and using the funds raised to repay short-term debt. In **public finance**, *overfunding* occurs when the government is selling more debt to the non-bank sector than is necessary to meet the **public-sector borrowing requirement** (PSBR), and *underfunding* when it is selling less than is necessary for that purpose. Under *full funding* purchases of government paper by the banks do not count towards the financing needs of the PSBR, which are fully met by sales to non-banks, that is, to other **financial intermediaries**, and the personal and corporate sectors.

funds at Lloyd's (FAL) Funds held in trust at **Lloyd's of London** to support a member's **underwriting** activities, comprising their **Lloyd's deposit**, their **personal reserve** and their **special reserve**.

funds broker (US) An intermediary for the arrangement of short-term lending between banks.

funds rate (US) See **Federal funds rate**.

funds statements See **sources and uses of funds**.

fungible A class of good or **security** that has the property of being substitutable or interchangeable with another in the same class. **Bearer securities**, **common stocks** and money, such as £5 notes, are fungible because, if of the same denomination, one can be replaced by another without loss or gain. Fungibility is important because it allows the pooling and offsetting of classes of items without the need to identify them individually by serial numbers or other means.

futures A vehicle for the purchase and sale of **commodities** and **financial instruments** at a date in the future. Futures take the form of a fixed and binding contract for a standard amount to be sold at a fixed price at a fixed future date. In the precise obligation involved, the future differs from an **option** and a **forward** transaction. A future is a **negotiable instrument**. See also **financial futures**.

Futures and Options Exchange (London FOX) (UK) The leading exchange in Europe for soft **commodities** (including cocoa, sugar, rubber, potatoes and grain). It was formed in 1987 as successor to the London Commodity Exchange, sharing a trading floor with the **International Petroleum Exchange**, and in 1991 took over the Baltic Futures Exchange (BFE), which itself had also been formed in 1987.

Futures Industry Association (US) The central body representing US operators in the **futures** market.

futures market A market dealing in **futures** and **options** on **shares**, **bonds**, foreign currencies and **commodities**.

futures option An **option** to buy or sell a **futures** contract.

GAB See **general arrangements to borrow**.

GAFTA See **Grain and Feed Trade Association**.

gai atsu (Jap.) The term describing foreign pressure for a change in Japanese financial and trade policies.

gaijin (Jap.) Literally, 'foreigner'. Used in Japanese stock market parlance to refer to a foreign investor.

gaimuin (Jap.) A **broker** in a small **securities** house.

gamma stocks See **alpha securities, stocks**.

Garn–St Germain Act 1982 (US) An Act that removed restrictions on the **asset** base of **savings and loan associations**, allowing these organizations to compete in the commercial lending market. **Building societies** in the UK have also been deregulated (see **regulation**) but are still restricted to the provision of financial services for individuals.

GATT See **General Agreement on Tariffs and Trade**.

GDP See **gross domestic product**.

gearing (UK) The relative importance of **loans** in the **capital structure** (US = *leverage*). There are several ways of measuring gearing. The usual way is the ratio of fixed-interest **debt** to shareholder interest plus the debt (see **net assets**). A corporation may borrow **capital** at fixed interest, and if it can earn more on that capital than it has to pay for it in interest, then the additional earnings accrue to the **equity** shareholders. Thus a firm with high gearing will be able to pay higher **dividends** per **share** than a firm with lower gearing earning exactly the same return on its total capital, provided that return is higher than the rate it pays for **loan**

capital. However, the contrary is also true; so the higher the gearing the greater the risk to the equity shareholder. See also **capital gearing, equity gearing, gearing effect**.

gearing effect (UK) **1**. The impact upon **earnings per share** of **capital structure**. See **gearing**. **2**. The multiplication of a change in the price of a **warrant** compared with that of a **share** that may be exchanged for it, or in the price of a share compared with an **option**.

Geldmenge (Ger.) **Money supply**.

Geldvolumen (Ger.) **Money supply**.

GEMU See **German Economic and Monetary Union**.

General Agreement on Tariffs and Trade (GATT) A convention entered into by most nations of the non-communist world in 1947 for the liberalization of world trade and for the establishment of an international trade organization. Provisions for the liberalization of trade – comprising chiefly an extensive reduction of **tariffs** and acceptance of the *most-favoured nation* principle (i.e. non-discrimination in the extension of tariff reductions) – and adoption of a code of fair trading – chiefly the disavowal of restrictive trade practices and non-tariff trade obstacles – proved well received; while those for the establishment of an international trade organization were not. Accordingly the tariff reductions were put into effect, and a secretariat was established in the United Nations European office in Geneva on 1 January 1948 to assist with the task of further implementing trade liberalization under the convention.

In course of time the secretariat and the convention signatories constituted themselves into an organization with the status of a specialized agency of the United Nations, and the title General Agreement on Tariffs and Trade, or GATT, became applicable both to the organization and to the convention itself.

The GATT has since greatly enlarged the scope of liberalization, notably through eight further negotiating rounds – two more at Geneva, one at Torquay and one at Annécy between 1947 and 1962; the Dillon round of 1967; a major round, the Kennedy round, ending in 1967; a major round between 1973 and 1979, denoted the Tokyo round; and an eighth round, the Uruguay round, beginning in 1986 and concluded at the end of 1993. Apart from further tariff cuts, reductions in non-tariff barriers and a long-lasting endeavour to reconcile French and US agricultural interests, the Uruguay round was distinguished by a proposal for a *Multilateral Trade Organization* (MTO) to enforce rules for international trade, itself a harking back to the International Trade Organization at the heart of the original convention of 1947, for which the GATT organization was only a substitute. As a result of these, world trade tariff barriers were reduced to a small proportion of their level in 1947.

As time went on, not only was the GATT joined in the work of liberalization by other bodies, such as the **Organization for Economic Co-operation and Development** and the **European Union**, but its own efforts focused more particularly on non-tariff hindrances, such as subsidies and incentives, government procurement, restrictive trade agreements, developing country problems, agriculture and trade in services. Membership in 1988 numbered 88 nations.

general arrangements to borrow (GAB) An addition to the central loan facilities the **International Monetary Fund** (IMF) created by the provision of special credits by 10 major IMF members, known thereafter as the Group of 10. The special credits granted were conditional on their use only for financial assistance to other members of the group. The GAB came into effect in 1962 and arose from a general strain on the IMF's **liquidity** and from a particular difficulty at that time in providing necessary loan assistance to the UK and the USA. A wider expansion of the IMF's funds would have necessitated new formal powers for the organization, which were thought undesirable. Subsequently the IMF concluded an agreement with Switzerland whereby that country extended credit in a similar way. In 1983 a revised GAB was formulated under which Switzerland, although not a member of the IMF, joined the GAB, and under which facilities were extended to non-members of the GAB. The GAB is denominated in **special drawing rights** (SDRs) and in 1988 totalled SDR 18,500m. The Group of 10 members are Belgium, Canada, France, Italy, Japan, the

Netherlands, Sweden, the UK, the USA and Germany (together with Switzerland).

general average See **average**.

general government A term normally used in public accounting matters to refer to central and local government, taken together, in a particular country. Thus the term refers in the UK to the government at Westminster and to all local authorities, i.e. district, county and borough councils; in the USA, to the federal government in Washington together with state, local and territorial governments; in Japan, to the central government of Tokyo together with prefectures and city, town and village authorities; in Germany, to the central government in Bonn together with *Länder*, city states and municipalities; in France, to the central government in Paris together with regions, departments and communes.

general insurance Insurance against fire, accident, theft, etc., as distinct from life.

general undertaking (UK) A document signed by the directors of a **company**, setting out their obligations to the **stock exchange** in terms of the provision of information and issue of **shares** for companies on the **unlisted securities market**. The version of this document used by companies going for a **full listing** is called the *listing agreement*.

gensaki (Jap.) A **bond** sale with a **repurchase** agreement; the difference between the sale price and the agreed repurchase price establishing the **yield**, which is expressed at an annual rate.

geometric average See **average**.

geometric mean See **average**.

geregelter Freiverkehr (Ger.) Second-tier official **unlisted securities markets** operating at the **stock exchanges** in Germany. There is also an unregulated third tier called the *ungeregelter Freiverkehr*. Finally, there is an **over-the-counter** telephone market in which both listed and unlisted shares are dealt, the *Telefonverkehr* (literally, 'telephone traffic'). See also *Freier Makler*.

German Economic and Monetary Union (GEMU) The process of integrating economic and monetary conditions in former East and West Germany, following the unification of the two countries in 1990.

German Futures and Options Market See **Deutsche Terminbörse**.

German stock exchanges All German exchanges are now grouped under Deutsche Börse AG, but share trading is not yet centralized, and there is no federal securities regulator, **regulation** being on a regional or *Länder* basis. The Frankfurt Stock Exchange accounts for about 75% of **volume** on the former West German exchanges, followed by Dusseldorf, Munich and Hamburg in that order. There are also exchanges in Stuttgart, Berlin, Hanover and Bremen. About 50% of volume is accounted for by foreign investors, and the shares in German companies are **heavy shares** because there is a minimum **par value** of DM50. The Frankfurt exchange has an active **trading floor** that is open for only two hours a day and operates on a **matched bid** basis for smaller companies, although there is continuous trading in the major **stocks**. There are plans for a computerized **futures** and **options** market in Frankfurt. See also **Deutsche Aktienindex**, *geregelter Freiverkehr*.

Gesellschaft (Ger.) **Company**.

Gesellschaft mit beschränkter Haftung (GmbH) (Ger.) A private limited company. See **incorporation**.

gesichert (Ger.) **Secured**.

Gewerbeertragesteuer (Ger.) See **local taxation**.

Gewerbekapitalsteuer (Ger.) See **local taxation**.

Gewinn (Ger.) **1**. Profit. **2**. Gain on a transaction, or a price.

gilts, gilt-edged securities (UK) Fixed-interest UK **government securities** traded on the **London Stock Exchange**. They are called gilt-edged because it is certain that **interest** will be paid and that they will be redeemed (where appropriate) on the due date. Some gilts are **dated securities**, some are **undated securities**, and some are index-linked (see **indexation**). Gilts are not a risk-free investment, of course, because of fluctuations in their market value. Gilt-edged securities do not include **Treasury bills**.

Ginnie Maes (US) A familiar term for mortgage-backed bonds issued by the **Government National Mortgage Association**.

Glass–Steagal Act 1933 (US) Legislation prohibiting **commercial banks** from acting as **investment banks** or owning a firm dealing in securities. The Act has been challenged by banks offering **money-market mutual funds** and other investment services and is expected to be the subject of reform.

global bond A **fixed-interest security** issued simultaneously in the USA, Europe and Asia. Principal issuers are **sovereign** governments and international organizations such as the **International Bank for Reconstruction and Development** but also **multinational companies**.

global custody A service provided by **investment banks** and other **financial intermediaries** to local **fund** managers for cross-border **settlement** and administration.

Globex An overnight electronic trading system developed in 1992 jointly by the **Chicago Mercantile Exchange**, the **Chicago Board of Trade** and **Reuters**, and dealing in **currency futures and options**. By 1993 little participation outside the founding exchanges and the **Marché à Terme des Instruments Financiers** (MATIF) was evident.

GmbH See *Gesellschaft mit beschränkter Haftung*.

GNMA (US) See **Government National Mortgage Association**.

GNP Gross national product. See **gross domestic product**.

going concern value See **goodwill**.

going public See **flotation**.

gold and foreign currency reserves See **reserves**.

Gold Demand Trends See **World Gold Council**.

gold standard A form of international **exchange** practised until the 1930s. Each country's national **currency** was linked by a fixed rate to gold and varied in volume with the amount of gold held. Thus a **balance of payments** surplus would lead to an increase in the **money supply**, thence to a rise in prices and so to a drop in exports and a rise in imports, eliminating the surplus. A balance of payments deficit acted in the opposite direction. Economic difficulties in the 1930s led to the abandonment of the gold standard.

gold warrant An instrument enabling the holder to buy or sell gold at a predetermined price and time, closely akin to call and put **options**. However, warrants are for periods of one year or more, are not subject to the **margin** requirements of **futures** and **options** exchanges and, having a close resemblance to conventional **securities**, are acceptable to portfolios unable to deal in other forms of **derivatives**.

golden share See **privatization**.

good till cancelled (GTC) An order for a **commodity** remaining open for execution so long as not specifically cancelled.

goodwill (UK) The value of a business to a purchaser over and above its **net asset** value (US = *going concern value*). It is normal practice to show goodwill in the **balance sheet** but to write it down for **depreciation**. See also **consolidated accounts**.

government broker The firm handling **new issues** of **gilts** for the **Bank of England**. Superseded by a number of **market makers** in gilts after the stock exchange reorganization (**Big Bang**) of 1986.

Government National Mortgage Association (GNMA) (US) A government agency that approves and guarantees mortgage-backed **securities** for the finance of low-cost housing. See also **collateralized mortgage securities**.

government securities All government fixed-interest paper, including **funded debt** and **Treasury bills**. See also **gilts**.

government stock A **bond** issued by government; a term most commonly used to refer to central government stock or, in the UK, **gilts**.

Gower Report See **Financial Services Act**.

grading The setting and checking of quality and type standards for **commodities** traded on a **commodity exchange**.

Grain and Feed Trade Association (GAFTA) The controlling body of the London Grain Futures Market, a commodity market for wheat and barley that trades on the floor of the **Baltic Exchange**. The market is managed by a GAFTA committee, the Grain Futures and Clearing House Committee; and prices are fixed by market members nominated each week by a panel of that committee. Deliveries of grain are from a store registered by the committee. GAFTA holds a reserve fund drawn from the income of the association and used for the settlement of claims against default. GAFTA has wide regulatory powers over market members.

Grain Market Report See **International Wheat Council**.

Gramm–Rudman Act 1985 (US) An Act of Congress, sponsored by senators Gramm, Rudman and Hollings, that required the US federal government to balance its **budget** by 1991. Despite various efforts, this object was not achieved.

granter See **options**.

Green Book 1. (UK) A handbook published by the **London Stock Exchange**, setting out the requirements for admission to the **unlisted securities market** and for subsequent reporting. **2.** (US) A familiar term for the economic forecast presented by the staff of the **Federal Reserve Board** to each meeting of the **Federal Open Market Committee**. One of three such information documents. See also **Beige Book**, **Blue Book**.

greenmail See **corporate raider**.

grey market A term describing a market in a **new issue** of **shares** before the shares have been received by subscribers.

gross domestic product (GDP) The money value (at market prices) of the goods and services produced by the economy in a period of time, usually a year or a quarter. No allowance is made for expenditure on the replacement of capital assets. Only goods for final consumption or investment are included, since the value of intermediate goods, e.g. raw materials, is included in the prices of final goods. GDP is distinguished from *gross national product* (GNP) by the exclusion of income on investment abroad. These national accounts aggregates, as they are called, may be valued at **current prices** or in **real** terms.

gross margin See **margin**.

gross national product See **gross domestic product**.

gross premium Of insurance, a **premium** less the amount paid in rebates or refunds, but before deductions for **commissions** and **reinsurance**.

Group of Five See **Plaza Agreement**.

Group of 10 See **general arrangements to borrow** (GAB).

Group of 30 (US) A 'think tank' originally sponsored by the Rockefeller Foundation composed of 30 high-level individuals drawn from central banks, commercial bank management, the economics profession and finance ministries in both developed and developing countries. The group was founded in 1979, with head-quarters first in New York, then in Washington, DC. The group's purpose is to prepare and publish studies on the basic function of international and economic systems, using the expertise of members and where appropriate that of outside contributors. A number of studies have been produced on such topics as **foreign exchange** movements, **exchange rate** policy and the role of the **International Monetary Fund** (IMF) and the World Bank (see **International Bank for Reconstructon and Development**). In 1993 a much discussed study was produced on **derivatives**. The chairman is Paul Volcker, former chairman of the US **Federal Reserve**.

Grundkapital (Ger.) **Share capital**.

Grundsteuer (Ger.) See **local taxation**.

GTC See **good till cancelled**.

Guarantee Fund for Futures and Options (Den.) A fund underpinning trade in the **Danish futures and options market**.

hammering (UK) The announcement, formerly with three blows of a hammer, of the bankruptcy of a member of the **London Stock Exchange**. In the USA the term means widespread selling short (see **position**) or hammering the market down when prices are thought to be too high.

Handel (Ger.) Trade.

Hang Seng Index See **Hong Kong stock exchanges**.

harakiri swap (Jap.) A **swap** carrying no **spread**, made for the purpose of increasing the initiator's market share.

hard currency See **currency**.

hard disk A magnetic computer-storage device capable of holding large volumes of data. In general it is permanently fixed inside the computer, in contrast to a **floppy disk**.

hard dollars See **soft dollars**.

hausse (Fr.) A rise in price.

hazard That element of an insurance **risk** that in the view of the insurer is capable of aggravating the loss.

heavy share (UK) A **share** that has a high unit price in relation to the average price of shares in the market. On the **London Stock Exchange** many shares are priced around £4, but a few are priced at £20 or more. For companies with similar earnings and prospects the **yield** may be the same but the price may be very different. In the UK investors seem to prefer to buy large numbers of shares at low prices, but in the US average unit prices are much higher. For this reason, to improve the marketability of its shares, a company that has experienced a rapid growth in the earnings may decide to make a **bonus issue** to reduce the price of its shares. See also **penny share**.

hedge A transaction tending to the opposite effect of another transaction, engaged in to minimize a potential loss on the latter. Hedging usually relates to **commodity**, **currency** and financial transactions. Thus an anticipated liability in a currency can be covered, where a rise in its price is apprehended, by a **forward** purchase of the same currency at a fixed price. Commodity and **security** transactions can be hedged by **futures** and **options** contracts, sometimes **put** and **call** simultaneously. In the commodities markets hedging is generally effected by taking a position in the futures market opposite to that held in the **physical** market. The word is used also to denote the instrument used to hedge.

'held covered' clause A clause in a marine **insurance** contract exonerating the **insured** from accidental misdescriptions of the goods, against an addition to the **premium**.

Herstatt risk The risk of loss in the capital value of a **currency** transaction, where one side of the bargain is completed, but completion on the other side is delayed. Named after the Herstatt Bank of Germany, which suffered loss in 1974 having settled the D-mark side of a transaction before closing for the night, leaving the dollar side unpaid in North America. See also **delivery versus payment**.

Hex The Helsinki Stock Exchange **share index**.

hire purchase (UK) A form of **consumer credit** in which the purchaser of a good or service pays the **principal** and interest in regular instalments over a period of six months to two years or more; usually an initial deposit is required, and full ownership passes to the purchaser at the end of the period. US = *instalment credit*. See also **finance house**.

historic cost See **costs, historical**.

historic-cost depreciation See **depreciation**.

hoekmen See **Amsterdam Stock Exchange**.

holder Of a **derivative**, the buyer. See **writer**.

holding company A company (see **incorporation**) that controls one or more other companies, normally by holding a majority of the **shares** of these **subsidiaries**. It is possible for a holding company to control a large number of companies with a combined **capital** very much greater than its own, since it needs to hold only half or even less of the shares of its subsidiaries. This is known as pyramiding. See also **consolidated accounts**.

home banking See **viewdata**.

home service See **industrial branch**.

Hong Kong Commodities Exchange Ltd Founded in 1977, the market deals in cotton, sugar, soya bean and gold **futures**.

Hong Kong stock exchanges The four **stock exchanges** in Hong Kong were modernized and unified in 1986, to become the Stock Exchange of Hong Kong (SEHK). They are regulated by the Securities and Futures Commission. Structural reforms including independence for the commission were recommended in a report by Ian Hay Davison following the October 1987 market crash and implemented. The Hang Seng Index of 33 leading stocks provides the basis for **options** and **futures** contracts on the futures exchange. There is also a more broadly based index, the Hong Kong Stock Index. A second-tier market has also been proposed.

horizontal spread A combination of **options**, namely a **long**-call **option** combined with a **short**-call option, or the same combination of *put* options, both with different expiry dates.

Hypothekenbank (Ger.) **Mortgage bank**.

IBBR See **London interbank offered rate**.

IBELs See **interest-bearing eligible liabilities**.

IBIS (Ger.) Interbank Information System. A screen-based securities quotation system.

IBMBR See **London interbank offered rate**.

IBNR See **incurred but not reported**.

IBNR claims reserve A fund (usually the **claims outstanding reserve**) set aside by an insurance company to meet **claims** that have arisen but not yet been presented to the company, i.e. **incurred but not reported** (IBNR). See also **technical reserves**.

IBRC See **Insurance Brokers' Registration Council**.

IBRD See **International Bank for Reconstruction and Development**.

ICCH See **International Commodities Clearing House**.

ichibu (Jap.) The *first section* of the **stock exchange**, dealing in prime **securities**.

IDA International Development Association. See **International Bank for Reconstruction and Development**.

IET See **interest equalization tax**.

IFA See **independent financial adviser**.

IFC International Finance Corporation. See **International Bank for Reconstruction and Development**.

ILU See **Institute of London Underwriters**.

IMF See **International Monetary Fund**.

immediate annuity An **annuity** commencing immediately on purchase.

impact loan (Jap.) A loan made in foreign **currencies**, provided by an **authorized foreign exchange bank**, the use of which is unregulated.

impôt (Fr.) Tax.

imputation system See **corporation tax**.

IMRO Investment Managers' Regulatory Organization. See **Financial Services Act**.

in camera In closed session of a law court.

in the money A term used in the **options** market where there is **intrinsic value** in the underlying **asset**.

inchoate instrument A money **instrument**, e.g. a **cheque**, **bill of exchange** or *promissory note* (see **note**), that is incomplete in all its particulars. A drawer of such an instrument can give authority to another party to insert the missing particulars, e.g. a drawer of a bill of exchange can leave the name of the drawee blank, authorizing a third party to find a drawee and add that person's name.

income share See **investment trust**.

income tax A compulsory transfer of a proportion of employment and investment income to the state. Gifts are taxed separately (see **inheritance tax**). Income for income tax purposes consists of wages, salaries, bonuses from employment, unincorporated business profits, **pensions**, rent, **interest** and **dividends**. In some countries the last three sources of income may be taxed under a different system; there may be a distinction made between earned income from employment and unearned income from rents and other investments. Some countries provide **tax allowances** or **tax credits** for **investment** (e.g. the **Enterprise Investment Scheme**) or investment income, and most do this also for pension provisions. **Capital gains** may be taxed under separate systems, while employee fringe benefits may also be taxed. In all countries income tax is progressive on successive slices of income, and allowances are given for dependants, etc. There is an international trend towards a reduction in the number of income tax bands and rates, though the UK added one in 1992/3. There were three rates of tax in the UK in 1994/5 on successive bands of taxable incomes: a *lower rate* at 20% (up to £3,000), a *standard rate* at 25% (£3,001–£23,700) and a single *higher rate* of 40% (£23,701 upwards). Some forms of investment income, e.g. **bank deposit** interest and **dividends**, have income tax deducted at source. People in employment are taxed under the Pay As You Earn (PAYE) system under schedule E. Under the PAYE system the employer deducts income tax by the use of code numbers that ensure that taxpayers receive the allowances to which they are entitled. The self-employed, including **partnerships**, are taxed under schedule D. See **Tax Reform Act**.

IFOX (Ire.) Irish Futures and Options Exchange.

incorporation The act of forming a company by carrying out the necessary legal formalities (see **memorandum of association**). A company is a legal person separate and distinct from the people who own it, usually with **limited liability**. In the UK under the Companies Act 1985 there are three classes of company: (i) limited and (ii) unlimited private companies and (iii) *public limited companies* (plcs). All companies are obliged to file certain information for public inspection and to circulate accounts to their shareholders, though these **disclosure** requirements are less onerous for smaller private companies. A plc may have an unlimited number of share-holders and may offer **shares** for public subscription (see **offer for sale**). Only plcs may qualify for listing on the **London Stock Exchange** or the unlisted securities market. Private companies may place certain restrictions on the transfer of shares but may not offer shares to the public (see **close company**). The **European Union**'s *Twelfth Directive* providing for single-member limited liability com-panies is now implemented in the UK. Company law sets out other provisions dealing with the powers, appointment and terms of directors, the protection of investors, including *minority interests* (see **consolidated accounts**), ownership and control, the regulation of shares, the disclosure of interests in shares, accounts, winding up (see

bankruptcy, **liquidation**) and other matters. The 1981 Companies Act allowed companies to acquire their own shares under certain circumstances, a practice known as buying in shares, which may be carried out to improve the dividend **yield**.

The broad outline of company law is similar in most countries, though there are important differences in detail; e.g. in Germany, public companies are required to have two-tiered boards. In the USA, the term for an incorporated business is corporation (Inc.), but there are not separate *legal forms* for private companies and public companies. Other business-legal forms include the **partnership**, **sole proprietorship** and **company limited by guarantee**. See also *Aktiengesellschaft, Bv, Gesellschaft mit beschränkter Haftung (GmbH), naamloze vennootschap, sociedad anónima, società per azioni, société à responsabilité limitée, société anonyme*.

incurred but not reported (IBNR) Losses believed by an insurer to be covered by a policy they have issued but not yet reported to them by the policy-holder, and not yet the subject of a claim. This can in particular be the case for **long tail business**. Insurers are legally required to constitute reserves in respect of IBNR.

indemnity The sum in compensation paid by an **insurance** company in the event of loss or damage under the contract.

independent financial adviser (IFA) A firm licensed under the **Financial Services Act** to advise on and to transact investment business on behalf of clients, acting on a wholly independent basis with no commitment to any producer of investment products. IFAs are legally obliged to give 'best advice'. i.e. to offer the product best suited to the circumstances of their client. Relevant investment products include **life assurance**, **pensions**, **unit trusts**, investment management and investment advice.

independent intermediary An independent insurance broker owing no allegiance to any insurance company, defined as a broker selling the products of more than one life company and of more than six general insurers, and legally bound to give 'best advice' to prospective policy-holders. None the less, the independent intermediary relies for their income on commissions paid by insurance companies on sales of policies. See also **independent financial adviser**.

index fund See **indexing**.

index-linking See **indexation**.

index number An **average** of a group of observations of a price or some other variable, expressed as a percentage of the average of the same variable in the base year against which the comparison is being made. In price indices the variables may be unweighted averages or **weighted averages**. See also **retail price index, share indices**.

indexation The indexation or automatic linkage between monetary obligations and the price level. **Securities** may be index-linked. The UK government introduced an index-linked security in 1981 for financial institutions and has subsequently issued others for private investors as well as institutions, e.g. the $2\frac{1}{2}$% *index-linked* Treasury stock 2011 in which both the interest and the **principal** are adjusted in line with changes in the **retail price index**. Some **National Savings certificates** are also index-linked (US = *inflation proofing*). General indexation, including the index-linking of bank and other loans, has been used in some countries, e.g. Brazil, to help control inflation in the past. In the UK the amount of **capital gains** and losses for tax purposes was subject to indexation, but in the November 1993 Budget the indexation of losses was abolished. See also **indexing**.

indexing Weighting a **portfolio** in the same proportions as the components of a **share index** such as **Standard and Poor's 500**. The performance of a fund consisting of company shares weighted in this way will mirror that of the index, thus ensuring that an index fund will not perform worse (or better) than the market as a whole. Not to be confused with **indexation**.

Indian Opportunities Fund An *offshore* (see **tax haven**) **open-ended fund** established to provide international investors with access to the Indian stock market free of **capital gains tax** or **withholding tax**.

Indian stock exchanges See **Bombay Stock Exchange**.

indice (Fr.) 1. Index, **index number**. 2. **Stock exchange** index.

indirect tax See **taxation**.

individual retirement account (IRA) (US) A pension plan (see **pensions**) under which employed people not covered by another retirement plan and whose income is below a specified minimum make tax–deductible contributions to a fund invested in **securities** and other forms of investments. Contributions are subject to a limit of $2,000 a year for an individual, more for married couples, and withdrawals before age $59\frac{1}{2}$ are subject to a penalty. See also **personal pension**.

industrial bank See **finance house**.

industrial branch Life insurance business conducted through the collection of **premiums** at the **policy-holder**'s home, also known as home service business. Now declining in relative importance.

inflation A fall in the purchasing power of money, reflected in a persistent increase in the general level of prices as measured by the **retail price index**.

inflation accounting Methods of keeping a record of financial transactions and analysing them in a way that allows for changes in the purchasing power of money over time. In periods of rapidly rising prices, with accounts maintained on a historical cost basis (see **costs, historical**), the replacement cost of assets may be much higher than their recorded costs, and **depreciation** provisions may be inadequate and **profit** overstated. *Current cost accounting* (CCA) is a form of replacement cost accounting that involves revaluing assets from historic costs to current costs.

inflation proofing See **indexation**.

Inhaber (Ger.) Owner.

Inhaberaktie (Ger.) A bearer share. See **bearer security**.

Inhabereffekten (Ger.) **Bearer securities**.

Inhaberobligation (Ger.) A bearer bond. See **bearer security**.

Inhaberpapier (Ger.) A **bearer security**.

inheritance tax (UK) A tax on the transmission of wealth on death and by gifts made in the seven years prior to death. Transfers in excess of £50,000 after March 1988 are subject to tax at a single flat rate of 40%. The tax replaced **capital transfer tax** in 1986.

initial public offering (IPO) (US) The offering of the **shares** in the **equity** of a company to the public for the first time. See also **new issue**.

initial yield See **yield**.

Inland Revenue (UK) The government department responsible for the collection and administration of **income tax**, **corporation tax**, **capital gains tax**, **inheritance tax**, **stamp duty** and petroleum revenue tax. (Similar functions in the USA are carried out by the *Internal Revenue Service* (IRS).) In the UK **value added tax**, **excise duty** and other taxes including customs duties (see **tariffs**) are the responsibility of another department, HM Customs and Excise. See also **taxation**.

innocent capacity **Reinsurance** activity undertaken by an obscure or newly established operator, neither familiar with nor expert in the workings of the market. Used chiefly in respect of the new operators drawn into the reinsurance market in the late 1970s and early 1980s in response to overcapacity in the **direct business** market.

INRA International Natural Rubber Agreement. See **International Natural Rubber Organization**.

INRO See **International Natural Rubber Organization**.

insider dealing The buying and selling of **shares** while in possession of price-sensitive information obtained unlawfully, e.g. through employment in the company whose shares are being dealt with (US = *insider trading*). Insider dealing is illegal in the UK, the USA, France and other countries.

insider trading See **insider dealing**.

insolvency See **bankruptcy**.

instalment credit See **hire purchase**.

Institute of London Underwriters (ILU) Founded in 1884, and with an international membership (confined, however, to those **underwriting** in the London market), the ILU is responsible for the standard clauses in marine and air cargo insurance; it services **Lloyd's** and non-Lloyd's marine committees, and it is a forum for professional discussion.

institutional investor An organization, as opposed to an individual, that invests funds arising from its receipts from the sale of **securities**, from **deposits** and from other sources; i.e. **insurance** companies, **investment trusts**, **unit trusts**, **pensions funds** and trustees (see **trust**). Institutional investors probably own over 70% of the **shares** of quoted UK companies.

instrument A term used to denote any form of financing medium, most usually those for the purpose of borrowing in the **money market**, e.g. **bills of exchange**, **bonds**, **certificates of deposit**, **Treasury bills** and *promissory notes* (see **notes**). Normally used to denote the document itself. **Financial instruments** are acquired, or bought, by payment to the existing owner of the **face value** of the instrument, normally less a **discount**. By the same token, the owner transferring the instrument is the seller. On original sale, or **issue**, the instrument is a means of raising a loan and thus of acquiring an **asset**. The term also applies to **derivatives**.

insurable interest A legal term referring to the value in the subject of **insurance** directly attributable to the **insured**; such value must normally exist both at the time of contracting the insurance and at the time of any **claim**, if the contract is to be valid.

insurance A method of compensation for financial loss in the case of death, illness, injury, accident, theft, destruction or damage through fire and other hazards, claims for negligence or incompetence, and other eventualities. The method is the creation of a fund out of payments, or **premiums**, by those exposed to the risk, out of which compensation is paid to those to whom the eventuality actually occurs. By the **law of large numbers**, the total of the premiums collected can be made to equal at least the total compensation paid out.

Insurance business is broadly divided between *general insurance* and *life insurance* (or life *assurance*, as it is often deemed to be more properly termed). Life assurance consists in provision for compensation against an inevitable occurrence, that of death, and in this respect differs from other insurance, which offers compensation against an eventuality that may or may not occur. Life assurance thus relies heavily on **actuaries**' computation of **mortality**. Deaths from accident and other non-natural causes of course occur, but this category constitutes so small a fraction of all deaths, and also can be so reduced by exclusion of people engaged in hazardous activities, that calculation of appropriate premiums by actuarial methods can be most precise.

Central to the financing of insurance is the investment of the fund generated by premiums. Insurance companies constitute one of the biggest **portfolio** holders on the **stock exchange**. The practice of general insurance dates back to earliest times. Life assurance did not take on its modern proportions until the theory of probability had been developed and combined with the principle of compound interest, in the early 18th century. General insurance contracts or policies are normally for a risk of a specified monetary value and for a specified period of time. Life assurance policies are for a specified monetary amount and are necessarily indeterminate in time; however, life policies may also be taken out for a specified period of years, in which case they are known as term policies. See **general insurance**, **life assurance**, **reinsurance**.

Insurance Accounts Directive A directive adopted by the Council of the **European Union** requiring consistent presentation of insurance company accounts in the Union.

Insurance Brokers' Registration Council (IBRC) (UK) A self-regulatory organization for insurance **brokers** recognized under the **Financial Services Act**.

insurance premium tax (UK) A tax of 3% on premiums for general insurance policies (i.e. including household and motor insurance but not life insurance, reinsurance, ships, aircraft or other commerical policies), introduced with effect from 1 October 1994.

insured The short term used to refer to the party to benefit under an **insurance** contract.

insurer An entity, either a company or a **mutual** society, engaged in the business of insurance.

intangible asset See **asset**.

integrated data feeds An **on-line** information system in which several services, e.g. NASDAQ (see **National Association of Securities Dealers Automated Quotation System**) and **Reuters**, are available on one screen.

Inter-Africa Coffee Organization An association of 25 African coffee-producing countries, responsible for approximately one-fifth (some 1m tonnes) of world output, formed after the suspension in 1989 of the stabilization measures incorporated in the International Coffee Agreements (see **International Coffee Organization**). In 1993 the organization, along with Latin American growers, reached an agreement to withhold 20% of output until a target price was attained.

inter-dealer broker (IDB) (UK) A **broker** who buys and sells **gilts** only from and to **market makers**.

inter vivos Between living persons.

interbank market The **money market** in which banks (see **banking**) borrow or lend money among themselves either to accommodate short-term **liquidity** problems or for the lending on of surplus funds. These loans may be arranged either direct or through **money brokers**. See **London interbank offered rate** (LIBOR).

Intercomalum An organization set up to promote and defend the aluminium industry of the former states of the Soviet Union. In 1993 a first contact with the then European Community (see **European Union**) arose out of a demand by European producers for strict quotas on imports from the states in question. See also **London Metal Exchange**.

interest 1. Payment for a **loan**. See also **rate of interest**. 2. A share in ownership; e.g. company A may have an interest (own **shares** in) company B.

interest-bearing eligible liabilities (IBELs) That proportion of commercial bank deposits defined as **eligible liabilities** that carry a rate of interest.

interest cover The number of times the interest payments made by a company to service its **loan capital** are exceeded by the income of the business.

interest equalization tax (IET) (US) A tax introduced in 1963, with the effect of raising the cost to US citizens of investing in issues by foreigners on the domestic US capital market, US market interest ratios being at that time lower than in most foreign markets. The tax, introduced for the purpose of defending the US balance of payments, duly discouraged foreign borrowers and also encouraged US borrowers to resort to foreign capital markets. The IET is generally regarded as one of the contributory factors leading to the emergence of the **Eurodollar market**. It was withdrawn in 1974.

interest rate See **rate of interest**.

interest rate future A form of **financial future** in which the contract is in respect of the interest rate on the underlying **asset**.

interest rate margin 1. The difference between a bank's lending and deposit interest rates. 2. The difference between the interest rate paid on a debt security and a reference interest rate. Most commonly used in the **Euromarket** for **floating rate notes** (see **note issuance facility**). Also termed **spread.** The reference rate is invariably the **London interbank offered rate** (LIBOR) and also the *London interbank bid rate* (LIBID) and **LIMEAN** (London interbank mean rate).

interest rate option See **option**.

interest rate swap A transaction under which two streams of interest rate payments are exchanged. The object is to enable a lower-class borrower to benefit from the better interest rate available to a higher-class borrower; the latter takes a small profit on the transaction. Interest rate swaps quickly came to be traded as

negotiable instruments in their own right, the **principal** not in fact changing hands, and this trade now forms the bulk of the market. Dealing is done chiefly by banks and securities houses. Trade in interest rate swaps began in 1982, and the market grew rapidly thereafter. By the end of 1985 some $200bn of swaps were reckoned to be outstanding. Standardized terms were introduced in 1985 by the International Swap Dealers' Association and the British Bankers' Association. In 1985 the asset-based swap was introduced, i.e. a swap of the interest on an **asset**, rather than a **liability** of the party concerned, namely the swap of an interest stream due to the party, rather than the stream payable by that party. See also **cross-currency interest rate swap**, **currency interest rate swap**, **swap**.

interest sensitive Economic and financial activities strongly influenced by movements in interest rates, e.g. house buying, hire purchasing, corporate borrowing.

interest yield See **yield**.

interim dividend See **dividend**.

intermarket spread swap A **swap** of securities made in the expectation of a change in the **spread** between the **yields** of the securities.

Intermarket Trading System (ITS) See **National Market System**.

intermediary A person or firm, other than the insurance company itself, engaged in the selling of insurance; e.g. an agent, an insurance **broker**, a bank, an accountant, a solicitor, a financial adviser or an estate agent. See **financial intermediary**.

intermediate offer A **new issue** of **shares** in which shares are placed with financial **intermediaries** (see **placing**). Private investors may apply for these shares through a **stockbroker**. See **offer for sale**.

intermediation See **disintermediation**.

internal rate of return See **discounted cash flow**.

internal repurchase agreement pool (US) The total of short-term investment balances, arising out of **repurchase agreements**, held by the **Federal Reserve** in the name of foreign **central banks** and international organizations.

Internal Revenue Service (IRS) (US) See **Inland Revenue**.

internal Rp pool See **internal repurchase agreement pool**.

International Bank for Reconstruction and Development (IBRD; World Bank) Founded, together with the **International Monetary Fund** (IMF), by the **Bretton Woods** Conference of 1944 as an international bank to finance the reconstruction and development of member countries. Operations started in 1946. The bank is financed partly by contributions paid by member countries, partly by bond issues. The national contributions constitute the bank's capital and relate to the individual countries' share of world trade. The bond issues finance the lending operations of the Bank. Operational revenues have come to be supplemented over the course of time by receipts of interest on, and repayment of the capital of, loans. In financing the economic needs of member countries, the Bank complements the IMF, which finances temporary **balance of payments** difficulties. Loans are made to governments or government-guaranteed entities. At first devoted to the reconstruction needs of industrial countries, the World Bank by the 1950s had focused its attention on the developing world.

In 1956 the Bank formed the *International Finance Corporation* (IFC), whose purpose was to promote growth in the private sector of developing countries and to mobilize domestic and foreign capital for this purpose. In 1960 the Bank formed the *International Development Association* (IDA) in order to assist the poorer developing countries (those with an annual per capita *gross national product* (see **gross domestic product**) of less than $731 in 1980 prices). Loans made to these countries carry no interest and are repayable over 50 years with an initial grace period of 10 years. The Bank's strategy since the 1960s has been to ensure that its aid reaches the broad masses of the people; this to be done by investments encouraging productivity and integrating the broad masses of the people as active partners into the development process. The capital of the Bank amounts to over $171bn. China became a member in 1990, and there are over 150 member countries. In 1980 the Bank introduced a new policy under its *Economic Structural Adjustment Programme* (ESAP) by which it makes loans to ease the balance of payments problems of the developing countries conditional on the adoption of free market economic policies specified by the Bank.

International Cocoa Agreement A series of intergovernmental agreements for the stabilization of the world cocoa market. The most recent, signed in September 1993 under the auspices of the United Nations, and replacing that of 1986, relies on production limits and consumption promotion measures; it is said to be the first United Nations commodity pact to make production management its cornerstone. A production committee has the task of fixing 'indicative figures for annual levels of global productions necessary to achieve and maintain equilibrium' in the cocoa market. A consumption committee seeks action by signatories 'to remove or reduce substantially' domestic taxes and import tariffs that deter consumption. The 40 signatories, both producing and consuming countries, account for three-quarters of world output and consumption. However, Malaysia, accounting for 10% of world production, and the USA, accounting for 25% of world use, did not sign.

International Coffee Council See **International Coffee Organization**.

International Coffee Organization An intergovernmental body established to administer a series of International Coffee Agreements, the first of which was negotiated in 1962 under the auspices of the United Nations and the remainder of which were negotiated at the headquarters of the organization in London. The latest of these, dating from 1983, has been successively extended to September 1994. The agreements for some time provided for stabilization of the market through production quotas, import controls, stock verification and a fund for the promotion of consumption. In 1973 these market stabilization measures were suspended, to be partly reinstated in 1976 and fully reinstated in 1983. However, in 1989 the measures were again withdrawn, not subsequently to be revived. The organization continues with its efforts, in force since the beginning, to further international co-operation between coffee-exporting and

-importing countries in order to achieve a reasonable balance between supply and demand that will ensure adequate supplies of coffee at fair prices to consumers and at remunerative prices to producers; and to act as a centre for studies and research on the production, distribution and consumption of coffee. There are 67 member governments: 47 from exporting countries accounting for over 97% of world production, the remainder from importing countries accounting for over 80% of world consumption. The organization consists of a council, an executive board and an executive director with appropriate staff.

International Commercial Exchange (US) The pioneer in **financial futures**, having first traded in these in 1970.

International Commodities Clearing House (ICCH) (UK) The major **clearing house** for **futures** dealings in the London **commodity market** in most **soft commodities** (except wheat and barley) and most metals, and also for **options** in certain soft commodities. First began operating in 1888, as the London Produce Clearing House, changing to its present functions and name in 1973. All members of the ICCH are members of the individual exchanges, and all transactions in the latter must be conducted through a member of the ICCH.

international commodity agreement An international agreement, normally concluded between governments, intended to influence the price of a **commodity**. The need for such price influence is seen to lie in the fact that commodities, particularly **primary** commodities, have in many cases long production cycles, responding poorly to demand fluctuations and thus causing price volatility, and that earnings on commodity sales constitute a major proportion of the export revenues of developing countries. Commodity agreements have been concluded in respect of, among other things, coffee, sugar, wheat, tin, cocoa, natural rubber and textiles. Agreements are normally implemented through **buffer stocks**, production controls and purchase guarantees.

International Development Association (IDA) See **International Bank for Reconstruction and Development**.

International Finance Corporation (IFC) See **International Bank for Reconstruction and Development**.

international liquidity See **liquidity**.

International Monetary Fund (IMF) Established by the **Bretton Woods** Conference in 1947, the purpose of the IMF is to foster international monetary co-operation through the stabilization of **exchange rates**, the removal of **foreign exchange** restrictions and the facilitation of international payments and of *international liquidity* (see **liquidity**). At the outset member nations declared their exchange rates, or **par values**, to which, within a margin of 1% in either direction, they held their currencies. The par values were quoted in terms of the US dollar, which was itself valued in terms of gold. However, following the breaking of the dollar's link with gold in 1971 and the abandonment of national fixed parities from 1972 onwards, the IMF rule was abolished in 1976.

The major function of the IMF has been lending in support of countries in **balance of payments** difficulties. For this purpose the IMF has been funded by contributions, or **quotas**, from member countries. Countries in difficulties obtain foreign currencies in exchange for their own, which they must repay within three to five years. Members in severe balance of payments difficulties are obliged to consult with the IMF on remedial domestic policies as a condition of further assistance. The funds of the IMF have been progressively increased over the years. A major increase occurred in 1962 under the **general arrangements to borrow** (GAB). A further large increase occurred through the creation, in 1970, of **special drawing rights** (SDRs).

In 1976 the use of gold as a constituent of the IMF's funds and as a **unit of account** was discontinued, and the IMF was authorized to sell its gold holdings. The IMF seeks the removal of restrictions on international monetary movements and publishes an annual record of these restrictions.

international monetary market See **Chicago Mercantile Exchange**.

International Natural Rubber Agreement See **International Natural Rubber Organization**.

International Natural Rubber Organization (INRO) An intergovernmental organization comprising six producer and 10 consumer members (the European Union being counted as one consumer country), based in Kuala Lumpur and formed to administer the International Natural Rubber Agreements. The first agreement was signed in 1979; the second came into force in 1988, being due to expire in December 1993. The object of the agreements has been to provide market stability, ensuring fair prices for both consumers and producers in the face of wide fluctuations in demand. This has been achieved by counter-cyclical buying and selling into and from a central buffer stock. Total natural rubber output and consumption in 1992 were some 5.6m tonnes, comparing with consumption of synthetic rubber of some 9m tonnes. However, demand fell during 1993, with technical difficulties inhibiting buffer stock purchases.

International Petroleum Exchange (IPE) (UK) A **commodity** market for petroleum; it instituted a **futures** contract for gas oil in 1981, following the dispersal of petroleum sales from the major world oil companies and following the success of a heating oil **futures** contract introduced by the **New York Mercantile Exchange** in 1958. The IPE is a member of the **International Commodities Clearing House**.

International Securities Market Association (ISMA) A Zurich-based organization for participants in the **Eurobond** markets. Formerly the Association of International Bond Dealers (AIBD).

International Securities Regulatory Organization See **Securities Association**.

International Stock Exchange See **London Stock Exchange**.

International Sugar Organization A successor to the International Sugar Council of prewar origin, the International Sugar Organization is an intergovernmental body comprising 26 sugar-producing and sugar-importing member countries, established under the auspices of the United Nations Conference on Trade and Development (UNCTAD). Until 1984, under successive International Sugar Agreements, the member states sought to stabilize world sugar prices through quotas and the holding of stocks. These efforts were discontinued in 1984; the aims of the organization since then have been to 'ensure and enhance international co-operation' in world sugar matters, to 'facilitate trade by collecting and providing information on the world sugar market' and to 'encourage and increase the demand for sugar'. In particular, the organization disseminates daily information on sugar market prices.

International Swap Dealers' Association See **interest rate swaps**.

International Swaps and Derivatives Association (ISDA) The trade association of dealers in **derivatives**.

international Trade Organization (ITO) See **General Agreement on Tariffs and Trade** (GATT).

International Union of Credit and Investment Insurers See **Berne Union**.

International Wheat Agreement (IWA) An international agreement signed in 1986 giving rise to the Wheat Trade Convention, administered by the **International Wheat Council**, and to the Food Aid Convention, administered by the **Food Aid Committee** (FAC).

International Wheat Council (IWC) Established in its present form in 1949, having existed since the early 1940s, the council is an intergovernmental organization of 48 members, including most wheat-trading countries. For many years concerned with market stabilization measures, the council's main task since the mid-1980s has been to promote collaboration, and in particular to administer the Wheat Trade Convention (WTC) of the **International Wheat Agreement** (IWA). The aims of the WTC are to further international co-operation in international trade in all grains (not only wheat), to contribute to the stability of international grain markets and to enhance world food security, particularly in the interests of developing member countries. For this purpose the council maintains an extensive information system covering different aspects of the world grains economy (including monthly market reports and a number of annual publications), and holds meetings and conferences where members may consult on world grain problems. Finance is provided by member governments in proportion to their votes. A small secretariat is based in London.

intervention mechanism A term used to describe the methods used by the **European Monetary System** (EMS) to maintain agreed **exchange rate** relationships. This is done in the first place by a very **short-term** financing **facility** under which the central bank of a country under exchange rate pressure may borrow from other central banks for 75 days, extendable under certain conditions up to three months. Further possibilities are **short-term monetary support** (STMS) and **medium-term financial assistance** (MTFA).

Intex Automated screen trading system software marketed by **Telerate**.

intrinsic value 1. The value believed by some to attach inherently to a natural object, e.g. a precious metal, regardless of its price at any given time. In economics, value is determined only by demand and is denoted by price; hence intrinsic value is inapplicable. **2**. In the **options** market, the amount by which the **striking price** differs from the current price of the underlying asset; i.e. in a *call option* the intrinsic value is an amount in excess of the current price; in a *put option* it is an amount below that price. See **time value**.

introduction (UK) A means of initial entry to a stock market for companies whose shares are already widely held but, until the introduction is effected, are not quoted or listed. For example, on the London **unlisted securities market**, where 10% or more of the share capital is already widely held by members of the public, permission to deal can be granted without the necessity for an **offer for sale**. See **placing**.

inventories A term for stocks of raw materials, work in progress and finished goods.

investment 1. The act of placing monetary resources into the creation of **assets**, in the manufacturing and services sectors of the economy. Only real *capital formation*, such as the production of machinery, adds to the stock of investment goods. **2**. The act of placing monetary resources into financial assets, namely the purchase of **shares** or **bonds**. Shifting money from a bank account to **securities** in this way simply moves **savings** from one form to another. **3**. The sum of money itself so invested, or the total of financial assets so acquired.

investment allowances, investment incentives Government assistance designed to encourage firms to invest in physical **assets** in total, in particular industries or in particular locations. Incentives may take the form of **capital allowances** for tax relief, cash payments or low interest rates.

investment balances See **money supply**.

investment bank (US) A **financial intermediary** that purchases new issues and places them in smaller parcels among investors. In the UK, a **merchant bank** or **issuing house**.

investment credit (US) A **tax credit** equivalent to 10% of the purchase price of investment goods by businesses. Intended to encourage investment in fixed **assets**, the investment credit was abolished in the **Tax Reform Act** 1986. (UK = **capital allowances**.)

investment currency pool (UK) See **dollar pool**.

investment grade See **Standard and Poor's ratings**.

Investment Managers' Regulatory Organization See **Financial Services Act**.

investment multiplier See **multiplier**.

Investment Services Directive (ISD) A **European Union** directive coming into force in 1996 that provides for securities dealers and **investment banks**, including portfolio managers and underwriters authorized in one member state to operate directly or via branches in any other EU state without further authorization. The Capital Adequacy Directive (CAD) sets out minimum **capital adequacy** requirements with which ISD firms must comply.

investment trust A company whose sole object is to invest its **capital** in a wide range of **securities**, i.e. a **closed-end fund**. An investment trust issues shares and uses its capital to buy securities and **shares** in other companies. A **unit trust**, in contrast, issues units that represent holdings of shares. Unit holders thus do not share in the **profits** of the company managing the trust. Investment trusts can also raise part of their capital by issuing fixed-interest securities, and the yield on the **ordinary shares** of the trust can thus benefit from **gearing**. The trust deed (see **trust**) may provide for the holdings of the investment trust to be sold at a certain date (for which there may be provisions for extension) and the proceeds distributed to shareholders; this is an investment trust with a limited life. In some investment trusts with a limited life there are two types of shares: *income shares* and *capital shares*. Holders of income shares receive all or most of the income from the **assets** of the trust, while holders of capital shares receive all or most of the capital value of the assets of the trust on **liquidation**. Such trusts are known as *split-level trusts* and allow shareholders to choose to receive their returns in the form of income or **capital gains**. The price of a share in an investment trust may be above (**premium**) or below (**discount**) the value of the underlying shares and other assets, i.e. the **net asset value** per share.

investor base The expected category of buyers of a **security** issue. Normally used in relation to **short-term** issues in the international market.

Investors Compensation Scheme (UK) Provides for payment of up to £48,000 to private investors if a firm authorized under the **Financial Services Act** goes into **default**.

invisible balance See **balance of payments**.

invisible trade See **balance of payments**.

IPE See **International Petroleum Exchange**.

IPO See **initial public offering**.

IRA See **individual retirement account**.

IRR Internal rate of return. See **discounted cash flow**.

irredeemable security See **redemption date**.

irrevocable letter of credit See **letter of credit**.

IRS (US) Internal Revenue Service. See **Inland Revenue**.

ISDA See **International Swaps and Derivatives Association**.

ISE International Stock Exchange. See **London Stock Exchange**.

ISE/Nikkei 50 Index A **share index** based on the prices of 50 Japanese **equities** traded both on the International Stock Exchange (see **London Stock Exchange**) and on the **Tokyo Stock Exchange**. The index reflects prices of the shares during the trading hours in Tokyo and London and is given on TOPIC (see **Teletext Output of Price Information by Computer**). See also **Nikkei Stock Average**.

ISMA See **International Securities Market Association**.

ISRO See **Securities Association**.

issue Initial sale of a **security**.

issue date The base date for calculating **interest** accrued on a **security**.

issue price The price, gross of any commissions, for any issue of **securities**, i.e. the price at which a **new issue** is offered.

issued capital The part of a company's **capital** that has been subscribed by shareholders. It may or may not be paid up (see **paid-up capital**).

issuing house (UK). A **merchant bank**, **stockbroker** or other **financial institution** that organizes a **new issue** of **securities**. The issuing house or securities house in conjunction with the issuing **broker** will advise the client on the timing and form of the issue and in return for a **commission** will **underwrite** or arrange underwriting for all or part of the issue. The issuing house is nowadays often referred to as a sponsor because it lends its reputation to the issue.

Istanbul Menkul Kiymetter Borsasi The **stock exchange** in Turkey, in its present form dating only from 1986. The number of companies listed (**listed companies**) at the end of 1992 was 145.

itayose (Jap.) A method of **stock exchange** dealing under which all orders entering prior to the official start of business are treated as having arrived at the same time.

ITO International Trade Organization. See **General Agreement on Tariffs and Trade** (GATT).

ITS Intermarket Trading System. See **National Market System**.

IWA See **International Wheat Agreement**.

IWC See **International Wheat Council**.

Jahresabschluss (Ger.) **1**. Year end. **2**. Annual account.

Jahresbericht (Ger.) Annual report.

Jahrgang (Ger.) A year; the period of a year.

Jakarta Stock Exchange In its present form dates from 1977 but has its origins dating back to the Dutch colonial era. Regulated (see **regulation**) by the Capital Market Executive Agency (BAPEPAM).

JASDAQ (Jap.) The Japanese equivalent of the US **National Association of Securities Dealers Automated Quotation System** (NASDAQ).

JGB An abbreviation used in English-speaking markets to denote a Japanese government bond.

***jikihone* bill** (Jap.) An **acceptance** under which an importer uses the yen counterpart of the **foreign currency** value of an import invoice.

Jingen Index See **China**.

jobber (UK) A dealer in **securities** who will buy and sell specific securities at all times, a **market maker**. Prior to the **Big Bang**, jobbers were one of two distinct classes of members of the **London Stock Exchange** who were permitted to deal only with **brokers** and not with the general public. The term is now obsolete.

jobber's turn See **spread**.

Johannesburg Stock Exchange (JSE) Established in 1886, the JSE is the only sizeable **stock exchange** in Africa. There are exchanges in Kenya, Nigeria and Zimbabwe, but the development of all these markets has been restricted until recently by **exchange controls** as well as by the relatively small size of the modern sectors of their economies.

joint and several liability A **liability** that falls at the same time on each one of two or more parties, and on all together. A plaintiff can choose to sue one or more of the parties (severally), or all together (jointly).

joint-stock bank See **commercial banks**.

jouissance (Fr.) The date of the start of **interest** payments.

jour de règlement (Fr.) **Settlement day**.

junior debt See **subordinated**.

junk bond (US) Company bonds of low-quality **security** backing sold with high **coupons**, rated below investment grade by the two US rating agencies, **Standard and Poor's** and Moody's, and giving a **yield** of at least 200 to 250 **basis points** above the yield on Treasury bonds. Junk bonds were pioneered in the mid-1970s by the New York house Drexel Burnham Lambert, and total issues in 1986 were estimated to amount to $32.4bn. However, this was a revival of a market dating back to at least the 1920s. See **leveraged buy-out**.

JSE See **Johannesburg Stock Exchange**.

JSE/Actuaries Index **Share index** for the **Johannesburg Stock Exchange**.

kabushiki kaisha (Jap.) A joint-**stock** company.

kaishime (Jap.) **Ramping**.

kamikaze pricing (Jap.) Deliberate low pricing of **securities** in order to secure a greater share of the securities market.

Kansas City Board of Trade A **commodity** market for grain, sharing with those in Chicago and Minneapolis a dominant influence, through their **futures** trading, on world prices. The market was established in 1856 and began trading in wheat futures in 1876, in value line stock index futures in 1982 and in wheat options in 1984.

Kapitalanlage (Ger.) **Investment**.

Kapitalertragsteuer (Ger.) **Withholding tax**.

Kapitalgewinn (Ger.) **Capital gain**.

Kassa (Ger.) For **cash**.

Kassenobligation (Ger.) A public-sector medium-term **note** issued by government as a security at a time of government borrowing; used in Germany and Switzerland.

Kassenverein (Ger.) The German **securities clearing house**.

Keidenran (Jap.) The federation of Japanese company associations. Equivalent to the UK Confederation of British Industry, the French Patronat and the German Bundesverband der Deutschen Industrien.

keiretsu (Jap.) A Japanese company group formed by interlocking shareholdings. *Keiretsu* normally contain a bank. They differ from *zaibatsu* in that the bank is not the group holding company, legislation having reduced a bank's permitted shareholding in a company to 5%.

Keogh plan (US) A pension plan (see **pensions**) under which contributions by unincorporated businesses or self-employed people are tax-deductible, and appreciation in the fund is tax free, but withdrawals are taxed as income. Originally established by the Self-Employment Individuals Retirement Act 1982.

kerb trading (UK) Trading that occurs after the close of the official market. In the USA the **American Stock Exchange** is sometimes referred to as the Curb Exchange.

key man insurance Insurance taken out by companies to provide compensation for the loss incurred through the absence through death, accident or ill-health of a vital employee.

key pad A small keyboard used to enter data into a computer.

kingaishin **fund** (Jap.) Funds, part of the *tokkin* fund system, placed with **trust banks**.

KISS Kurs Information Service System. See **Deutsche Aktienindex**.

KLCE See **Kuala Lumpur Commodity Exchange**.

KLSE See **Kuala Lumpur Stock Exchange**.

knock-for-knock A practice whereby motor insurers agree, in the event of an accident, each to repair their own insured vehicles, so saving administrative and possibly legal expense. The insured's no-claim bonus is normally not affected.

koko (Jap.) A public corporation engaged in the financing of a particular economic sector, e.g. housing. Funds derive from the Industrial Investment Special Account and from borrowing from the Trust Fund Bureau and from the Post Office life insurance and annuity accounts.

Kommunalobligation (Ger.) A loan to local authorities by a *Hypothekenbank*.

Kontrahent (Ger.) A contracting party.

Konzern (Ger.) A German company grouping of considerable size, the nucleus of which is a holding company having outright ownership, or a majority shareholding, of the remaining members of the group. Featured largely in German industry before the Second World War, subsequent legislation having disbanded many groups in pursuit of decartelization policy.

Korea Stock Exchange (KSE) Established in its present form in Seoul in 1956, with antecedents back to 1911. It is one of the largest and most modern **stock exchanges** in the Far East, in 1992 second only to the Japanese and Hong Kong exchanges in **equity** market **capitalization**.

Kuala Lumpur Commodity Exchange (KLCE) A **commodity** market set up in 1980 for trade in rubber and crude palm oil. A major world market for **hedging** in RSS1 (Ribbed Smoked Sheet No. 1) quality, a long-established grade of natural rubber.

Kuala Lumpur Stock Exchange (KLSE) Dates from 1973 with the ending of the joint **stock exchange** of Malaysia and Singapore, which had been established in 1964. There is also an **unlisted securities market**.

Kuala Lumpur Tin Market A **commodity** market set up in 1984, dealing only in **physical** transactions in tin.

Kuponsteuer (Ger.) A tax on interest receipts of foreign holders of German **bonds**.

Kurs (Ger.) The official **stock exchange** price of a **security**.

Kurs Information Service System See **Deutsche Aktienindex**.

Kursmakler (Ger.) An official **broker** in the German **stock market**, acting as intermediary between banks, admitted to deal on the exchange, but not acting for members of the public; also responsible for fixing prices.

kurzfristig (Ger.) **Short term**.

ladder option An **option** during the life of which the holder can incorporate gains in the underlying security price. Also known as a *step-lock option*.

lagged reserve requirement (LRR) (US) A system in which banks are required to hold reserves with retrospective effect, i.e. in relation to the level of deposits in a recent past period. The maintenance period, normally of one week, is usually in respect of the preceding two weeks.

LAN See **local area network**.

Land, Länder (Ger.) The eight major territorial subdivisions, or states, into which West Germany was divided after the Second World War, having wide powers of self-government and conforming closely to the pre-1914 principalities, kingdoms and city-states. On German reunification in 1990, the five *Länder* of former East Germany were added. To these must be added the self-governing 'city-states' of Berlin, Bremen and Hamburg.

langfristig (Ger.) **Long term**.

LAPR Life assurance premium relief. See **unit-linked life assurance**.

last trading day The last day on which **futures** trading can be done for a particular **delivery month**. After that day physical delivery is mandatory.

LAUTRO Life Assurance and Unit Trust Regulatory Organization. See **Financial Services Act**.

law of large numbers The mathematical law that states that the larger the number of times that several possible outcomes occur, the greater the likelihood that the frequency of occurrence of each particular outcome will coincide with the average frequency that can be established by theoretical calculation. Used in the calculation of **risk** in insurance.

LBO See **leveraged buy-out**.

LDP See **London daily prices**.

leaning into the wind (US) An expression used to describe the policy of the **Federal Reserve**, practised particularly in the 1950s and 1960s, of lowering interest rates at times of low economic demand and raising them at times of high demand.

lease-back A contractual arrangement in which an **asset** is sold and immediately leased back (see **leasing**) to the seller. It is a means of raising **finance** from an institution such as an insurance company and then renting it back on a long lease.

leasing An agreement between the owner of property (lessor) to grant use of it to another party (lessee) for a specified period at a specified rent. Leasing of business equipment, for example, may have tax advantages because the leasing company may receive tax relief on **depreciation** or **investment allowances** that it can pass on to the lessee. Leasing may in effect be a form of **hire purchase**, because ownership of the **asset** may be transferred to the lessee for a small sum at the end of the lease, and the distinction between the two becomes blurred. Leasing is also a form of **off-balance-sheet finance**.

legal person See **incorporation**.

legume (Fr.) An edible vegetable **commodity** (e.g. peas and beans).

lender of last resort An institution, normally a **central bank**, that stands ready to lend to the commercial banking system when the latter is in overall shortage of funds. The latter position will arise when extra large payments out of the banking system, such as seasonal tax payments (e.g. periodic **corporation tax** payments by companies), reduce the banking system's holdings below the level appropriate to its **reserves**. The central bank will, in such cases, lend at short term to the banking system until such time as funds return through normal depositors. Lenders of last resort in the USA and the UK are the **Federal Reserve** and the **Bank of England** respectively. The Federal Reserve normally lends through **repurchase agreements**. The Bank of England lends to the **discount houses**. As part of its function as a regulator of **credit** and **money supply** a central bank will, on occasion, induce a shortage in the commercial banking system so as to force the system into resort to it ('into the bank') and to require commercial banks to borrow from it at high rates of interest, so bringing about a general rise of interest rates and discouraging subsequent lending.

letter of credit A non-**negotiable** order from a bank to a bank abroad, authorizing payment to a named person of a particular sum of money or up to a limit of a certain sum. Letters of credit are often required by exporters who wish to have proof that they will be paid before they ship goods, or who wish to minimize delay in payment for the goods. A confirmed letter of credit is one that has been recognized by the paying bank. Letters of credit may be irrevocable or revocable, depending on whether or not they can be cancelled at any time.

leverage (US) See **gearing**.

leveraged buy-out (US) The acquisition of one company by another, financed mainly by bank loans and **bonds**. **Corporate raiders** in the USA launched **take-overs** using **junk bonds** and bank loans on many occasions in the 1980s.

levy A duty applied to imports into the **European Union** of agricultural produce from third countries, the effect of which is to raise the price of such produce to a level consistent with that of prices of the same product sold within the Union.

liability 1. An obligation to make a financial payment, namely repayment of a bank loan, redemption of *loan stock* (see **stock**), payment of a **commercial bill**, payment of a business invoice. It may be either direct or implicit, i.e. the implicit obligation of a bank to repay the **deposits** held with it. The liabilities of a company include its **bank loans** and **overdraft**, its short-term **debts** for goods and services received (*current liabilities*) and its **loan**

capital and the **capital** subscribed by **shareholders**. Antithesis of **asset**. Most frequently used in **money markets**, **banking** and business accounting. **2**. Of insurance, the insurance of the risk of claims in respect of misjudgment and incompetence to which employers and the professions (e.g. doctors and accountants) are exposed. The term also used to denote such exposure.

liability management The management of the **liability** side of a bank's balance sheets, i.e. of its **deposits.** The term denotes efforts by a bank to overcome liquidity shortages by increasing the total of its deposits, rather than by reducing its loans, or **assets**. Such increases are actively sought through the issue of **instruments** such as **certificates of deposit**, rather than passively awaited in the form of new conventional deposits by bank customers.

LIBID *London interbank bid rate.* See **London interbank offered rate**.

LIBOR See **London interbank offered rate**.

licensed deposit taker (LDT) A financial institution, other than a bank, authorized under the **Banking Act** 1979, and similar US legislation, to take **deposits** from the general public.

life assurance A branch of insurance in which compensation is made available to designated survivors of a deceased person, or to a person on their own survival of a fixed term of years, in return for payments, or premiums. Life assurance is based on the mathematics of probability, which determine the level of premium to be paid, and on those of compound interest, which determine the growth over time, through investment, of the fund constituted by the intake of premiums (see **insurance**, **mortality**). The two together ensure a fund adequate to provide the compensation required. Basic life assurance therefore covers the whole life of the insured person and is so named. However, life assurance may be taken out for less than the whole life and is then named *term assurance*. In this case the insured sum is paid only in the event of the insured person dying within the term.

An integral part of life assurance financing is the fund of collected premiums, invested in its turn for capital growth and income. Over the course of time insurance companies become more expert investors, and in recent decades stock market values grew strongly. The fund was thus found increasingly to be surplus to payment needs. A further important refinement then emerged in the shape of *endowment assurance*. This is a development of term insurance in which the lump sum is payable either on death during the term, or certainly at the end of the term. A further variation of this has been endowment assurance with profits, in which the lump sum payable is raised in line with the growth in profits through the allocation to the policy of further sums, known as *bonuses*; these bonuses are declared regularly, normally annually, under the name *reversionary bonuses*. A further bonus, formally discretionary but normally declared, is determined at the end of the policy, or at the prior death of the holder. All bonuses are held as credits until death or termination of the policy. Given the certainty of an eventual lump-sum payment, endowment policies quickly lent themselves to the purchase of assets against this expectation. Thus endowment policies came to be used as a means of paying off mortgages for home buying; a later development was the concept of **unit-linked life assurance**.

Premiums are normally paid annually or at lesser intervals and are known as *regular premiums*. In some cases, particularly with unit-linked life assurance, one large premium only may be paid at the outset of the insured period; this is termed a *single premium*. In the latter case the life policy is more usually termed a **bond**.

Life Assurance and Unit Trust Regulatory Organization (LAUTRO) See **Financial Services Act**.

life assurance premium relief (LAPR) A tax relief given on premiums paid for 'qualifying' life assurance policies issued in the UK up to March 1984. Policies 'qualify' by reason of conformance with certain requirements regarding size, regularity and duration of premium payments, size of final pay-out, and others. The relief was withdrawn in the 1984 Budget for all policies issued thereafter. See **life assurance, unit-linked life assurance**.

lifeboat operation See **secondary bank**.

LIFFE See **London International Financial Futures Exchange**.

LIMEAN London interbank mean rate. The mean (see **average**) between **London interbank offered rate** (LIBOR) and *London interbank bid rate* (LIBID).

limit The permitted range within which prices may move, within a specified period, usually a day, in **commodity markets**.

limit order See **order**.

limited company See **incorporation**.

limited liability The restriction of an owner's loss in a business to the amount of **capital** that they have invested in it. Should a **company** be put into **liquidity**, the owner as **equity** shareholder can lose, at most, only the value of their shares, although director shareholders may be subject to other **liabilities** such as personal guarantees for bank borrowing.

line 1. See **line of credit**. **2**. A large block of shares. **3**. Acceptance of an **insurance risk** by an **underwriter**, whether as an assumption of the whole of the risk or of a part.

line of credit 1. An agreed amount of loan arranged between a bank and its customer, normally to be **drawn down** in stages. See **overdraft**. **2**. A loan from the **International Monetary Fund** to a member country, the total amount of which is fixed, but normally available in stages.

liquidate The act of cancelling, or closing out, a **futures** contract where the owner of the contract is **long**; normally done by physical sale of the underlying asset or by purchase of an offsetting contract. The term is also used, although more rarely, for **short** positions, where the term **cover** is more usual. See also **liquidation**.

liquidation The termination, dissolution or winding up of a limited company (see **incorporation**). Liquidation may be initiated by the shareholders or directors (voluntary liquidation) or by its creditors. If the company is solvent (see **bankruptcy**) the ordinary shareholders will receive any surplus after the company's liabilities have been met.

liquidity 1. In general, availability of funds to meet claims. An economic agent is considered to have high liquidity, or to be highly liquid, if all its financial holdings, or **assets**, are in cash; and to have low liquidity if its holdings are all in forms, such as property, commodities and long-term securities, that are difficult to convert into exact amounts of ready cash. **2.** In **banking**, liquidity refers to a commercial bank's ability to meet withdrawals of deposits, and relates to the bank's holdings of cash and short-term assets. **3.** In **balance of payments** contexts, liquidity relates to a country's ability to cover a shortfall on its overall external accounts, and refers essentially to that country's **reserves**. International liquidity is the total of all national reserves. **4.** In **monetary control** terminology, liquidity denotes the total amount of money and very short-term financial assets in the economy. **5.** In **securities markets**, liquidity refers to the quantity of tradable **instruments** available. The greater the number of **stocks** at issue, the more **market makers** there are; and the more widely held the stock, the greater the liquidity of the market in any given stock is likely to be. Stocks on the **London Stock Exchange** are classified into *liquid* and *less liquid* categories. See also **normal market size**.

liquidity ratio 1. The proportion of the total **assets** of a bank that are held in the form of cash (see **cash ratio**) and **liquid** assets. There is no longer a mandatory liquidity or reserve asset ratio for UK banks, although all larger banks are required to deposit 0.5% of **eligible liabilities** with the **Bank of England**. See also **capital adequacy**, **Federal Reserve System**. **2.** The ratio of liquid assets to the current **liabilities** of a business. This is also called the cash ratio.

liquidity trap A monetary situation enunciated by J. M. Keynes in which **interest rates** fall so low that only a rise can be anticipated. Since, however, any rise would only depress the price of **bonds**, the compulsion to remain in **cash** persists. At this point no increase in the **money supply** can increase people's preference for cash (liquidity preference) or therefore have any effect on incomes.

Lisbon Stock Exchange The principal **stock exchange** in Portugal. There is another one in Oporto. The exchanges are regulated (see **regulation**) by the Bank of Portugal, the **central bank**.

listed company A company whose **shares** are listed on an official **stock exchange**. Thus, a *quoted* company.

listed security A **security** that has been officially accepted for trading and **quotation** on a recognized **stock exchange**. The term 'listing' comes from the published list issued by the stock exchange authorities and known in the UK as the *Stock Exchange Daily Official List* (see **official list**).

listing See **listed security**.

listing agreement See **general undertaking**.

Little Board See **American Stock Exchange**.

Liverpool Cotton Association (UK) A **commodity** market in cotton, set up in 1841, for many years a world centre for cotton **physical** and **futures** contracts. However, government intervention in the physical market in later years greatly impeded futures transactions. None the less 20m bales are traded annually, and some 50% of all contracts made in the rest of the world are estimated to be drawn up under Liverpool rules.

Lloyd's adviser An adviser required to be retained by a corporate member of **Lloyd's of London** to furnish analyses to syndicates and to negotiate the member's participation in syndicates.

Lloyd's broker See **Lloyd's of London**.

Lloyd's Names' Associations Working Party A co-ordinating body created to promote common policies among the **Lloyd's of London action groups**.

Lloyd's of London An insurance institution based in London, the capital of which is provided by a large number of individual members each assuming unlimited personal liability for claims. The institution offers **general insurance** and **reinsurance** and some limited **life assurance**. Members **underwrite** an amount of **policies** in proportion to the deposit they make with the institution. Members are grouped in **syndicates** in which insurance policies are underwritten on behalf of the members by a professional underwriter. Business is accepted primarily from Lloyd's **brokers**. In 1987 there were 32,000 members, grouped into 370 syndicates, with a total **premium** income of over £3bn. As a result of severe losses incurred in 1989–91, active membership fell below 20,000, with a consequent shrinkage of available capacity from £11.5bn to £8.75bn. A programme of measures to isolate prior losses from current business, to reduce trading costs, to settle members' claims against underwriters and agents, to reduce hardship incurred by specially affected members, to attract corporate capital with limited liability, and to reorganize individual members' underwriting on a pooled basis (*Members' Agents Pooling Arrangement*) was undertaken. By reason partly of these measures, and partly of the stringencies imposed by losses, the number of syndicates fell to 228. However, total resources of Lloyd's, before current and future liabilities, rose from £16bn in 1988 to £24bn at the end of 1992.

Lloyd's was founded in the 18th century, taking its name from Edward Lloyd, the owner of the coffee house in which business was first conducted. It is now wholly international, deriving most of its business from abroad. See also **action group**, **active underwriter**, **allocated capacity**, **Association of Lloyd's Members**, **central fund**, **CentreWrite**, **errors and omissions**, **external member**, **funds at Lloyd's**, **Lloyd's adviser**, **Lloyd's Names' Associations Working Party**, **managing agent**, **members' agent**, **Newco**, **Old Years**, **overall premium limit**, **Premium Trust Fund**, **reinsurance to close**, **ring fence**, **stop loss insurance**, **syndicate**, **year of account**.

LME See **London Metal Exchange**.

load fund A **mutual fund**, the units in which are sold by commission brokers.

loading 1. Of insurance, that part of the premium that provides for administrative expenses, contingencies and profit. **2.** Of banking, an additional charge made to the customer's account to recover the cost of additional services or account-handling difficulties. **3.** Of unit trusts, the charge incorporated in prices and premiums to defray administrative expenses. **4.** Of loans, the charging of interest. See **front-end loading**.

loan The lending of a sum of money. Loans may be secured or unsecured (see **securities**), **interest** bearing or interest free, long term or short term, redeemable or irredeemable (see **redeemable security**). Loans may be made by individuals, governments, companies, banks, **insurance** and **hire-purchase** companies, **building societies** and other **financial intermediaries**, or by **pawnbrokers**, or by the issue of **securities**. See also **finance, term loans**.

loan capital Fixed-interest borrowed funds, e.g. **debentures**.

loan certificate (Nor.) **Commercial paper**.

loan guarantee See **credit guarantee**.

loan participation certificate (US) A device introduced by US banks on the occasion of high market interest rates in 1969, consisting of a loan to which a depositor had partial proprietary rights, thus enabling the banks to pay interest on their liabilities above the maximum level set by the supervisory authorities.

loan selling A term used to describe the issue of **debt instruments**, particularly **Euromarket securities** such as **floating rate notes** and **Euronotes** in **note issuance facilities**. Also sale of outstanding loans, particularly in Third World countries with external payments difficulties, by the lending bank to another bank or financial institution. The transaction is normally at a **discount**.

loan stock See **stock**.

local (US) A dealer in **financial futures** or in **traded options** who is independent and acts on their own account.

local area network (LAN) A connected set of **microcomputers**, which allows individual users to access computer programs, data, storage space (e.g. **hard disks**) and peripheral equipment such as printers and **modems**, usually found on a central unit called the file server. The LAN includes the connecting wiring and the necessary computer software.

local authority bill A **bill of exchange** drawn on a local authority.

local authority stock A **bond** issued by a UK local authority.

local taxation Taxation levied by (or for) local rather than central government. In the UK local government rates were proportional to the estimated rentable value of business and domestic premises. From 1990 (in England) rates on domestic property were replaced with the *community charge*, a per capita tax for each occupant aged 18 or over. The community charge was extremely unpopular and was replaced in 1993/4 by the *council tax*. This tax is based on the values of property in 1990, defined by a series of bands. There is a rebate for people living alone and various other reliefs. Business properties continue to be based upon local valuations as before but are set by government on a uniform basis throughout the country, hence their name the *uniform business rate* (UBR). In the USA the states levy **sales tax**. In France the principal local tax on business is the *taxe professionelle*, which is based on the rentable values of buildings and equipment but also includes a **payroll tax**. In Germany regional government (*Länder*) levies a tax on business that has three elements: a **profits** tax (*Gewerbeertragesteur*), a tax on **assets** (*Gewerbekapitalsteuer*) and a tax on the capital value of buildings and land (*Grundsteuer*). See also **poll tax**.

loco A **commodity market** term referring to the location of dealing in a commodity, e.g. tin may be traded *loco* London.

Loi Monory (Fr.) A law introduced by H. René Monory in 1978 to stimulate **stock exchange** investment in the **securities** of domestic companies. Individuals may deduct their share purchases up to a specified limit from their taxable income.

Lombard rate (Ger.) **1**. A generic term for lending against **security**, normally against a **financial instrument**. **2**. The interest rate at which the **Bundesbank** lends in the normal course of events to the German commercial bank system. Such lending is always against **security**. Lombard rate is normally set about a half-point above **discount rate**.

Lombardsatz, Lombardzinssatz, Lombardzinsfuss (Ger.) **Lombard rate**.

Lomé Convention See **European Development Fund**.

London and New Zealand Futures Association (UK) A **commodity** market, set up in Bradford in 1953, dealing in **futures** contracts for New Zealand crossbred wool. A member of the **International Commodities Clearing House**.

London Bankers' Clearing House See **clearing house**.

London Cocoa Terminal Market Association Ltd A **commodity** market, dealing principally in **futures** contracts, opened in 1928 and stemming from the Cocoa Association of London, formed two years earlier. Futures trading lapsed during the price controls of the Second World War but resumed in 1951. The market, along with that in New York, is the largest in the world. Much **arbitrage** trading is conducted between the two markets. The London market is a member of the **International Commodities Clearing House**.

London Commodity Exchange See **Futures and Options Exchange**.

London daily prices (LDP) Prices assessed each day for white sugar at the **United Sugar Terminal Market** in London, then transmitted and used widely across the world for **physical** trade in the commodity. There is no trading as such on the London market; the price is arrived at by the market's price committee in the light of reported business and dealings in the **futures** market.

London FOX See **Futures and Options Exchange**.

London Gold Futures Market Ltd A market in **futures** contracts in gold, set up in 1982 by the members of the **London Gold Market** in consultation with the **London Metal Exchange** and the **International Commodities Clearing House**. With a dollar unit of **currency**, the market is firmly established alongside other gold futures markets in the USA, Australia, Hong Kong and Tokyo.

London Gold Market Ltd A long-standing market comprising five dealers – Rothschild, Midland Montagu, Mocatta & Goldsmid (part of the Standard Chartered Group), Mase Westpac (owned by Republic National Bank of New York) and Sharps Pixley (owned by Deutsche Bank). The group meets twice daily at Rothschild's to fix the London price of gold. The price has long been a highly influential guide to the world market, although in recent years Zurich has become a strong rival. The market has in latter years formed itself into a company, in which each member has an equal share, although chairmanship at the fixing sessions resides permanently with Rothschild.

London Grain Futures Market Set up in 1925, the market is now a **commodity** market for European Union varieties of wheat and barley, and deals in **futures** contracts. The market is controlled by the **Grain and Feed Trade Association** (GAFTA), which sets the rules for the conduct of the market, fixes opening and closing prices and acts as a **clearing house**. The market generates ruling prices for most trades throughout the European Union.

London interbank bid rate (LIBID) See **London interbank offered rate** (LIBOR).

London interbank offered rate (LIBOR) (UK) The rate of **interest** offered on **loans** to first-class banks in the London **interbank market** for a specified period (usually three or six months). Owing to the heavy volume of interbank dealing, the three-month and six-month rates have come to be widely used as a basis of reference for the setting of many other interest rates. It is closely related to **base rate** but is closer to *prime rate* in US terms. The rate may apply to sterling or **Eurodollars**. The corresponding rate for **deposits** is the *interbank market bid rate* (IBMBR), the *interbank bid rate* (IBBR) or the *London interbank bid rate* (LIBID). Some other financial centres have interbank bid and offer rates, e.g. the *Paris interbank offered rate* (PIBOR) and the *Tokyo interbank offered rate* (TIBOR).

London International Financial Futures Exchange (LIFFE) An exchange established in London in September 1982 for trading in **financial futures** and **options**. The decision to set up a London market followed the success of the financial futures market in Chicago (see **Chicago Board of Trade**) and of that started in Sydney in 1979. The market is centred on a clearing house through which all transactions pass and that acts as a financially independent guarantor and regulator of the exchange. The exchange is also under the supervision of the **Bank of England**, which may, if needed, intervene. The market began by trading in four **currency futures** contracts (sterling, D-marks, yen and Swiss francs against the dollar) and three **interest rate futures**. Given the large size of the closely similar **forward** market, the currency futures became less popular than the interest rate futures. By 1985 LIFFE was trading in three more futures contracts and two **option** contracts, the subjects of these including short-term sterling, long-term **gilts**, the FT/SE Index (see **Financial Times share indexes**) and US **Treasury bonds**. Options on three-month sterling interest rate futures were introduced in November 1987; trade in Japanese government bond futures began in July 1987.

London Jute Association Set up in 1875, the association is not a marketing body but administers the contracts under which jute is sold throughout the world. There are few, if any, **futures** transactions.

London Meat Futures Exchange Ltd Set up in 1984, this is a **commodity** market for pigmeat, dealing in **futures** contracts. A member of the **International Commodities Clearing House**.

London Metal Exchange (LME) With origins dating back to the 18th century, and incorporated in 1881, the exchange is the London **commodity** market for trade in metals and the world **futures** and cash market for trades in aluminium, aluminium alloy, copper, lead, nickel, tin and zinc. The market is daily for cash and contracts up to three months; and weekly, and then monthly, for contracts up to 15 and 27 months. Dealing in aluminium and nickel began in 1978 and 1979 respectively; dealing in aluminium alloy began in 1993; dealing in the other metals is of long standing. Membership is wholly international and comprises 17 main ring members, i.e. those authorized to deal on the 'ring', or trading floor; 23 broker members, i.e. brokers authorized to place contracts, on behalf of clients, with ring dealers; and 80 trade members, i.e. companies active in metals business, having rights of direct consultation with the market authorities on market arrangements such as contract specifications.

London Potato Futures Market A **commodity** market, trading in **futures** contracts, set up in 1980. Futures dealings are possible given the exemption of potatoes from **European Union** pricing rules, although the UK Potato Marketing Board attempts to control production. Dealing is in all varieties of potatoes, with some **arbitrage** in the Bintje variety possible with the Dutch market, the only other potato futures market in Europe. The market is a member of the **International Commodities Clearing House**.

London Rubber Terminal Market Association A commodity market established in 1974 for dealing in **futures** contracts. The Rubber Terminal Market superseded the Rubber Settlement House, which had conducted futures trade for the previous 50 years. The market is a member of the **International Commodities Clearing House**.

London Soya Bean Meal Futures Market A commodity market, established in 1975, for trade in **futures** contracts in soya bean meal. The market provides **hedging** facilities, principally for trade between the UK and the rest of Europe; there is some **arbitrage** between the London and the Chicago markets. The market is a member of the **International Commodities Clearing House**.

London Stock Exchange (LSE) (UK) The London market in which **securities** are bought and sold. Its correct name is the International Stock Exchange of the United Kingdom and the Republic of Ireland Ltd (ISE). Members are formed into a declining number of firms that, following the **Big Bang**, now include major **merchant banks**, **clearing banks** and other financial intermediaries, some of which are foreign owned. All business is now conducted by telephone or for small orders through an **automated screen trading system**, and the **trading floor** (including regional trading floors) is no longer used. The **Stock Exchange Automated Quotation System** (SEAQ) allows **market makers** and others to see competing quotations on their screens, and **stockbrokers** to select the best **bid price** or **offer price** for their clients. Prior to October 1986 the rules of the exchange did not permit **jobbers** to deal directly with the public, but only through stockbrokers; but now firms operate in **dual capacity**. On 31 December 1992, 7,300 securities were listed on the main market of the stock exchange (see **unlisted securities markets**), of which 4,692 were company securities, the remainder being public-sector securities and **Eurobonds**. The total market value of these securities was £2,605,093.5m. See also **alpha securities**, **stocks**, **alternative investment market**,

Financial Services Act, normal market size, offer for sale, Securities Association, stock exchange.

London Sugar Futures Market A **commodity** market, dealing in **futures** contracts for raw sugar and white sugar, the descendant of the first London sugar futures market, formed in 1888. Closed during both world wars, the market reformed after each, the latest occasion being in 1957 when postwar sugar controls were relaxed. The market is not a **physical** market but a daily price-fixing one. The London daily price, based on business in physical sugar and the tone of the futures market, is used worldwide as the basis of sales contracts. There is **arbitrage** with the futures market in New York, which is roughly equivalent in size. The market is a member of the **International Commodities Clearing House**.

London Traded Options Market (LTOM) An options markets merged in 1991 with the **London International Financial Futures Exchange** (LIFFE).

London Underwriting Centre A centre established in 1993 for non-marine **underwriters** of 22 major **general insurance** and **reinsurance** companies offering the convenience of one-stop business for brokers. The centre regards itself as complementary to **Lloyd's of London** and claims a capacity of £6bn, as against Lloyd's £8bn.

London Vegetable Oil Terminal Market A **commodity** market, opened in 1967, dealing first in soya bean oil, coconut oil and sunflower seed oil, and from 1973 trading only in soya bean oil; concerned primarily with **futures** contracts. The market is a member of the **International Commodities Clearing House**.

long 1. Of **commodity** and **securities markets**, having assets normally under a **futures** or **forward** contract, available for sale on the prescribed date, e.g. having bought a futures contract. 2. Of securities and currencies, having a holding larger than normal quantities. See also **position**. 3. An abbreviation for **long term**.

long-dated securities See **dated securities**.

long-form report (UK) A detailed confidential report for the

sponsor (see **issuing house**) of a company being prepared for flotation (see **float**) by the reporting accountants. The long-form report is intended to satisfy the sponsors so that they can lend their name to the issue and identify matters that need to be rectified before going public. The report will provide the basis for the *short-form report* included in the **prospectus**.

long hedge A **hedge** effected by the purchase of a **futures** contract.

long tail business Of insurance, certain forms of insurance, particularly in **liability** business, claims under which may arise long after the policy is issued. Example are claims in respect of ill-health from exposure to asbestos or to certain drugs.

long term 1. Of a **security**, having a **maturity** of long duration, usually of more than 15 years. 2. Of a bank loan, repayable between five and 10 years. 3. Of a **money market instrument**, having a maturity between three months and one year. 4. Of insurance, life insurance **annuity**, **permanent health insurance**, pension fund management (see **pensions**) and capital redemption business.

loss adjuster An independent expert called in where necessary by **insurers** to assess an **insured**'s claim and to negotiate a settlement with the latter. Normally used for large claims.

losses occurring policy An insurance policy specifying the **insurer**'s obligation to pay claims made in respect of losses incurred during the period of validity of the policy, regardless of the date of the claim or of the act causing the loss.

lot A minimum quantity unit traded in a **commodity market** or in a **securities market**.

loyalty bonus See **privatization**.

LSE See **London Stock Exchange**.

LTOM See **London Traded Options Market**.

LUC See **London Underwriting Centre**.

lump sum 1. The amount calculated by **discounted cash flow** for the immediate purchase of an **annuity**. 2. The amount generated throughout the term of a **life assurance** policy used for the purchase of a **pension**. See also **equalization of pensions**.

lunga scadenza (It.) **Long term**.

Luxembourg Stock Exchange (LSE) The LSE is managed and self-regulated (see **regulation**) by the Société Anonyme de la Bourse. The volume of trading on the **stock exchange** is small, but Luxembourg is an important centre for the **settlement** of trading in **Eurobonds** (see **Centrale de Livraison de Valeurs Mobilières**).

Maastricht Treaty A treaty signed in February 1992 by the member states of the then European Community (EC) intended to inaugurate 'a new stage in the process of European integration'. The treaty declared the member states henceforth to be members of a **European Union** (EU), of which all inhabitants were citizens. Employing, like the Single European Act (SEA), the method of amending and expanding the original three treaties of the Community, the Maastricht Treaty provided for: (i) the establishment of full Economic and Monetary Union; (ii) the implementation of a common foreign and security policy; (iii) the development of close co-operation on justice and on home affairs; (iv) the strengthening of the common commercial, transport, capital and payments, environmental and other existing policies of the Union; (v) the endorsement of the principle of subsidiarity. Lastly (vi) there was attached to the treaty a protocol on social policy.

(i) The existing arrangements for the **European Monetary System** (EMS) were taken to be stage one of progress towards full Economic and Monetary Union. During stage two, beginning on 1 January 1994, general economic and financial convergence was to take place; a European Monetary Institute (EMI) was to be established with the task of taking over the functions of the European Monetary Co-operation Fund and of preparing for the third stage in consultation with the member states' central banks, *inter alia* in specifying the arrangements for the European System of Central Banks (ESCB). In stage three, to start not later than 1 January 1999, the move to a single currency, the ECU, was to be made, with provisional derogations for member states not meeting the requisite convergence criteria; the ESCB and the European Central Bank (ECB) were to enter into their functions, and the EMI was to be liquidated.

(ii) There was to be close consultation between member states, with the presidency representing the European Union in matters where a common policy has been agreed in the Council, after liaison with the European Parliament. The Western European Union was to advise on and implement the European Union's actions and decisions in the field of security and defence.

(iii) The Union was to come to joint positions and, where appropriate, take joint action on: asylum, immigration, anti-drug addiction, anti-international fraud, and customs, police and judicial cooperation policies.

(iv) A number of tidying and reinforcing adjustments were made.

(v) In response to widening fears of overcentralization of Union action, the principle of 'subsidiarity', i.e. that the Union institutions should undertake actions only where these can be better performed than by the the member states acting individually, was explicitly recognized.

(vi) The relevant documents consist of an agreement 'On Social Policy concluded between the Member States of the European Community with the Exception of the United Kingdom and Northern Ireland', which is annexed to a Protocol on Social Policy that explicitly recognizes the abstention from the agreement of the UK. (The documents are popularly miscalled 'the social chapter', in fact an existing section of the original EC Treaty.) The agreement records the intention of the signatory states to pursue so far unfulfilled aspirations of the Social Charter (see **European Union**), to which the UK was not a signatory.

Ratification of the Maastricht Treaty proved difficult, owing, it was surmised, to a general feeling that its provisions had gone too far, outpacing the member states' wishes for integration. A referendum in Denmark in June 1992 vetoed ratification. In September 1992 a referendum in France approved ratification by the smallest of margins a 'oui, mais'. The UK Parliament began a long-drawn-out wrangle over the 'social chapter'. The treaty was referred to the German constitutional court. Eventually a new referendum permitted Danish ratification in May 1993, UK ratification following two days later. That of Germany ensued in October 1993.

However, by then other events had weighed against attainment of the treaty's aim of strengthening and deepening the European

Union. Severe currency turbulence led on 'Black Wednesday', 16 September 1992, to the withdrawal of the UK and Italy from the Exchange Rate Mechanism (ERM); and a repetition of the disorder in August of the following year compelled the extension of the ERM divergency margins to 15% on either side of the central parity, signalling the virtual lapsing of the whole system, amid grave doubts about the move to Economic and Monetary Union. Apart from this, continued dissatisfaction with the working of the common agricultural policy, coupled with external factors such as German unification and events in Eastern Europe and the former Soviet Union, combined to distract attention from issues of further Union integration.

Madrid Stock Exchange The **stock exchanges** in Spain are located in Madrid, Barcelona, Bilbao and Valencia. Draft legislation of 1988 (the Ley del Mercado de Capitales) provides for the electronic linking and automation of the exchanges and for a new regulatory body, the Comisión Nacional del Mercado de Valores (National Capital Market Commission). Spanish and European Community/Union banks and other financial institutions were allowed to own up to 30% of stockbroking firms in 1990, and by 1992 all barriers to entry had been removed.

mailbox number See **electronic mail**.

mainframe computer The largest size of computer.

mainstream corporation tax See **corporation tax**.

maintenance period (US) The period in which the banks must meet the reserve requirement set down by the **Federal Reserve**, i.e. in which the average level of a bank's deposits in its reserve account at the Federal Reserve bank must be at least equal to the amount required. The maintenance period is normally of two weeks, termed statement weeks, running from a Thursday to the second Wednesday following.

major market index (MMI) (US) A **futures** contract established by the **Chicago Board of Trade** in 1983 and based on movements in the Dow-Jones Industrial Average Index (see **Dow-Jones indexes**) of the stock exchange prices of 20 of the most heavily capitalized companies in the USA. The contract is licensed by the **American Stock Exchange**, which trades **options** in the index. In 1993 the contract was transferred to the **Chicago Mercantile Exchange**.

Makler (Ger.) **Broker**.

Maklergebühr (Ger.) **Broker**'s fee.

managed currency A **currency** whose **parity** is maintained at a declared level by the **central bank** of the country concerned.

managed futures fund (US) A **mutual fund** dealing in **derivatives**. These funds grew from a total size of $4bn in 1986 to some $25bn in 1992.

managed unit trust (UK) A unit trust invested solely in other unit trusts belonging to the same group; first introduced in the UK in 1985. The purpose is to provide a lower-risk investment vehicle than a normal unit trust, a choice not easily made by the investor in the face of the more than 1,000 unit trusts in existence. The Department of Trade has laid down that managed unit trusts must be invested in at least five out of a possible choice of at least eight individual trusts, and be invested as to not more than 50% in any one. Doubts over **conflict of interest** have remained, although biased purchases and sales would be speedily reflected in performance. Also known as *master trust* and *fund of funds*.

management buy-in See **management buy-out**.

management buy-out (MBO) The acquisition of all or part of the **share** capital of a company by its directors and senior executives. Competitive pressures upon large companies in the 1980s have led to the disposal of many weak or peripheral subsidiaries in this way. The management are usually assisted by **loans** from a venture capital (see **risk capital**) or other financial organization, and both expect to seek public **flotation** in due course. In a *management buy-in* an outside team of managers acquires a company in a similar way. A *buy-in management buy-out* (BIMBO) combines interests of both existing and new outside management.

managing agent The agent responsible for managing one or more

Lloyd's of London syndicates, and for employing the **active underwriter**.

Manila Stock Exchange (MSE) Established in 1927, with a trading floor also in Makati. The **stock exchange** and the regulatory body, the Securities Exchange Commission, are based on the US model, as is the **over-the-counter market**.

MAPA Members' Agents Pooling Arrangement. See **Lloyd's of London**.

marché (Fr.) **Market**.

marché à options (Fr.) **Options market**.

marché à primes (Fr.) Market for a form of **call option**, giving the holder the right to buy certain **securities** on any one of three consecutive monthly dates ahead. Holders may abandon their option before **settlement** on payment of a penalty (the *prime*).

marché à terme (Fr.) The *forward* or monthly account market.

Marché à Terme des Instruments Financiers (MATIF) (Fr.) The French financial **futures** market, established in 1986.

Marché au comptant (Fr.) The **cash**, **spot** or **physical market**.

marché conditionnel (Fr.) A generic term for the **options** market, the **marché à primes**, the *stellage* market and the double option market (*opération du double*).

marché de l'argent (Fr.) **Money market**.

Marché des Options Négotiables de Paris (Fr.) The French **traded options** market, established in 1987.

marché des valeurs (Fr.) **securities market**.

marché hors-cote (Fr.) The third-tier unofficial **unlisted securities market**, not regulated by the **Commission des Opérations de Bourse**.

marché monétaire (Fr.) **Money market**.

margin 1. Generally in finance, the *gross margin* is the difference between the price at which something is bought and the price at which it is sold; thus the contribution towards **overheads** and other costs. **2.** In banking, the difference between the interest **rate** paid to depositors or for funds on the **money market** and the rate charged to borrowers. **3.** A deposit as partial surety that a **contract** will be fulfilled, as in **commodity markets** and **financial futures markets**. Expressed as a percentage of the price paid (or sold), the *margin requirement* may necessitate further payments by the client if prices move against them. **4.** (US) The proportion of the price of a **security** paid when giving an **order** to a **broker**, the rest being on **credit**. **5.** The permitted divergence between national **currencies** in the **European Monetary System**.

margin call A requirement for an increase in the original deposit, or margin, placed on a **futures** or **option** contract, when the buyer has increased the size of the contract, or when market prices have become heavily adverse.

margin requirement See **margin**.

margin trading A term describing the process by which **commodity speculators** trade in **futures** by subscribing only the **margin**, i.e. the deposit, on a contract valued many times higher than the margin; thus permitting, if successful, a profit far exceeding the original outlay.

marginal cost See **capital, cost of**.

marker barrel The unit of petroleum sales of Saudi Arabia, used as a reference in assessing changes in the general oil price. The specification is: Saudi Arabian Light, API 40, Ras Tanura.

market Business or trade in any **commodity**.

market capitalization The total value at market prices of the **securities** at issue for a company or a stock market or sector of the stock market. Calculated by multiplying the number of shares issued by the market price per **share**.

market clearing price The price at which all goods or services available in a market will find buyers.

market instrument Short-term **debt instrument**.

market maker A **broker–dealer** who is prepared to buy and sell specified **securities** at all times and thus makes a market in them. Prior to the **Big Bang**, this function was carried out by **jobbers**, who were not allowed to deal with the public. Since the Big Bang all members of the **stock exchange** may deal with the public as broker–dealers. Some specialize as market makers and others as **stockbrokers**.

market order An instruction from a client to a **broker–dealer** to buy or sell a **security** or **commodity** at the price prevailing at the time of execution of the transaction. See **order**.

marketable See **negotiable**.

Marktbewertung (Ger.) **Market capitalization**.

mark-to-market The daily valuation of **derivatives** prices in comparision with those of the underlying instruments.

Marshall aid A programme of financial aid to Western European countries instituted by the USA after the Second World War; so called because the programme resulted from a proposal made by the US Secretary of State, General George C. Marshall, in June 1947. The form and distribution of aid were made according to the requirements set out by the recipient nations, grouped together in the **Organization for European Economic Co-operation**.

Maruyu (Jap.) A postal savings investment system, operated by the Postal Savings Bureau (PSB), under which deposits up to Y3m, defined as 'small savings', were free of tax; the system was withdrawn in April 1988. The PSB, founded in 1875, had by 1988 some 300m deposits, valued at Y286 trillion, mostly held in 10-year deposits at government-guaranteed interest rates. The system was abolished partly to create uniformity of treatment for savings, and partly to deal with the growth of illicit accounts, a trend illustrated by the fact that the number of accounts was 2.5 times the country's population.

masse monétaire (Fr.) **Money supply**.

master trust See **managed unit trust**.

MAT Of insurance, an abbreviation for *marine, aviation and transport*, a recognized class of insurance business.

match (US) See **matched sale–purchase agreement**.

matched bargains or bids A method of **securities** trading in which bids and offers (see **bid price**, **offer price**) are matched together. Used on the **German stock exchanges**, it is said to have greater **transparency** than the more common **quote-driven** systems. See also **order driven**.

matched sale–purchase agreement (US) A sale of **money-market instruments** by the **Federal Reserve** for immediate effect, coupled with a simultaneous **forward** purchase of the same instruments, having as a result a distribution of the reserves of the banking system. Identical in effect to **repurchase agreements**, but used by the Federal Reserve to overcome the legal bar to its borrowing from the public, and thus to reverse repurchase agreements. First employed in 1966.

material facts A term used to define the information that an **insured** must disclose under a contract of **insurance**. See also '**prudent insurer**', *uberrimae fidei*.

mathematical reserves Reserves held by **long-term insurance** businesses to cover all liabilities other than those already due for settlement. A frequent measure of the strength of the company is the excess of net assets over mathematical reserves.

MATIF (Fr.) See **Marché à Terme des Instruments Financiers**.

maturity The period between the creation of a financial **claim** and the date on which it is to be paid. Often refers to the date of payment, e.g. the date on which a **bond** becomes due for repayment.

maturity balance (US) The mix of **maturities** of **securities** (**Treasury bills**, **Treasury bonds**) and **Federal agency securities** held by the **Federal Reserve** for use in its **open market operations**.

MBO See **management buy-out**.

mean See **average**.

median See **average**.

medical insurance See **permanent health insurance**.

medium term 1. Of a **security**, having a **maturity** of a medium duration, usually between five and 15 years. **2**. Of a bank loan, for repayment between three and five years. **3**. See **finance**.

medium-term financial assistance (MTFA) Loans of a **term** of two to five years, available from **European Union** countries to a member country in **balance of payments** difficulties. The loans are made by donor countries up to a specified ceiling to which individual countries are committed, no one recipient country being entitled to receive more than 50% of the ceiling; financial and economic conditions may be placed on the recipient country in return for the loan.

medium-term note (MTN) **Euro–commercial paper**, issued with a maturity of several years.

MEFF A term used in English–speaking markets to denote the Spanish **futures** exchange, the Mercado Español de Futuros Financieros.

megabyte One million **bytes**.

members' agent An agent responsible for advising **external members** of **Lloyd's of London** on the choice of syndicates and for administering the member's business affairs at Lloyd's.

memorandum of association The document that forms the basis of registration of a company, listing the subscribers to the **capital** and the number of **shares**, the name and address of the company and, where appropriate, its powers and objects. The memorandum also states that the **liability** of its members (see **shareholders**) is limited (see **incorporation**) (US = *articles of incorporation*). The *articles of association* set out the rules by which the company will be administered, e.g. the voting of directors and the calling of meetings (US = *corporate bylaws*).

Mercado de Valores de Buenos Aires See **Buenos Aires Stock Exchange**.

Mercado Español de Futuros Financieros See **MEFF**.

mercato ristretto (It.) A regulated market dealing in unlisted securities (see **unlisted securities markets**), based in Milan and five other centres. In its present form, regulated by CONSOB (see **Commissione Nazionale per le Società e la Borsa**), the *mercato ristretto* dates from May 1978. See also *terzo mercato*.

merchant banks Institutions that carry out a variety of financial services, including the acceptance of **bills of exchange**, the issue and **placing** of **loans** and **securities**, **portfolio** and **unit trust** management, **foreign exchange** dealing and some **banking** services. Several houses, often through subsidiaries, provide **risk capital**, deal in gold **bullion**, **insurance** and **hire purchase**, and are active in the **Euromarket**. Merchant banks advise companies on **mergers** and other financial matters, and many of them are well known, e.g. Rothschild, Baring, Hambro, Lazard and Schroder. There has been a recent trend, especially following the **Big Bang**, for merchant banks, including London firms on the **stock exchange**, to participate in financial **conglomerates**, so as to be able to offer a full range of financial services, including retail services. See **accepting house**.

merger The fusion of two or more separate companies into one. In current usage merger is a special case of combination, where both the merging companies wish to join together and do so on roughly equal terms, as distinct from a **take-over**, which occurs against the wishes of one company and is preceded by a contested bid. See also **leveraged buy-out**.

Mexican Stock Exchange The Bolsa Mexicana de Valores in Mexico City, established in 1894, has grown rapidly and now has the largest **market capitalization** in Latin American.

mezzanine A term signifying an intermediate stage in a financing operation. It usually refers to **unsecured debt** and **equity** in ranking for payment in the event of **default** (see also **subordinated**). It may carry an **option** on some other claim to a stake in equity (an *equity kicker*).

Mibtel See **Milan Stock Exchange**.

microcomputer The smallest class of computer, also called *personal computer* or *PC*. PCs can be used for data processing on their own or as terminals connected to other PCs, **minicomputers** or **mainframe computers** through a **local area network** or via a **modem** and telephone lines.

Middle East See **Tel Aviv Stock Exchange**.

Midwest Stock Exchange Established in 1882 under the name Chicago Stock Exchange to deal in local railway, bank and energy company securities. In 1948, when the second largest stock exchange in the USA, it changed its name to the above. However, the market declined in relative size over succeeding years, in the face of strong competition from the **New York Stock Exchange**, the **American Stock Exchange** and the **over-the-counter market**. In 1993 the exchange reverted to its original name.

MIF Milan **futures** market.

Milan Stock Exchange Of little international interest or importance until 1985; prices doubled on the exchange in that year mainly as a result of the emergence of **mutual funds** in Italy in the early 1980s. Only some 230 companies are quoted, and a large proportion of these are controlled by 50 groups. The exchange is to be the subject of deregulation (see **regulation**), and **brokers** at present are not allowed to deal on their own account as **market makers**, though CONSOB (see **Commissione Nazionale per le Società e la Borsa**) has made proposals. Much security trading in Italy is carried out off the exchange by banks. The two widely quoted **share indices** are the *Mibtel* and the *Comit Index* published by the Banco Commerciale Italiano.

milliard Originally the common term in English and French for *one thousand million*. Now superseded, at least in English, by the term *billion*.

Minex See **Electronic Broking Service**.

minicomputer A computer midway in size and data-processing capacity between a **microcomputer** and a **mainframe computer**. With recent increases in the power and storage capacity of personal computers the borderline between micros and minis has narrowed.

minimum contract size See **lot**.

minimum lending rate (MLR) The interest rate at which the Bank of England lent to relieve shortages in the **money market**. The rate could be set at such a level as to foster a rise or a fall in the general level of money market interest rates, but was generally neutral to the trend, being in fact fixed by a formula relating to **Treasury bill tender rate** in the period 1972-8. MLR replaced **bank rate** in 1972 but was discontinued in 1981, the Bank of England reserving the right to restore it periodically in the future.

Minneapolis Grain Exchange A **commodity** market for grain, established in 1881, dealing in **futures** contracts for spring wheat and white wheat, and in the **cash** market for barley, maize, drum wheat, flaxseed, oats, rye, soya beans, spring wheat and sunflower seeds. Together with the Kansas and Chicago exchanges, it sets the world price for grains.

minority interests See **consolidated accounts**.

MIRAS See **mortgage interest tax relief at source**.

mismatch See **floating rate note**.

MITI (Jap.) Ministry of International Trade and Industry.

mittelfristig (Ger.) **Medium term**.

mixed policy A policy for the **insurance** of a ship under which the vessel and its cargo are insured for a particular voyage and for a particular period of time.

MLR See **minimum lending rate**.

MMDA See **money market deposit account**.

MNC See **multinational company**.

MNE See **multinational company**.

mobilization (Fr.) The act of converting a **claim** into a **negotiable asset**, i.e. by discounting a bill of exchange.

mode See **average**.

modem A device providing an interface between a computer and a telephone line or other line used for transmitting data.

MONEP See **Marché des Options Negotiables de Paris**.

monetarism See **monetary school**.

monetarist An adherent to monetary theories, particularly those of Professor Milton **Friedman**.

monetary base That part of the **money supply** that, in the view of the **monetary school**, is the most dynamic in its effects and is the ultimate source of money supply growth. Defined in the USA as total bank reserves plus notes and coin held by the public. In the UK, **till money**, bankers' balances with the **Bank of England**, and notes and coin in general circulation are regarded as the monetary base, in close conformity with the US definition. Definitions vary according to country, but all are broadly in line with the above.

monetary control The operation by a central bank of measures to regulate the size of the **money supply**. In some countries, such as France and the UK, monetary control is a matter of government policy, and the central bank acts in accordance with this. In other countries, such as Germany and the USA, the central bank is entirely independent, though the government may make its views known.

Monetary Control Act (US) An Act of 1980, making all US banks members of the **Federal Reserve System**.

monetary policy The policy of a government or central bank in monetary affairs, having regard to broad goals such as economic growth and restraint of inflation. See also **monetary control**, **money supply**.

monetary school The school of monetary theory based on the teachings of Professor Milton **Friedman** of Chicago University, also referred to as *monetarism*. See also **money supply**.

Monetary Union See **Maastricht Treaty**.

monetization The financing of a budget deficit through sale of short-term government **debt**, namely **Treasury bills**, to the banking system (UK) or to the **Federal Reserve** (US), and similarly to banking purchasers in other countries. Purchase of Treasury bills by banks adds to their reserves and thus to their capacity to create money. Purchase of Treasury bills by the Federal Reserve from the banking system similarly adds to the latter's reserves.

money The means of facilitating the exchange of goods and services and the accumulation of financial wealth, commonly recognizable as banknotes, coins and bank deposits. The theory of money ascribes to it three functions: a medium of exchange; a unit of value; and a store of wealth. Money is thus a convenient proxy for all goods and services, enabling these to be exchanged more readily than if they were bartered each against the other; by its division into convenient units, the value of goods and services can be denoted by specific amounts of money; accumulated stores of money are reservoirs of purchasing power, or of wealth. The amount of money available to a community has commonly been held to have some influence on the relative value, or price, of goods and services. In the 1970s and later, increased emphasis was placed on this characteristic, leading to the emergence of the theories of the **monetary school**, or monetarism. These theories led to governments' greater resort to **monetary policy** and **monetary control** and to various theories of, and attempts to define, the nature of money (see **money supply**), as well as to define the effect of changes in the quantity and circulation of money on the level of national income and of price.

money as money does A theory of money measurement, assigning weighting to money forms based on frequency of use in transactions, to be employed when adding them together. Also known as the MQ approach.

money at call See **call money**.

money broker A **broker** operating in the **interbank market**, acting as intermediary between banks wishing to borrow and banks wishing to lend. Money brokers also operate in the **foreign exchange**, **Eurodollar** and **Eurobond** markets.

money market The market in short-term (normally up to one year) financial **claims**, e.g. **bills of exchange**, **Treasury bills**, **interbank** money and **discount house deposits**. The market is wholesale, i.e. in large quantities traded not by individuals but by banks, discount houses, finance houses, the **Bank of England**, the **Federal Reserve** and others; and most transactions are by **discount**. In the UK the money market is frequently referred to as the *discount market*, mainly because many of the transactions are carried out by the discount houses.

money market deposit account (MMDA) (US) A form of retail bank account introduced in 1982, based on holdings in the money market, interest on which was free of official maxima. There were restrictions on withdrawals. Also known as a *supersaver account*.

money market mutual fund A type of **mutual fund** created in the USA in the early 1970s, designed to take advantage of the rise in interest rates by investing in **short-term money market instruments**. From 1974, when their **assets** were first recorded, money market mutual funds grew rapidly, rising from $2.2bn to over $200bn in 1982, thereafter stabilizing.

money purchase Of a pension, when constituted by an annuity derived from the investment, at retirement date, of a capital fund accumulated through contributions during working life. Contrasted with occupational pension schemes, where the pension is a guaranteed proportion of earnings, obtained through investment in the same way, but supplemented where necessary by additional contribution by the company or scheme manager. All **personal pensions** are money purchase schemes.

money stock The total amount of **money** existing in the economy. When multiplied by its **velocity**, termed the **money supply**, for which it is used, loosely, as a synonym. See also **monetary control, monetary school**.

money supply The quantity of money in circulation in the economy. This conventionally consists of all **private-sector**-held notes and coin, excluding those held within banks, and all bank **deposits**, excluding those held by banks themselves. The money supply in the UK is normally categorized as *total money supply*, that is, including all deposits held in the UK in all currencies; and *sterling money supply*, i.e. only those deposits denominated in sterling. The money supply was initially further subdivided into: $M1$ = notes and coin, plus **sight deposits**; and $M3$ = $M1$ plus *time deposits*.

In the course of time, further definitions were added to the above main categories, as follows. $M2$ is an intermediate aggregate, designed to distinguish *transactions balances* (deposits held for purposes of expenditure) from *investment balances* (deposits held as long-term savings). Only transactions balances were considered to form part of the money supply. These, redefined as *retail deposits*, included all bank deposits of less than £100,000 from which early withdrawals could be made, all early withdrawable shares and deposits in **building societies** and all deposits with **National Savings Bank** ordinary accounts. Thus: $M2$ = $M1$ plus retail deposits. MO is a narrower category, subsequently introduced, which consisted effectively of the **monetary base**, i.e. the central stock on which all money supply expansion is based, namely notes and coin, including that held by banks, plus operational balances held by banks with the Bank of England.

Before this, a definition still wider than that of $M2$ had been essayed. $PSL1$ (private-sector liquidity) = $M3$ (time deposits up to two years) plus all **money market** and **certificate of deposit** holdings; and $PSL2$ = $PSL1$ plus all shorter-term holdings of building society and National Savings instruments (excluding holdings of money-market instruments by building societies themselves). In further search for definition, two more aggregates were added: $M4$ = $M1$ plus most bank deposits plus holdings of money-market instruments; and $M5$ = $M4$ plus building society deposits.

UK definitions are similar to those of other countries. In the USA, $M1$ = notes and coin (US = *currency*), sight deposits (US = *demand deposits*), travellers' cheques of non-bank issuers, **NOW accounts**, and ATS (automatic transfer service) and CUSD (credit union share draft) accounts. US *monetary base* = bank reserves plus notes and coin held by the public.

moneyness The degree to which a financial **asset** may be deemed, in theory, to be a form of money.

Montreal Stock Exchange See **Toronto Stock Exchange**.

Moody's Investors Service See **Standard and Poor's Ratings**.

moratorium An agreed suspension of repayments of **principal** and/or **interest** spread over a longer period. A number of countries have negotiated moratoria or rescheduling (which is effectively refinancing) on international loans.

Morgan Stanley Capital International World Index (MSCI Index) A global index of equity prices based on 1,375 **shares** from 19 countries and covering roughly 60% of the **market capitalization** of world **stock exchanges**. The *Financial Times* (see **Financial Times share indices**) and other organizations also publish world indices. See also **share indices**.

mortality Mortality rates are calculated, e.g. per 1,000, of death by age groups, by area groups or other classifications. Mortality tables as used by insurance companies show average expectation of life according to age group.

mortgage A legal agreement conveying conditional ownership of **assets** as security for a loan and becoming void when the **debt** is repaid. A common form of **loan** for home purchase in most countries, the home being the asset providing the **security**.

mortgage-backed security A **security**, normally a bond or note, the **servicing** of which is provided by the returns on mortgages (or housing loans). A portfolio of mortgages, insured against default and held by a trustee, constitutes the security or collateral to the bond or note issue.

mortgage debentures See **debentures**.

mortage interest tax relief at source (MIRAS) Interest payable on a **mortgage** being free of tax, **mortgagors** in the UK, under an arrangement introduced in the 1983 Budget, deducted an amount equivalent to the standard rate of tax from their payment of interest to the **mortgagee**, thus taking for themselves their tax relief; the Inland Revenue subsequently refunded the mortgagee. Tax relief at higher rates was claimed in the mortgagor's normal tax return. Tax relief was later restricted to the *standard rate*, then the *lower rate*, and from 1995/6 it will be restricted to 15%. See also **income tax**.

mortgagee The lender of funds under a **mortgage**.

mortgagor The borrower of funds under a **mortgage**.

Moscow Central Stock Exchange A stock exchange set up in the early 1990s, one of the 109 exchanges registered throughout Russia in 1993.

Moscow Interbank Currency Exchange A currency exchange made the basis of a bond market, in which, in 1993, 24 primary dealers traded in government bonds.

moving average A sequence of **averages** calculated for the time series that damps down the fluctuations in values for that series. In a 12-month moving average, for example, the values for the latest month are added to the 12-month total, the value for month one is subtracted, and the result is divided by 12. Used in **technical analysis**.

MQ See **money as money does**.

MSCI Index See **Morgan Stanley Capital International World Index**.

MSP See **matched sale–purchase agreement**.

MTN See **medium–term note**.

MTO Multilateral Trade Organization. See **General Agreement on Tariffs and Trade** (GATT).

multi-component Euronote facility A **Euronote facility** providing for the issue of Euronotes in a number of different currencies according to the issuer's choice.

multi-option facility The term given to a short-term borrowing package comprising a number of different **instruments**. These may include bankers' **acceptances**, **Euronotes** and **commercial paper**. Most facilities are based on an **underwritten credit**, of which part may be 'available', i.e. to be drawn on at will, and part may be 'unavailable', i.e. to be drawn on only at notice, a lower commitment fee being payable on this portion.

Multi-Year Rescheduling Agreement (MYRA) An arrangement for the postponement to various years of the due dates for repayment of loans from commercial banks to developing countries, first instituted in 1985. The arrangement was intended to substitute clear and dependable repayment programmes for the *ad hoc* maturity postponements frequently practised.

Multilateral Trade Organization (MTO) See **General Agreement on Tariffs and Trade** (GATT).

multinational company (MNC) A company having production and other facilities in a number of countries outside the nation of origin. Also, and more correctly, called multinational enterprise (MNE), or *transnational corporation*. According to the United Nations there are about 35,000 multinationals controlling some 170,000 affiliates, though the largest 100 account for about 40% of cross-border **assets**.

multiplier An increase in national income or some other money aggregate divided by the increase in expenditure generating that increase in income. In the *investment multiplier*, an increase in capital expenditure of £100m on roads, for example, will result in increased wages, salaries of employees and profits of contractors. These sums will be partly spent and partly saved, thus generating further increases in income and so on. The extent to which each increment of income is spent or saved will determine the final increase in national income, though if resources are not available to meet increased demand prices may rise. See **money supply**.

Muttergesellschaft (Ger.) **Parent company**.

mutual 1. A company without **issued capital** stock, legally owned by those who have deposited funds with it, perhaps by paying premiums on an **endownment policy**. Common among **savings banks** and **insurance** companies. Profits, after retention of reserves, are distributed to depositors. Contrast **proprietary company**. **2**. In the USA, also an open-ended investment trust. See **mutual fund**.

mutual fund (US) A pooled system of group investment, equivalent to a **unit trust** in the UK, first developed in the USA in the 1930s. Total **assets** of mutual funds grew rapidly until the 1970s, then stagnated until the 1980s, when growth again accelerated (total funds rising from some $135bn in 1980 to well over $350bn by 1985). The funds are invested chiefly in **stocks** (company shares) and bonds, both of companies and of the public authorities. A major category emerging in recent times has been the **money-market mutual fund**. See **open-ended fund**.

mutual offset An arrangement under which markets in different time zones agree to link so as to market each other's product and provide a facility for, or towards, **24-hour trading**.

mutual savings banks (US) Banks accepting interest-bearing **deposits** and owned by their depositors. Also called **thrifts**.

naamloze vennootschap (NV) (Neth.) A public limited company.

NAFTA See **North American Free Trade Agreement**.

naked Said of the holding of a **security** that is not covered, or **hedged**. An expression more frequently used in reference to **derivatives**.

name **1**. The parties to the commercial transaction underlying a **bill of exchange**, as recorded on that document (in the **clausing**). **2**. An external underwriting member of **Lloyd's of London** insurance market.

NAPF See **National Association of Pension Funds**.

NASD See **National Association of Securities Dealers**.

NASDAQ International See **National Association of Securities Dealers Automated Quotation System**.

NASDAQ OTC Price Index A series of **share indices** measuring changes in the prices of shares quoted on the **National Association of Securities Dealers Automated Quotation System**. There are seven indices, including a composite index based on 5 February 1971.

NASDIM See **National Association of Securities Dealers and Investment Managers**.

National Association of Pension Funds (NAPF) The representative organization of providers of occupational pension schemes (see **pensions**).

National Association of Securities Dealers (NASD) (US) See **National Association of Securities Dealers Automated Quotation System**.

National Association of Securities Dealers and Investment Managers (NASDIM) (UK) A now defunct body, formed in 1979 as the Association of Licensed Dealers and until 1987 the leading representative body for some 800 licensed securities dealers, who are now members of one of the *self-regulating organizations* recognized under the **Financial Services Act**.

National Association of Securities Dealers Automated Quotation System (NASDAQ) (US) A series of computer-based information services and an **order** execution system for the US **over-the-counter market**. The system was set up in 1971. NASDAQ provides quotations by over 500 active **market makers** on the **securities** of over 4,000 companies that are actively traded, an average of eight dealers for each security and a minimum of two.

There are some 180,000 NASDAQ terminals in use, of which 25,000 are outside the USA. NASDAQ was designated a UK *recognized investment exchange* in 1988 (**Financial Services Act**). Brokers and institutional traders, having selected the market maker who offers the best price on their screens, may execute their deals by telephone or teletype or, since 1984, may enter orders directly through the Small Order Execution System (SOES). The SOES allows dealers to fill orders for 500 shares or less and 1,000 shares for NASDAQ **National Market System** issues. NASDAQ International has operated from London since early 1992 and allows investors to trade US stocks before the **New York Stock Exchange** opens.

The National Association of Securities Dealers (NASD) is a self-regulatory organization (under delegated powers from the **Securities and Exchange Commission**) that set up and now regulates NASDAQ and the OTC market.

national bank (US) A **commercial bank** that receives its charter from (is registered with) the Comptroller of the Currency (who is a federal government official) and is required to be a member of the **Federal Reserve System** (Fed). A *state bank* receives its charter from a state banking regulatory authority and may opt or not to join the Fed.

national debt The outstanding borrowings of the government, including overseas borrowing. Most of it consists of government and government-guaranteed **securities**. See also **public-sector borrowing requirement**.

National Market System (NMS) (US) A system providing information on the quoted price of **stocks**, the latest price paid, the high and low for the day and the current **volume**. NMS brokers are required to report this information through the system within 90 seconds of the trade. Congress mandated the creation of a NMS in its amendments to the 1934 Securities Exchange Act in 1975, which created the **Securities and Exchange Commission**. The purpose of the NMS was to increase competition by linking the US stock exchanges together in a way that would ensure that prices for any given stock would be the same at all of them. However, the **New York Stock Exchange** (NYSE) allows its members to trade on the exchange only the stocks listed on the exchange, and only on the **National Association of Securities Dealers Automated Quotation System** does the NMS operate fully. However, for certain stocks the Intermarket Trading System (ITS) has since 1980 linked a number of stocks quoted on the NYSE, on the **American Stock Exchange** and one or more of the regional exchanges.

National Savings Bank (NSB) (UK) A **savings bank** administered by the Department for National Savings and operating through the post office network. Formerly known as the Post Office Savings Bank (POSB).

National Savings certificate (UK). A **bond** issued by the UK government. There have been over 40 different issues of these certificates, on which interest, an index-linked increase (see **indexation**) or a bonus is payable on **maturity** or earlier. The certificates can be cashed at any time, and interest is tax free.

National Securities Clearing Corporation (US) A clearing house jointly owned by the **New York Stock Exchange**, the **American Stock Exchange** and the **National Association of Securities Dealers**, set up in 1977. It works through the Securities Industry Automation Corporation (SIAC), which provides the automation, data-processing and communication facilities.

NAV See **net assets**.

NCI See **new Community instrument**.

near money Financial assets that are highly liquid but do not have a direct role in transactions and therefore cannot be fully regarded as **money**.

nearby month See **front month**.

Negotiable 1. Subject to agreement between the parties involved in a transaction. 2. A negotiable instrument, e.g. a crossed **cheque** or **bearer** share, is one in which the title to ownership is transferred freely from hand to hand. 3. The propensity of a financial claim, e.g. a **bill of exchange**, **certificate of deposit**, **Treasury bill** or **bond**, to be traded in financial markets, e.g. in the **money market**. The term is interchangeable in this sense with *transferable* and *marketable*.

negotiable order of withdrawal See **NOW accounts**.

Nennwert (Ger.) Nominal value. See **par value**.

net assets, net asset value (NAV) The value of a company according to the **balance sheet**. It is calculated by taking fixed **assets** plus current assets less **liabilities** owed to all except the owners of the company, and therefore is the same as **shareholders' equity** and is also called *net worth*. Assets are valued at *historic cost* (see **costs, historical, depreciation**). The market value may be greater than the net asset value. See also **balance sheet**, **capital employed**, **investment trust**, **working capital**.

net borrowed reserves (US) **Borrowed reserves** less **excess reserves**, i.e. the amount of banks' reserves borrowed from the **Federal Reserve** less the amount of reserves they hold over and above the required minimum.

net current assets See **working capital**.

net premium Of insurance, a **premium** less the amount paid for **reinsurance**, and/or less the amount paid in **commission** or **brokerage**.

net present value See **discounted cash flow**.

net price On **stock exchanges**, net prices are net of **commission**.

net profit See **profit**.

net tangible assets (NTA) Fixed **assets** plus current assets minus intangible assets, such as **goodwill**, and minus current **liabilities**.

net worth See **net assets**.

Neuausgabe (Ger.) **New issue**.

new Community instrument A loan financed by direct international borrowing of the European Commission, initiated in the 1970s. The Commission, which had until then organized borrowings through separate bodies established for the purpose, e.g. the **European Investment Bank** (EIB), became aware that, given its own standing, it would command advantageous rates itself in the international capital market. The funds thus raised are re-lent to public and private bodies in the **European Union** (formerly European Community) on the same terms and conditions as by the EIB, and the lending programme is managed by the EIB.

new issue The sale of **securities**, e.g. **loan stock** or **equity**, to raise new or additional **capital**, either by way of a **placing**, an offer for *subscription* (see **offer for sale**) or a **rights issue**. The term may also refer to the **flotation** of the existing securities of a company on a **stock exchange** or an **unlisted securities market** for the first time, though such an issue may also involve the raising of additional capital. See **new issue market**.

new issue market That part of the **capital market** that provides new long-term capital, specifically the **stock exchange**. Borrowers in the new issue market may be raising capital for new investment or may be converting private capital into public capital; this is known as *going public* (see **flotation**). See also **new issue**, **rights issue**.

new time (UK) Trading on the **London Stock Exchange** in the following **account** period during the last two days of the current one.

New York Cotton Exchange A **commodity** market for cotton, founded in 1870, dealing principally in **futures**. The exchange is the world's most active market for futures trading in cotton. The market also trades in liquified propane gas futures. It also transacts **options** in cotton futures.

New York Mercantile Exchange (NYMEX) A **commodity** market, founded in 1872 as the Butter and Cheese Market of New York, reincorporated in 1887 under its present name; it now deals in **futures** in crude oil, heating oil, leaded regular gasoline, platinum and palladium. NYMEX introduced the first petroleum futures contract, that on heating oil, in 1978. A merger with the **Commodity Exchange of New York** was projected in 1993, presaging a merger of two of the world's largest markets in energy and precious metals.

New York Stock Exchange (NYSE) (US) The leading New York **stock exchange** and largest in the world in terms of **market capitalization** (see also **American Stock Exchange**). Some 2,000 companies and 5,000 **securities** are listed on the NYSE. It is the oldest exchange in the USA, dating from 1792, and is also referred to as the Big Board. There are about 500 broking firms, with some 1,366 members or seats. These members trade as **specialists** in particular **stocks** on the **trading floor**, as **floor brokers** on behalf of clients or as **floor traders** on their own account. The NYSE is a self-regulating body, though it has to ensure compliance with the requirements of the **Securities and Exchange Commission**. See also **Dow–Jones indexes**.

New Zealand Futures and Options Exchange (NZFOE) Established in 1985, this exchange trades **financial futures**, **currencies** and wool using an automated trading system.

New Zealand Stock Exchange (NZSE) This exchange has its origins in the 1870s. The trading floors were closed in 1991 in favour of a screen-based trading system. Fixed **commissions** were abolished in 1986. The market **share index** is the NZSE 40. The exchange is regulated by the Securities Commission and the Stock Exchange Association.

Newco An insurance company, proposed in 1993 by the authorities of **Lloyd's of London**, which would have the task of reinsuring the liabilities of **Old Years**.

newly industrialized countries (NICs) Not counted as developing or Third World countries, although they have not yet achieved the status of an advanced country. See also **dragons, emerging markets, tigers**.

NFA (US) National Futures Association.

nibu (Jap.) The second section of the **stock exchange**, devoted to dealing in lower-rated **securities**.

niche player A term used to describe a financial institution, generally small, concentrating on a specialized sector, rather than the full range, of the market. Also known as a *boutique*.

NIF See **note issuance facility**.

Nikkei/Dow-Jones Average See **Nikkei Stock Average**.

Nikkei Stock Average A **share index** based on an unweighted (see **weighted average**) average of the prices of 225 **equities** quoted on the **Tokyo Stock Exchange**. Published since 1949, the index was originally called the Nikkei/Dow-Jones Average. Nikkei is the popular name for Nihou Keizai Shimbun, which calculates the index. The Nikkei 300 is capital-weighted and somewhat less volatile. See also **ISE/Nikkei 50 Index**.

NMS See **National Market System, normal market size**.

No. 145 government bond Most recently issued Japanese government bond as at mid-1993, and therefore the 'benchmark' bond, defining going yields. (Japanese government bonds are numbered in sequence.)

nominal The characteristic of an aggregate or level expressed in current money terms, i.e. inclusive of the effect of inflation; e.g. nominal **money supply, rates of interest**. Always implies a relation to a previous size or level. See also **par value, real**.

nominal interest rate The **rate of interest** on a **fixed-interest**

security, expressed as a percentage of the **par value** as opposed to its market price. See **yield**.

nominal value See **par value**.

nominal yield See **yield**.

Nominalwert (Ger.) **Nominal** price.

nominee A person or **company** holding **securities** on behalf of another in order to preserve anonymity or to simplify **settlement**. Many **stockbrokers** have set up *nominee companies* in which their clients have *nominee accounts* recording their beneficial interest in **shares** legally owned by the nominee companies. Such a system avoids the necessity for the broker to send **share certificates** through the post and could be the basis for the *paperless settlement systems* now being considered in several countries. See also **Transfer and Automated Registration of Uncertified Stock (TAURUS)**.

nominee account See **nominee**.

nominee company See **nominee**.

non-bank Any financial transactor outside the commercial banking system. See **commercial banks**.

non-borrowed reserves (US) Those reserves of the US commercial banks that are not derived from borrowings from the **Federal Reserve**, i.e. reserves accumulated through ordinary banking business.

non-obligatory expenditure Expenditure of the **European Union** not specifically laid down in the founding treaties. In regard to these, the European Parliament, which has the right of final adoption or rejection of the Union budget, may propose amendments that may be sustained despite disagreement by the European Council. See also **obligatory expenditure**.

non-proportional treaty Of insurance, an agreement for the reinsurance of a varying amount of claims. See also **excess of loss treaty**, **reinsurance treaty**, **stop–loss treaty**.

non-recourse finance A loan whose servicing and repayment is dependent solely on the profitability of the underlying project, and not on other funds potentially in the possession of the borrower. See also **factoring**.

non-underwritten A **note**, particularly a **Euronote**, that is not **underwritten**. Where issued by a non-bank, such Euronotes are classified as **Euro-commercial paper**, and such issues are know as *Euro-commercial paper programmes*. The term is interchangeable with **uncommitted**.

normal market size (NMS) (UK) A system for classifying **stocks** quoted on the **London Stock Exchange** by **liquidity**. The new system replaced the old **Stock Exchange Automated Quotation System** categories (alpha, beta and gamma; see **alpha securities**) on 14 January 1991. NMS for each stock is calculated by multiplying the value of the average daily customer **turnover** in the previous year by 2.5% to give an estimated average value of the normal institutional **bargain**; this is then divided by the price of the stock to give that normal bargain size in terms of the number of shares. This number of shares is allocated to 12 NMS *bands*; e.g. if the NMS interim number of shares is between 1,334 and 2,400, the NMS band is 2,000; if it is between 2,401 and 3,750, it is 3,000. All stocks that fall into an NMS band of 2,000 or more are called *liquid*, while others are called *less liquid* (equivalent to the old gamma stock grouping). The system is used to set the size of transactions for which **market makers** quote prices and for the publication of market data.

North American Free Trade Agreement (NAFTA) An agreement for a tariff-free area arising out of the Free Trade Area (FTA) established between the USA and Canada in 1989, and extended to Mexico by signature of the three heads of government in 1992, with ratification by the three legislatures sought in 1993. Two accords allaying the fears of US trade unions, consumer groups and environmentalists were attached by President Clinton to the agreement in 1993.

***nostro* account** See *vostro* account.

note 1. An **instrument** recording a promise to pay a specific sum of money by a given date; a *promissory note*. See also **commercial paper**. 2. An inscription on an unpaid bill of exchange by a notary comprising their initials, the date and other details, used by the notary to draw up a **protest**. 3. A banknote.

note issuance facility (NIF) A form of medium-term **Euro-credit**, under which the borrower issues a series of short-term **instruments** against a banker's guarantee over the whole **term**, given in the form of either an **underwriting** or a **back-up credit** arrangement. Where the borrower is a bank, the instrument is usually a short-term **certificate of deposit**; where the borrower is a **non-bank**, the instrument is normally a *promissory note* (see **note**). **Maturities** of the instruments are usually three or six months. NIFs are variously known as RUFs (revolving underwriting facilities), *note purchase facilities* and **Euronote facilities**. The advantage of an NIF to the investor is the high **liquidity** of the instrument, in that it has a short term and the investor need not partake in the next issue in the series. The willingness of banks themselves to buy the instruments, and the comparatively narrow **margins** offered, have made NIFs attractive to borrowers, particularly in view of the flexible **drawdown** available.

The instruments are sold either to a group of purchasing banks or to a *tender panel*, invited by the syndicate of banks managing the facility, or they are sold through a **placement**, ensured by a sole placing agent. The **syndicate** either underwrites the issue or makes back-up credit available. The first well-publicized NIF was an issue by the New Zealand government, for $750m, in 1981. By 1985 there were estimated to be new issues worth $33bn, giving a total of $60bn NIFs in place.

note purchase facility See **note issuance facility**.

notice day The day on which notice must be given in the **commodity market** of the intention to supply a commodity due under contract for delivery in that month (rather than to **cover** the contract or to **liquidate** it by purchase of an offsetting contract).

novus actus interveniens A legal term requiring that human intervention, coming between the insured **risk** and the loss itself, shall be deemed to be the proximate cause of the loss. See also **proximity rule**.

NOW account (US) A personal interest-bearing savings account at a bank or **savings and loan association** on which a *negotiable order of withdrawal* (NOW; in effect a **cheque**) may be drawn, making it an interest-bearing chequing account (see **current account**). NOW accounts were legally permitted throughout the USA from January 1980, although until recently the interest rate payable was capped at $5\frac{1}{2}\%$.

NPV Net present value. See **discounted cash flow**.

NSB See **National Savings Bank**.

NV See *naamloze vennootschap.*

NYMEX See **New York Mercantile Exchange**.

NZFOE See **New Zealand Futures and Options Exchange**.

NZSE See **New Zealand Stock Exchange**.

OAT See *obligation à trésorerie*.

obiter dictum An incidental observation of a judge, not necessarily binding in the case being heard, but of possible application in subsequent matters.

obligation 1. A debt. 2. A **debt instrument**, normally a **bond**.

obligation (Fr.) A **bond**.

Obligation (Ger.) A **bond**.

obligation à trésorerie (OAT) (Fr.) A French **Treasury bill**.

obligation au porteur (Fr.) A bearer **bond**. See **bearer security**.

obligation convertible en action (Fr.) A **convertible bond**.

obligation de caisse (Fr.) A bank bond issued at medium term, not traded on the **stock exchange**.

obligation d'état (Fr.) A government **bond**.

obligatory expenditure Expenditure of the **European Union** directly deriving from the founding treaties. The European Parliament, which has the final decision on approval or rejection of the Union budget, may propose amendments to obligatory expenditure; but if these are not agreed by the European Council, then its only recourse is to reject the budget as a whole. Main examples of obligatory expenditure are those under the common agricultural policy. See also **non-obligatory expenditure**.

occupational pension scheme See **pensions**.

OEIC See **open-ended investment company**.

Oesterreichische Kontrollbank The semi-official Austrian financial institution, supported by government funds, issuing bonds in particular in the international and **Eurobond** markets.

Oesterreichische Termin und Optionsbörse The Austrian **futures and options** exchange.

off-balance-sheet finance Where a business **asset** is not purchased and subject to **depreciation**, but is acquired by **leasing** or **hire purchase**, it may not appear on the **balance sheet**. Rental payments will, of course, be taken into account in the **profit and loss account**, but the indebtness of the company and **capital employed** will be understated. However, in the USA and UK companies may be required to capitalize leased assets. See also **market capitalization**.

offer for sale (UK) Shares may be offered to the public at a fixed price in an advertised offer for sale (US = *public offering*). Those who purchase the shares are said to have subscribed, i.e. it is an offer for subscription. More rarely an offer for **tenders** will be called for. In a tender, potential investors are invited to specify the number of shares they are prepared to buy at a specified price at or above the issuer's stipulated minimum price. The **issuing house** will set a price, the **striking price**, at which the whole issue can be sold at the highest price. Those who have made a tender offer at or above the striking price will receive the number of shares they ask for (unless the issue is **oversubscribed**); those whose offer price is below the striking price will receive no shares. Issues over a certain size (£50m) have to be offered to the public in their entirety, under the rules of the **London Stock Exchange**, instead of by a **placing** or an **intermediaries offer**. See also **introduction**.

offer price The price at which a **dealer** or **market maker** will sell **commodities** or **shares** (US = *asked price*). **Unit trust** managers also quote an offer price at which they will sell units to the general public. Cf. **bid price**.

office A company or **mutual** society engaged in insurance.

official list (UK) The daily list of **securities** admitted for trading on the **London Stock Exchange**. It does not include securities quoted on the **unlisted securities markets**.

official prices Of the **London Metal Exchange**, the prices reached in the first trading session of each day, which are then made public and used as a reference for most world trade in the metals for the following 24 hours. Also known as settlement prices.

offre publique d'achat (Fr.) A **cash take-over** bid.

offre publique d'échange (Fr.) A bid for a **take-over** based on an exchange of **shares**.

offshore banking See **tax haven**.

offshore financial centres See **tax haven**.

offshore funds See **tax haven**.

ohne Dividende (Ger.) **Ex-dividend**.

ohne Kupon (Ger.) *Ex-coupon*. See **ex-dividend**.

OKB See **Osterreichische Kontrollbank**.

Old Lady of Threadneedle Street Popular nickname for the **Bank of England**.

Old Years Term used at **Lloyd's of London** to refer to the 1985 business year and to all preceding years. The feature of these years was that they embraced the severe losses arising out of US legislation on asbestosis and environmental pollution, and other losses. US asbestosis and environmental legislation had occasioned US employers and producers massive costs in compensation payments, going back up to 40 years, and in remedial works. US courts had so interpreted the wording of insurance contracts, also up to 40 years old, that insurers were required to pay employers' and producers' costs.

OM The Stockholm **options** exchange.

on-line A part of a computer system, e.g. a printer, is on-line when it is connected to and ready for use by the computer.

one-month money Money placed, i.e. an **instrument** 'bought' in the **money market**, with a **maturity** of one month.

one-year money Money placed, i.e. an **instrument** 'bought' in the **money market**, with a **maturity** of one year.

OPEC See **Organization of Petroleum Exporting Countries**.

open cover A policy for the **insurance** of ships' cargoes similar to a **floating policy** except that the duration of the policy is unlimited.

open-end credit See **revolving credit**.

open-ended fund An investment company in which units may be purchased from or sold to the fund manager, i.e. a **unit trust** or **mutual funds** company. The fund is open in the sense that its size depends upon its success in selling units, in contrast to an **investment trust**. Units are bought and sold at a price that reflects the market value of the securities they represent, plus a management charge equal to the difference between the **bid price** and **offer price**.

open-ended investment company An **open–ended fund** listed on a **stock exchange** at a single unit price; like an **investment trust** but it can issue or redeem (see **redemption**) **shares** to match demand in a similar way to a **unit trust**. Common in continental European countries and the United States and likely to be permitted in the UK from 1995.

open market desk (US) A familiar term for the section of the New York Federal Reserve Bank that conducts open market operations on behalf of the Federal Reserve Board, and specifically of the Federal Open Market Committee. More exactly referred to as the *domestic open market desk*. See **Federal Reserve**.

open market operations Dealings in the **money market** by a central bank, with the object of influencing short-term interest rates, in pursuit of **monetary control** policies. The term is used to distinguish such activities from other policy measures available to central banks, such as **reserve asset** requirements, bond sales and direct lending.

open-mouth operations (US) Expression used to describe the **Federal Reserve**'s use of public statements to induce a change in **money–market** conditions. The term is a play on the official usage: **open market operations**.

open outcry, open outcry system The practice in a **stock**

exchange or **commodity market** whereby trading is done by oral calling of bids and offers by market members to the point where prices are settled and deals are concluded.

open position A **position** that is not **covered**, or **hedged**. Of trade in **commodities**, a position, or holding of contract, that has not been **liquidated**.

open year The business of **Lloyd's of London** syndicates is conducted on a three-year cycle; i.e. the results of any one year's transactions are not finalized until the third year thereafter; e.g. the accounts of business done in 1993 are not closed until the end of 1995. This procedure provides for the fact that claims on policies issued in one year continue to arise for some time after the end of the year, and facilitates the choice of a fair premium for **reinsurance to close**. The first and second years in the three-year cycle are known as 'open years'. The term is also used on occasion to refer to a **run-off account**.

opening price The price at which a **security** is quoted when a **stock exchange**, or other market, opens for business in the morning (see **bid price**, **offer price**). **Market makers** will adjust their prices from the level they reached when trading stopped on the previous day (see **closing prices**) in line with their expectations of the strength of supply and demand.

operating factors (US) Circumstances, such as the **Federal Reserve float**, influencing the **liquidity** of the US banking system, which must be taken into account when conducting the **Federal Reserve**'s **open market operations**.

operating system The set of programs or software that controls the basic functions of a computer. Additional software is normally necessary to use the computer to carry out specific tasks such as word processing.

operating target (US) The monetary aggregate (see **non-borrowed reserves, reserves, Federal funds rate**) taken by the **open market desk** as its guide in its open market operations.

opération du double (Fr.) **Bourse** transaction under which *put* (*option de vente*) and *call* (*option d'achat*) **options** are simultaneously held.

OPIC See **Overseas Private Investment Corporation**.

OPL See **overall premium limit**.

option 1. A contract giving its beneficiary the right to buy or sell a financial **instrument** or a **commodity**, including gold, at a specified price within a specified period. The option can be freely exercised or disregarded, there being no obligation to transact. Where the right is to buy, the contract is termed a *call option*; where the right is to sell, it is termed a *put option*. The holder of the option is able to take advantage of a favourable movement in prices, losing only the premium payable for the option should prices move adversely. The writer, or seller, of the option is correspondingly more exposed to risk. 2. In the **foreign exchange** market, a binding contract to buy or sell a currency at a specific price, the date of the transaction being left to the choice of the holder of the contract.

Trade in option contracts (hence *traded options*) was long practised between banks but developed, particularly in currency options, after these began to be traded on the Philadelphia Stock Exchange in 1982. Trade in securities options, or *interest rate options*, began later. Currency options were introduced on the **London International Financial Futures Exchange** (LIFFE) and the **London Stock Exchange** in 1985. Options on three-month sterling **futures** were introduced on LIFFE in November 1987; trade in Japanese government bond futures began in July 1987. Chief centres for trade in options are the **Chicago Board Options Exchange**, the **American Stock Exchange**, the **European Options Exchange** in Amsterdam and markets in Australia, France, Sweden and Switzerland. See also **futures options**, **over-the-counter market**.

option d'achat (Fr.) *Call* **option**.

option de vente (Fr.) *Put* **option**.

Options Clearing Corporation A **clearing house** for **over-the-counter derivatives**, based in New York.

Optionsschein (Ger.) A right held by shareholders in a new issue to buy more shares at an agreed price, the right itself being tradable.

order An instruction from a client to a **broker–dealer** to buy or sell a **security**. An order may be a market order to buy or sell at the best price the dealer can obtain at the time of execution. Alternatively, the client may impose a stop order to buy or sell only if the price rises or falls to a specified level. Stop-loss orders are intended to protect the client from loss or to limit the client's loss in a falling market (US = *limit order*).

order driven A **stock exchange** system in which prices react to orders, as in the *auction system* in the **New York Stock Exchange**, where **brokers** and dealers bid for stock (*open outcry* or *auction*) around a *specialist* who maintains a market in chosen stocks by buying and selling for their own account and for broker clients. As distinct from **quote driven**. See also **matched bargains**.

ordinary branch Of insurance, life insurance business other than **industrial branch** business.

ordinary share (UK) A share in the **equity** capital of a business; holders of ordinary shares being entitled to all distributed **profits** after the holders of **debentures** and **preference shares** have been paid (US = *common stock*).

Organization for Economic Co-operation and Development (OECD) The successor to the **Organization for European Economic Co-operation** (OEEC), the OECD was constituted in 1961 out of the original membership of the OEEC, comprising most Western European countries, together with Canada and the USA, to which Finland, Japan, New Zealand and Australia were subsequently added. The OECD thus represents the industrialized world as a whole. The purposes of the OECD are to promote growth and high employment consistent with financial stability in its member countries; to foster international trade; and to contribute to the economic progress of the developing countries and of non-member countries. The OECD is based in Paris and operates through a number of major committees attended by ministers of the member countries. An early achievement was the further promotion of the code of liberalization adopted by its predecessor, which contributed substantially to the removal of **exchange controls**. The Economic Policy Committee has latterly become an important venue for international consultation and agreement on policy response to the economic situation. The OECD publishes a wide range of reports, among them regular assessments of the worldwide economic situation and of the economies of individual members. The Development Assistance Committee centralized the OECD's activities in respect to the developing world and established, among other things, a standard of aid contributions to which all members should aspire (0.7% of *gross national product*; see **gross domestic product**).

Organization for European Economic Co-operation (OEEC) An organization set up in 1948 in response to the offer of **Marshall aid** from the USA. Open to all European countries, membership comprised 17 nations of Western Europe; the Eastern European countries, including the Soviet Union, refused to join. The task of the OEEC was to reach common agreement on the allocation of Marshall aid to individual countries. This was done through a range of technical committees for separate industries and economic sectors, in accordance with the European Recovery Programme established by the council of the OEEC. In concert with this, the US Congress voted funds as far as possible in the amount deemed necessary. Under the programme, which continued from 1948 to 1951, some $12.1bn was disbursed by the USA, equivalent to some $55bn in 1988 prices. As a result of these efforts, total OEEC industrial production expanded by 50% between 1947 and 1952/3, and the volume of exports to third countries doubled. Other measures included a co-ordinated reduction of quantitative restrictions on trade, in conformity with the convention of the **General Agreement on Tariffs and Trade** (GATT); the introduction in 1950 of a code of liberalization, placing trade in goods, services and capital on a multilateral rather than a bilateral basis; and the establishment of the European Payments Union (EPU), extending payments for trade from a bilateral to a multilateral system. The EPU was succeeded in 1958 by the European Monetary Agreement (EMA), further extending **convertibility** and establishing a

European fund for *ad hoc* credit; automatic credits were ended. By 1960, with a further major rise in output and trade, it was decided that broader purposes were now appropriate, and the convention was signed for the transformation of the OEEC into the **Organization for European Co-operation and Development** (OECD).

Organization of Petroleum Exporting Countries (OPEC)

An intergovernmental organization of oil-producing countries, established in 1960 and comprising Algeria, Ecuador, Gabon, Indonesia, Iran, Iraq, Kuwait, Libya, Nigeria, Qatar, Saudi Arabia, the Union of Arab Emirates (UAE) and Venezuela. During the 1960s the member countries nationalized the management of the oilfields, until then operated by the major international oil companies. In the course of the 'Yom Kippur' Arab–Israeli conflict of October 1973, the OPEC countries reduced output and embargoed supplies to Western countries, with a consequent sharp rise in oil prices. The cutbacks in production continued after the conclusion of peace, and developed into a co-ordinated programe of production and export restrictions designed to raise prices permanently. In the event oil prices rose from some $3 a barrel in 1972 to some $15 a barrel in the mid- to late 1970s, and to some $33 a barrel in 1981. This caused a major wave of worldwide inflation and recession, and, given the Arab countries' propensity to concentrate their substantial new wealth in short-term bank deposits, a severe imbalance in international monetary resources.

However, by the mid-1980s the stringent measures of energy conservation, the switch to other fuels and the opening up of major new oilfields that had occurred in importing countries had effectively ended the OPEC domination of prices. By the mid-1990s oil prices per barrel had stabilized in the $15–$20 range.

OSC Ontario Securities Commisison. See **Toronto Stock Exchange**.

OTOB See **Oesterreichische Termin und Optionsbörse**.

out of the money A situation where the **exercise price** of an **option** is adverse to the market price, i.e. where the exercise price is higher than the market price in the case of a *call option* and the reverse of this in the case of a *put option*. See also **in the money**, **intrinsic value**.

outright forward In a **forward currency contract**, a single sale or purchase, as against a **forward–forward**, or a **swap**, sale or purchase.

outright purchase/sale (US) The purchase or sale by the **Federal Reserve** of **money–market instruments** (**Treasury bills**, government **bonds**) for retention or for indefinite disbursement, thus creating a drain on or an influx into the reserves of the banking system.

over-the-counter (OTC) market 1. A group of licensed dealers who provide two-way trading facilities in company **securities** outside the **stock exchange**. The term originated in the USA in the 1870s when **stocks** were first bought across bank counters. The term is often used to refer generally to **unlisted securities markets** and specifically (US) to the elaborate electronic dealing system, with **market makers** across the country, called the **National Association of Securities Dealers Automated Quotation System** (NASDAQ). However NASDAQ trades also in large-company stocks including those listed on other stock exchanges. 2. More generally any securities trading activity carried on outside stock exchanges, e.g. OTC **options**, which are options written by a single seller for a single buyer under a private and confidential arrangement, as distinct from *traded options*.

overall premium limit (OPL) The maximum amount of insurance a member of **Lloyd's of London** can **underwrite**, i.e. the maximum amount of premiums they can accept. The OPL is calculated as a multiple of the member's **funds at Lloyd's**.

overdraft (UK) A **loan** facility on a customer's **current account** at a bank permitting the customer to overdraw up to a certain limit for an agreed period. **Interest** is payable on the amount of the loan facility taken up, and it may therefore be a relatively inexpensive way of financing a fluctuating requirement. See also **line of credit**.

overfunding See **funding**.

overheads Costs that do not vary with output in the short run, e.g. rent, administrative salaries.

overlay manager See **currency overlay manager**.

overnight money Money placed in the **money market** for repayment the next day.

overnight repo See **repurchase agreement**.

overseas banks (UK) **1**. Banks operating in the UK but foreign-controlled. There are over 600 such banks in the UK. **2**. UK-owned banks that conduct their business mainly abroad.

Overseas Private Investment Corporation A US government agency set up to encourage US private investment in emerging countries.

overseas sector A term used in economic and **money supply** contexts to denote foreign transactors, i.e. individuals, companies and governments resident abroad that are trading with, or involved in investment transactions with, national residents. See also **private sector**, **public sector**.

oversubscribed, oversubscription A **new issue** is said to be oversubscribed when investors are prepared to purchase more shares at the offered price (or the **striking price**) than are available. In these cases the **issuing house** either conducts a ballot or lucky draw in which the successful applications are selected at random, or it scales down applications for above a certain minimum quantity of **shares**. See **offer for sale**.

overtrading A business is said to be overtrading when it has insufficient **working capital** to meet its debts when they fall due.

own resources A term derived from the French *ressources propres* to denote the autonomous revenues of the **European Union**, in contrast to direct contributions from member states. The European Union's own resources consist of the proceeds of the common external tariff, agricultural **levies** and 1% of **value added tax** collections, all of which pass to the Union as of right under a decision taken in 1970.

P&L See **profit and loss account**.

pagare (Sp.) *Promissory note*. See **note**.

pagare de empresa (Sp.) **Commercial paper**.

paid-up capital That part of the **issued capital** of a company that has been paid in by the shareholders. Partly paid shares are those on which only a proportion of the issue price of the shares was paid on subscription. This may arise where shares are issued in partly paid form, the second part being payable a few months later to increase the attractiveness of the issue.

pair (Fr.) **Par**.

paper A vernacular term for any **security**, most generally applied to those in the **money market**. Used more specifically for **notes** issued by companies for trading at a **discount**, namely **commercial paper**.

paperless settlement systems See **Transfer and Automated Registration of Uncertified Stock** (TAURUS).

par 1. A **security** is issued at par, its *nominal* or *face* value, and may thereafter trade above or below par, or still at par. **2**. The official fixed **rate of exchange** of a currency, as it was notified to the **International Monetary Fund** (IMF) up to the time of the abolition of fixed exchange rates in 1978. The second amendment to the articles of agreement of the IMF, adopted in 1978, declared the withdrawal of par values, subject to their reintroduction, calculated however in terms of **special drawing rights** (SDRs) or any other denominator except gold or US dollars, on a 85% vote of the members.

par banking (US) The practice of paying the full nominal value by one bank of a cheque drawn on another made universal in the USA by the **Federal Reserve** in the early 20th century.

par bond A bond trading at **par**, the latter generally as defined by the price of new issues or by prevailing yields.

par casier (Fr.) One of the three types of quotation on the French **stock exchange**, the others being *à la criée* and *par opposition*. *Par casier* involves the deposit of orders for **securities** in specified repositories, or 'pigeon-holes' (the meaning of *casier*), in the market, which are then collected and used to determine a **market clearing price**. The method is normally used in the **spot** market.

par opposition (Fr.) One of the three forms of quotation on the French **stock exchange**, the others being *par casier* and *à la criée*. The method of *par opposition* is to strike a price **arbitraging** the **forward** and the **spot** market.

par priced A security issued or trading at its **par**, or *nominal* or *face* value.

par value The price at which a **share**, or other **security**, is issued, which may of course be greater or less than its market price. Alternatively *nominal* or *face* value, though these terms are more usually applied to **currency**; e.g. a silver coin may be worth more than its face value. See also **parity**.

parallel markt (Neth.) The now definct second-tier **unlisted securities market** of the **Amsterdam Stock Exchange**. There were two sub-tiers in the Dutch second-tier market: one for companies that have been officially admitted, and one for companies that have not met all the requirements. The term *parallel markets* is also widely used to refer to other second tiers or unlisted securities markets.

parallel money markets Markets in short-term securities other than **Treasury bills**, **bills of exchange** and **bonds** and including **Eurocurrency**, **certificates of deposit**, loans to local authorities and interbank loans. See **interbank market**.

parent company A company that owns 50% or more of the **ordinary shares** of a **subsidiary** company.

pari passu With equal ranking.

Paris Bourse (Fr.) The principal **stock exchange** in France, from 1991 incorporating the **regional stock exchanges** in Bordeaux, Lille, Lyon, Marseille, Nancy and Nantes. A member of the stock exchange in France is called an *agent de change* and will be a member of the **Chambre Syndicale des Agents de Change**, which, with the official **Commission des Opérations de Bourse**, supervises the securities markets. The *bourse* operates a partially **automated screen trading** system called CAC, based on CATS (see **Toronto Stock Exchange**). In theory **commission** for stockbrokers is based on a fixed scale, but in practice **net prices** are often quoted. The *CAC General Index* is based on 250 **shares**; and the *CAC 40*, the most commonly quoted Paris index, is used as a basis for **futures** contracts. French and foreign banks are now permitted to buy stakes in broking firms. See also **Compagnie des Agents de Change**, **Marché à Terme des Instruments Financiers**, *second marché*.

Paris interbank offered rate The French equivalent of **London interbank offered rate** (LIBOR).

parity A term interchangeable with **exchange rate**, most often used by international institutions, a further alternative term being **par value**. See also **International Monetary Fund**.

parquet (Fr.) A generic term for the Paris **stock market**, originally the name only of the official market as distinct from the **coulisse**.

part (Fr.) 1. In general, a **share** of any possession. 2. A company share. 3. A **shareholding**. 4. A financial interest. 5. A contribution.

participating preference shares (UK) See **preference shares**.

participation (Fr.) A **shareholding**.

particular average See **average**.

partly paid shares See **paid-up capital**.

partnership An **unincorporated business** based on a contractual relationship between two or more people who share risks and profits. Each partner is liable for the **debts** and business actions of the others, to the full extent of their own resources (although they are taxed as an individual). See also **fiscal transparency**.

pass (US) See **coupon pass**.

pass through (US) An arrangement whereby the interest and capital repayments on the mortgages underlying a **collateralized mortgage security**, and received by the servicing agent, are forwarded to the security holder. This may be a straight pass through, where the transfers proceed as the underlying payments are received, or a *modified* pass through, where the transfers to the security holder are guaranteed, irrespective of the payments received by the security agent.

passif (Fr.) **1**. **Liability**. **2**. The liability side of a **balance sheet**.

Patronat (Fr.) The federation of company associations equivalent to the UK Confederation of British Industry.

pawnbroker (UK) A person who lends money against a pledged article that the lender is free to sell if the **loan** is not repaid with **interest** within a stated period.

Pay As You Earn (PAYE) See **income tax**.

pay-out ratio See **dividend cover**.

payback, payback period The period over which the cumulative net revenue from an **investment** project equals the original investment. Its main defects are that it does not allow for the time value of money or for **cash flows** over the whole life of the project. See also **discounted cash flow**.

PAYE Pay As You Earn. See **income tax**.

paying agent An intermediary, usually a bank, responsible for transmitting payments of interest and capital, received from the **fiscal agent**, to holders of **bonds**, normally international in character (e.g. **Eurobonds**), against presentation of **coupons** and bond certificates.

payroll tax A tax (see **taxation**) levied on employers' wage and salary bills.

PC Personal computer. See **microcomputer**.

P/E ratio See **price–earnings ratio**.

peg A fixed level of exchange rates or interest rates, normally established by government intervention. To peg: to achieve such a level. See also **crawling peg**.

penny share (UK) A share **quoted** on the **London Stock Exchange** priced at less than £1, e.g. 18p. Penny shares seem cheap and are for this reason popular with some speculators, but what is really important is the **yield** of a share and the prospects for the company. See **heavy share**.

pension (Fr.) A borrowing in the French money market, the **security** against which is held by the lender.

Pension Benefit Guarantee Corporation See **Employee Retirement Income Security Act**.

pension mortgage Use of the tax-free lump sum payable on the maturing of a **personal pension** scheme to pay off a **mortgage**. There is a tax advantage in that contributions to a pension scheme attract tax relief, whereas premiums on a life assurance policy, the other method of financing a mortgage, do not. A disadvantage is that a smaller amount remains from the lump sum to buy an **annuity**. See also **life assurance**.

pensions Regular income after a certain age and usually after retirement from work, provided by a state scheme or private scheme. Most countries have state schemes as well as private schemes. In Britain the flat-rate retirement pension is paid to men over 65 and women over 60 who have paid appropriate National Insurance contributions, and there is also a State Earnings-Related Pension Scheme (SERPS). There are two broad types of private scheme: *occupational pension schemes*, provided by employers, either contributory or non-contributory; and *personal annuity schemes*, for the self-employed or others not members of an occupational scheme. Under these schemes individuals pay contributions into a fund managed by a **life assurance** company, or other **institutional investor**, which provides a cash lump sum at retirement age; if it is to qualify for tax relief, all the premiums must be used to purchase an **annuity**. Occupational pension schemes may also be *self-administered*, i.e. managed by the employer.

Pension schemes may be *funded* (a capital reserve system), with contributions paid into a fund that is invested in **securities** and other **assets** and from which pensions are ultimately paid. Such funds, which received special tax treatment, are important operators in securities markets (see **institutional investor**). Pension schemes may also be *unfunded*, as in the UK National Insurance scheme and most other state schemes, where pensions for retirees are paid out of the contributions of those in work.

See also **Employee Retirement Income Security Act**, **equalization of pensions**, **individual retirement account**, **Keogh plan**, **personal pension**.

per mille 'Per thousand': a term used to express very fine interest rates, thus '5 *per mille*' equals 0.5%.

per se By itself; in itself.

peril Of insurance, one of several possible occurrences, all of which constitute the **risk** against which insurance is provided.

peripherals See **local area network**.

permanent health insurance Cover for the cost of medical and hospital treatment in the case of illness, provided against regular payments of premiums. Permanent health insurance is distinct from accident insurance. The business is normally transacted by life insurance companies. Also known as *medical insurance*.

perpetual annuity An annual sum of money paid over an indefinite period of time.

perpetual FRN (floating rate note) A floating rate note having no **maturity**, i.e. not to be repaid; used chiefly as an investment **instrument**.

personal annuity schemes See **pensions**.

personal equity plan (PEP) (UK) A scheme introduced in the Finance Act 1986 to provide tax relief on the proceeds of personal investments in **equities** listed on the **stock exchange**. In any one year a maximum of £6,000 per annum plus £3,000 in a single company PEP per individual may be invested. There is no tax on

capital gains, and **dividends** are free of **income tax** if reinvested. To qualify for these benefits, the shares must be held from the start of the plan until 31 December of the following year. The plan must be administered by a financial institution, and some **investment trusts** and **unit trusts** have PEP status.

personal financial planning (PFP) Commercially provided advice on the financial affairs of individuals looked at as a whole, but with emphasis upon **pensions**, **life assurance**, **taxation** and **investment**. PFP concentrates on the creation and protection of **capital**, the maximization and balancing of capital growth and income in accordance with the wishes and tax circumstances of the client. PFP also aims to make provision for contingencies including house purchase, tax liabilities, the acquisition of shares in partnerships or other enterprises, school fees, sickness and disablement, retirement and death. PFP is not normally concerned with maximizing **earned income**, but it is concerned with the form in which that income is taken, in other words, with the mix of the renumeration package. PFP services are provided by **financial intermediaries** that also provide their own savings media, such as the **commercial banks**, and by specialist consultants, **insurance brokers**, accountants and solicitors, all of these advisers being subject to the provisions of the **Financial Services Act**.

personal identification number (PIN) A number unique to an individual required to gain access via a **key pad** to computer-controlled equipment such as a security lock or an **automatic teller machine**.

Personal Investment Authority (PIA) (UK) A new self-regulatory organization for the regulation of retail financial products. The PIA replaced FIMBRA and LAUTRO and some of the present activities of IMRO and the SFA in 1994. See **Financial Services Act**.

personal loan (UK) A **bank loan** made without **collateral security** to a private customer, usually for specific purposes. A **term loan**.

personal pension A pension deriving from a pension account in the name of a single individual, as compared with an occupational pension or company scheme. Personal pensions were made available to UK employees under the Social Security Act 1985; until then employees had access only to occupational pensions. Personal pensions are all **money purchase** schemes; taxation and contribution rules are the same as for self-employed pension schemes. Personal pensions can move with individuals when they change jobs, thus the term *portable pensions*. In the USA personal pensions were introduced in 1975 as **individual retirement accounts** (IRAs).

personal reserve Moneys arising from **Lloyd's of London** members' **underwriting** profits that they place with their **funds at Lloyds**. **Members' agents** are empowered to insist on a minimum amount, but there is no upper limit.

petroleum revenue tax (PRT) (UK) A tax on the profits of oil companies deductible from **corporation tax**. It was introduced to increase revenue from the profits earned on the development of oilfields in the North Sea.

Pfandbrief (Ger.) A loan instrument issued to refinance mortgages or public-sector projects, closely regulated under law. *Pfandbriefe* may be issued only by authorized banks, themselves fully liable for the issue. Underlying mortgages may not exceed 60% of the property value; public-sector projects must be secured by public-sector loans. *Pfandbriefe* must also be covered by separate funds with at least equivalent yields; holders have first claim on assets in case of default. *Pfandbriefe* are vetted by a state-appointed trustee.

physical A **commodity**, sold on a **commodity market**, available for immediate or very early delivery. So called because the commodity is physically at hand, as against commodities that are the subject of **futures**, **forward** and **option** contracts of sale. The term is used synonymously with 'actual', 'cash' and 'spot'.

physical price The price of a commodity immediately available for sale and delivery. Also known as cash or actual price. See also **forward**, **futures**, **option**.

PIA See **Personal Investment Authority**.

PIBOR See **Paris interbank offered rate**.

PIN See **personal identification number**.

pink sheets Listings of **bid prices** and **offer prices** for **market makers** in **over-the-counter markets**. Published in the USA by the National Quotation Bureau, which also publishes *yellow sheets* for corporate bonds.

pit trader A **dealer** in an area of or on a platform on the floor of a **stock exchange** or **commodity market** trading by **open outcry**.

placement See **placing**.

placement (Fr.) An **investment**.

placing (UK) The sale of new shares to institutions or private individuals, as distinct from an **introduction** or **offer for sale** (US = *placement*). The placing of shares is common for **private companies**, where it may be carried out by the company directly with investors (a private placing) or with the help of a **stockbroker**. For **public** companies wishing to place shares as a route towards a **listing**, a **sponsor** will be used; this is sometimes called a public placing (see **introduction**). **Stock exchange** authorities allow listed companies to use placing only for small issues, since not all investors have the opportunity to buy at the same price. For larger issues an offer for sale is required, but this is a more costly means of raising capital. See also **intermediaries offer**.

plastic money See **credit card**.

Plaza Agreement (1985) An agreement reached at a meeting at the Plaza Hotel, New York, in September 1985 of the *Group of Five* – the USA, the UK, Japan, France and West Germany – to the effect that measures would be taken to establish greater international currency stability, and exchange rates more closely reflecting the economic situation of the countries involved.

Plc See **incorporation**.

plus value (Fr.) **1. Appreciation** of capital. **2.** Surplus value, i.e. the Marxian concept of the true value of labour as contrasted with the value of wages paid.

poison pill A defensive action to discourage a hostile **take-over bid**, such as the sale of a major **asset**. See **corporate raider**.

polarization (UK) The new regulatory framework in the investment industry (see **Financial Services Act**) does not allow banks, **building societies** and other **financial intermediaries** to sell their own financial products, such as **unit trusts**, and present themselves at the same time as advisers on such products. They must polarize: act either as independents, offering advice on, and sales of, all competing products; or as agents, selling only their own services. Some institutions have chosen one route, some the other. See also **independent financial adviser** (IFA), **independent intermediary**.

policy A contract for **insurance**.

policy-holder The possessor of an insurance **policy**.

poll tax A tax levied equally on each adult member of a community; hence the unofficial name given to the community charge in the UK (see **local taxation**).

pooling of interests See **consolidated accounts**.

portable pension (UK) See **personal pension**.

portfolio 1. A group of **securities** held as an investment. 2. A branch or class of insurance business.

portfolio insurance A **stock exchange** technique whereby offsetting transactions in the **futures** market are used to compensate for changes in the current market.

portfolio investment See **balance of payments**.

portfolio theory Economic analysis of the means by which investors can minimize risk and maximize returns. Central to **portfolio** theory are the notions that risk can be reduced by diversifying holdings of **assets**, while returns are a function of expected risk. Statistical analysis of **share** prices is used to provide guidance on portfolio composition. See also **alpha coefficient**, **capital asset pricing model**.

POSB Post Office Savings Bank. See **National Savings Bank**.

position 1. The extent of a person's financial commitment to a **stock**, **commodity** or **currency**. If a **dealer**, for example, sells 100 **shares** they do not own, they have sold short or have a short position of 100 in the shares. If they own 100 shares, they have long position of 100 of the stock on their books. They will take a **bear** position, i.e. a short position, if they expect the price of the stock to fall and can buy the stock to meet their sale more cheaply later on; and a **bull**, or long, position if they expect the price to rise. 2. The acquisition by the arranging bank of one-half of a **swap** deal in order to complete the deal with the intention in due course of finding a counter-party.

Post-Market Trading (PMT) An **automated screen trading** system operated by the **Chicago Mercantile Exchange** in collaboration with **Reuters**.

Postal Savings Bureau See **Maruyu**.

Potato Terminal Market (Neth.) A **futures** market, set up in 1958, operating in Rotterdam and Amsterdam, dealing in the Bintje variety. The only **commodity** market dealing in potato futures of note in Europe, apart from the **London Potato Futures Market**.

pound cost averaging (UK) The accumulation of **assets** by investing a regular sum of money at regular intervals. A regular investment of this kind will buy more **shares** when prices are low and fewer when prices are high, and may therefore be preferred to the regular acquisition of a fixed number of shares. (US = *dollar cost averaging* or *constant dollar plan*.)

PPP See **purchasing power parity**.

pre-emptive rights (UK) The right of shareholders of a **company** to have first refusal to purchase any new **shares** issued by the company. These rights have legal backing in the UK. See also **rights issue**.

preference shares (UK) Holders of preference shares precede the holders of **ordinary shares**, but follow **debenture** holders, in the payment of **dividends** and in the return of **capital** if the issuing company is liquidated (see **liquidation**). Preference shares (US = *preferred stock*) normally entitle the holder to a fixed rate of dividend, but *participating preference shares* also entitle the holder to a share of residual **profits**. Preference shares carry limited voting rights and may be redeemable or not (see **redeemable securities**). *Cumulative preference shares* carry forward the entitlement to preferential dividends, if unpaid, from one year to the next.

preferred stock (US) See **preference shares**.

Preis (Ger.) The price of an individual **share**; as against *Kurs*, the going market price for the class of shares.

pre-market Trading between members of a **commodity market** before the trading session on the floor begins.

premier cours (Fr.) **Opening price**.

premium 1. In **insurance**, the sum of money paid, either once (single premium) or continuously (regular premium), to buy an insurance policy. 2. In the **forward** and **futures currency** and **commodity** markets, the amount by which a later-date price exceeds an early-date price. 3. Of **securities**, the amount by which the **secondary market** price exceeds the **issue** price or **par value**. 4. Of **options**, the initial down payment, normally of 10%, required. 5. The amount by which the price of an **investment trust** share exceeds the **net asset value**.

premium income The total flow of insurance policy premiums into an insurance company.

premium pool 1. An arrangement whereby several insurance companies derive business jointly through a single **broker**. See also **dollar pool**.

Premium Trust Fund The fund into which all premiums received on insurance and reinsurance policies issued by **Lloyd's of London** must be paid, and from which claims and other underwriting liabilities are paid. The fund is administered under a trust deed approved by the **Department of Trade and Industry**.

present value See **discounted cash flow**.

Prestel See **viewdata**.

prêt (Fr.) A **loan**.

price–earnings (P/E) ratio (PER) The quoted price of an **ordinary share** divided by the most recent year's **earnings** per share, also known as the *multiple*. In the UK the net distribution method is usually used in calculating the PER, in which earnings are defined as the net-of-tax dividends plus **retained earnings** (see also **corporation tax**). High P/E ratios reflect favourable investors' assessments of the future earning power of the company.

price index See **share indices**.

primary 1. Of the stock market, that part of the market concerned with new **issues**; compare **secondary market**. **2.** Of the **Federal Reserve System**, a **dealer** in government **securities** through whom **open market operations** are conducted. **3.** Of **insurance**, business conducted by an **insurer** with the general public, rather than **reinsurance**. **4.** Of the **commodities market**, a product in its natural state, having undergone little or no refining or processing, e.g. raw wool, metal ores.

primary dealer 1. A **securities** dealer with whom the **open market desk** deals, in conducting its open market operations (US). **2.** A securities dealer appointed by the Bank of England to deal as a **market maker** in **gilts** (UK).

primary market See **new issue market**.

prime (Fr.) **1.** An insurance premium. **2.** An additional payment.

prime rate See **base rate**.

principal 1. A person acting on their own account, and buying and selling at their own risk, as distinct from someone acting as an **agent** for another, e.g. a **broker**. **2.** The amount of a debt, i.e. the capital sum, excluding any **premium** or **interest**.

prise de contrôle (Fr.) A take-over.

private In economic and financial language, a term used to denote non-state or non-governmental matters. See also **public**.

private company (UK) See **incorporation**.

private placing See **placing**.

private sector The part of the economy that does not belong to the government, central or local, or to trading corporations and other non-trading entities owned by the government. The private sector comprises chiefly privately owned financial institutions and companies, and individuals. A distinction is also made between the banking private sector, i.e. those financial institutions that are banks, and the non-banking private sector. The term is used widely in economic and **money supply** contexts. See also **overseas sector**, **public sector**.

private trading system (US) A screen-based trading system used by **institutional investors** and **broker-dealers** not wishing to use the **stock exchanges** on grounds of cost, secrecy or other reasons.

private unrequited transfers A term used in **balance of payments** statistics to cover remittances by foreign workers to relatives and others in their countries of origin. Also includes charitable donations and other non-commercial transfers.

privatization The sale of government-owned **equity** in nationalized industry or other commercial enterprises to private investors. Privatization, which used to be called *denationalization*, may involve the retention of either a majority or a minority holding by government, though the UK government in several cases has retained a *golden share*, which is intended to give it power of veto in an unwelcome take-over bid, e.g. one from overseas. A large proportion of state-owned industry has been privatized in the UK since 1981, with the declared objective of promoting competition, efficiency and individual share ownership. Inducements, such as *loyalty bonuses* (e.g. a 10% free issue of shares to investors who retain their holdings beyond a certain date), not normally employed in the **new issue** market, have been used. Privatizations have included British Gas, British Telecom, Jaguar and the electricity and water companies. Many other countries, including France and **newly industrialized countries** in **Eastern Europe**, have embarked upon a privatization programme. Recent examples are Banque Nationale de Paris and Singapore Telecom. See also **privatization voucher**.

privatization voucher A voucher exchangeable for a share in a privatized company, with a nominal value of Rbls10,000, distributed to Russian citizens as part of the privatization programme. By the end of 1992, 150m such vouchers had been issued. These were quickly utilized, given the privatization of 3% to 4% of Russian manufacturing companies each month in the period, with the emergence of some 35m shareholders.

prix d'émission (Fr.) The **striking price** in a sale of **securities** by **offer for sale** by **tender**.

prix d'offre (Fr.) The **reserve price** in a new issue of **securities**.

profit *Net profit* before tax is the residual after deduction of all money costs, i.e. sales revenue minus wages, salaries, rent, fuel and raw materials, **interest** on **loans**, and **depreciation**. *Gross profit* is net profit before depreciation and interest. In manufacturing companies it is common to describe some elements in costs as the **cost of sales**, and in distribution the term 'gross **margin**' is used in calculating profit.

profit and loss account (P&L) (UK) A financial statement showing revenue, expenditure and the **profit** or loss resulting from operations in a given period.

profit-sharing scheme (UK) Arrangements for giving employees a share in the **profits** of the company they work for. These may take several forms. Employees may be granted *share options* under which they may purchase shares at a fixed price that may, after a time, be substantially less than the market price. The scheme may be restricted to certain classes of employee, as in *executive share options*. Alternatively employees may be allowed to purchase shares under a save-as-you-earn scheme. Other forms of profit sharing include **employees stock ownership plans**, under which shares are distributed free, and schemes whereby a proportion of profits are set aside and distributed not to shareholders but to employees, either on a discretionary basis or as a percentage of earnings. Some profit-sharing schemes are eligible for relief from **capital gains** tax and **income tax**.

programme trading (UK) US = *program trading*. Computer-generated purchases or sales of **securities** that occur when large premiums open up or disappear between the prices of securities and the prices of the same securities on the **futures** market. A form of **arbitrage**.

project finance The assembly of funds necessary for large-scale civil engineering and construction operations, including large housing projects. These are chiefly **loan** funds, with possibly some admixture of **equity** finance, of a **maturity** matched as far as possible to the duration of construction; together with such government grants and credits as may be available; and backed, particularly in the case of foreign operations, by public or private **credit guarantees** and political risk insurance. Where projects on foreign soil are concerned, optimum use of **foreign exchange** is necessary. Significant finance is invariably obtained from international sources such as the International Development Association (IDA; see **International Bank for Reconstruction and Development**), the **Export-Import Bank**, the development banks and the **Eurobond** and **Eurodollar** markets. Project finance is normally conducted by a consortium of banks, contractors and investment vehicles.

promissory note See **note**.

prompt date The delivery date set in a **commodity futures** contract.

property income certificate (PINC) (UK) A **share** in the ownership of a single building, giving holders the benefits of income and capital growth, but which can be traded. The trading of shares in individual buildings through PINCs is expected to be conducted on a new unitized property market or markets, but developments have been held up by problems in clarifying the tax status of this new investment vehicle.

proportional treaty Of insurance, an agreement for the **reinsurance** of a fixed proportion of claims. See also **quota share reinsurance treaty**, **reinsurance treaty**, **surplus treaty**.

proprietary company 1. An insurance company with issued

capital stock; compare **mutual** company. **2**. In Australia, a **limited company**.

prospectus A document containing company information in connection with a **new issue**. With only a few exceptions, it is unlawful for a company to invite anyone to apply for shares unless the application form is accompanied by a prospectus containing certain information set out in the Companies Act 1985 (see **incorporation**) or, in the case of a **London Stock Exchange** company, in compliance with the regulations in the **Yellow Book**.

protest A document drawn up by a notary, certifying that a **bill of exchange** has not been paid on the due date.

provisions Sums set aside in the accounts (and charged against profits) to provide for anticipated loss or expenditure, e.g. a bad debt. Provisions may not be made where the loss or expenditure is highly uncertain, as in a possible lawsuit, but noted as a *contingent liability*. Where losses do not materialize the provisions may be *written back*. Where, for example, a bad debt has proved impossible to recover it will be *written off*, i.e. removed from asset book values.

proviso clause (US) A clause inserted in 1966 in the written **directive** given to the **open market desk** after each meeting of the **Federal Open Market Committee**, instructing the desk to maintain **free reserves** at a given level, provided that growth of **bank credit proxy** was not excessive.

proximity rule The rule in **insurance** law that only the immediate, or proximate, cause of loss or damage is to be taken into account when deciding whether the insured **risk** has occurred.

proxy Shareholders unable to be present at a shareholders' meeting (see **annual general meeting**) may authorize (give proxy to) another person (including the chairperson or other director) to vote on their behalf, either as they think fit or according to specific instructions.

PRT See **petroleum revenue tax**.

'prudent insurer' A term used to define the extent of the duty of disclosure of material facts incumbent on the **insured** under a contract. The insured must disclose all those facts likely to be considered by a prudent insurer when deciding whether to insure a **risk**.

prudential ratios See **capital adequacy**.

PSB Postal Savings Bureau (Jap.). See **Maruyu**.

PSBR See **public-sector borrowing requirement**.

PSL Private-sector liquidity. See **money supply**.

PTS See **private trading system**.

public A term used in economic and financial language to denote state activities, in contrast to those of the general public, for which the term *private* is used. The two terms are to an evident degree anomalous; a term such as *state*, *official* or *governmental*, as against 'public', would have been more precise.

public dividend capital A form of UK long-term government finance for nationalized industries on which dividends are paid, rather than interest. The capital is not repayable. Since dividends are paid out of profits and these have rarely materialized in nationalized industries, little of this capital has been supplied.

public finance The provision of money for public expenditure by **taxation** and borrowing. See also **budget**.

public limited company (plc) See **incorporation**.

public offering See **offer for sale**.

public placing See **placing**.

public sector The part of the economy that consists of the central government, local government, the nationalized industries and other entities owned by central and local government. The term is used widely in economic and **money supply** contexts. See also **overseas sector**, **private sector**.

public-sector borrowing requirement (PSBR) (UK) A term used for the overall financial deficit of general government and the public corporations (state-owned enterprises), i.e. the amount needed to be borrowed, in a given financial year.

public subscription See **offer for sale**.

pumping (US) The action of the **Federal Reserve** in injecting a heavy addition to bank reserves, and thus provoking a fall in interest rates, before announcing a cut in the **discount rate**. This enables the Federal Reserve to state that the lower discount rate was necessary in order to bring it into line with prevailing market rates. The stratagem, generally provoked by political considerations, has been described as a 'shortfall of candour'.

purchase Acquisitions of ownership of an **instrument** or **bond** through payment of its **face value** with either a **discount** or a **premium**.

purchasing power parity (PPP) exchange rates Exchange rates based on the relative prices of the same basket of goods in each country, instead of indicated by market or fixed rates. PPPs are used because exchange rates may be *over-* or *undervalued* in terms of relative domestic purchasing power. A currency may, for example, be overvalued in relation to its real purchasing power because of capital movements or **speculation**.

pure risk Of insurance, a risk in which a loss will certainly arise if a given contingency, or **peril**, occurs; and therefore a risk, in contrast to **speculative risks**, which is insurable, since the occurrence can be calculated by the **law of large numbers**.

put option See **option**.

pyramid investment scheme A scheme whereby each member subscribes a small sum, in return for which, provided only that the membership grows continuously, they will later receive a much larger payment. Such schemes must inevitably collapse, with large losses for the later subscribers. In 1993 the Caritas scheme in Romania, involving 3m people, about a sixth of the population, appeared to be on the point of breakdown.

pyramiding See **holding company**.

quanto option An **option** on an underlying foreign security in which immunity from **exchange rate** risk is guaranteed.

quantum theory of money A theory devised by the Yale University Professor of Political Economy, Irving Fisher (1867-1947), to the effect that changes in the quantity of money available in an economy directly influence the general level of prices. The theory is expressed in the equation $MV = PT$, where M is the quantity of money, V is the velocity with which it circulates within the economy, P is the general level of prices, and T is the total number of transactions in the economy. The equation is a truism but is given significance by Fisher in his contention that V is constant and that T reflects the physical activity of the economy. Thus $M = P$. The theory was challenged by Keynes on the grounds that V could in fact vary with M, but it was revived by Milton **Friedman** and made the point of departure for his **monetary school**.

quota An agreed fixed proportion of a financial obligation, thus: **1**. Of the **International Monetary Fund** (IMF), that part of the organization's resources subscribed by each country and determined in relation to the country's participation in international trade. **2**. Of **reinsurance**, that portion of the **cedant**'s risks that must be reinsured under a **quota share reinsurance treaty**. **3**. Of **international commodity agreements**, quantities of the commodity under consideration that contracting countries undertake to import, or quantities that exporting contracting countries undertake not to exceed.

quota share reinsurance treaty A **proportional treaty** under which an insurer places an agreed proportion of any particular class of **risks** with a **reinsurer**, ceding to the reinsurer an equivalent proportion of the relevant premiums and receiving from them a refund, in the same proportion, of relevant claims paid.

quotation A price for **securities** at which a **market maker** will trade. See also **bid price**, **offer price**.

quote driven A **stock market** system (usually in relation to an electronic system) in which prices are initially determined by quotations of **dealers** or **market makers**. Ultimately prices are determined by supply and demand as in any other market, but the term is useful to distinguish between the systems in use on, e.g., the **New York Stock Exchange,** which are **order driven**, and those on the **National Association of Securities Dealers Automated Quotation System** and now the **London Stock Exchange**, which are quote driven. Electronic quote-driven systems are leading to the demise of the traditional **trading floor**.

quoted company A company (see **incorporation**) whose shares are listed on an official **stock exchange**. Compare **unlisted company**.

quotient cours bénéfice (Fr.) **Price—earnings ratio**.

Quotron A company now part of **Reuters** providing screen-based **equity** price quotations. Recently many competitors have emerged in the market for **real-time** stock market information, including those readable by hand-held mobile telecommunications equipment. See also **Telerate**.

rallonge See **short-term monetary support** (STMS).

rally A sharp increase in the price of a **stock**, or in the general level of prices, following a decline.

ramp, ramping The purchase of securities for the sole purpose of increasing their price. A practice used in the **Euronote** market; also practised in the company share market in the course of a take-over bid – although it is illegal for a company to buy its own shares.

ratchet See **earn-out**.

rate 1. An abbreviation of **interest rate** and applied mostly in the **money market**, e.g. interbank rate, bank bill rate, CD (see **certificate of deposit**) rate. 2. An abbreviation of **rate of exchange**, e.g. dollar rate, DM rate. 3. Of **commercial paper** in the USA, France, Australia and Canada, to assess the creditworthiness of the issuer; done by a **rating agency**. 4. To assess the creditworthiness of a **security** issuer, done by a rating agency.

rate anticipation swap A **swap** of securities made in the expectation of a change in interest rates.

rate of exchange The value of a **currency** in terms of another, i.e. the number of units of that currency required to obtain one unit of the other.

rate of interest The proportion of a sum of money that is paid over a specified period of time in payment for its **loan**. It may be a fixed rate of interest or a **floating rate**.

rate support grant A generalized grant from the UK central government to local governments, supplementing the latter's finances with the object of enabling them to attain comparable standards of service at comparable cost to local taxpayers.

rates See **local taxation**.

rating See **Standard and Poor's Ratings**.

rating agency A firm or organization set up to **rate** issuers of **commercial paper**, or **securities**. In the UK, USA and other countries there are many rating agencies. In France the Agence d'Evaluation Financière (ADEF) was set up as a joint venture between the government agencies and institutional investors. In Australia rating is done by Australian Ratings. See also **credit rating**.

reaction function (US) The adjustment by the **Federal Reserve** of its **monetary control** to broad changes in the general economy.

real The characteristic of an aggregate or level that is expressed in money terms divested of the effect of inflation from a previous date, e.g. real **investment**, **rates of interest**, **money supply**.

real bills doctrine See **elastic currency**.

real-estate investment trusts (REITs) (US) Publicly **quoted** trusts (see **investment trust**) issuing **bonds** secured by a package of commercial property. First launched in 1982, REITs had by 1993 moved from a **market capitalization** of $3bn to one of $25bn. This growth was attributed to the popularity of the instrument with developers, given its low yield compared with that required by buyers of new-built property, a low yield level sustained by heavy demand from **mutual funds**. REITs are a form of **securitization**.

real time A computer and communications system in which the generation of data and the inputting and processing of that data occur virtually simultaneously, so that the output of the system, e.g. a **share price index**, will reflect real changes (in prices) as they occur.

receivables Amounts due to a business, i.e. owed by **debtors**.

receivership See **bankruptcy**.

reciprocal insurance See **reinsurance**.

recognized investment exchange See **Financial Services Act**.

recognized professional body (RPB) See **Financial Services Act**.

Red Book (UK) A familiar term for the **financial statement and budget report** issued on Budget day.

red herring (US) A preliminary **prospectus** issued to test the market for a **new issue**; does not include a firm price.

redeemable security Stocks or **bonds** that are repayable at their **par value** at a certain date, dates or specified eventuality. Most fixed-interest **securities** are redeemable, though **consols** bear no redemption date.

redemption The repayment of a **loan** or the **par value** of a **security** at **maturity** on the repurchase of a security such as a **unit trust** certificate.

redemption date The date at which a loan is repaid.

redemption yield See **yield**.

rediscount The act of a **central bank** in **discounting paper** submitted to it by **money market** operators. So called because the paper has already been discounted in the market, and the central bank is acting in its capacity of **lender of last resort**; often referred to simply as discounting.

reducing-balance methods of depreciation See **depreciation**.

réescompte (Fr.) **Rediscount**.

refinance 1. To take over or guarantee an existing loan; frequently by an official agency, such as the **Export–Import Bank** (US) or the **Export Credit Guarantee Department** (UK), *vis-à-vis* commercial banks providing export credit. 2. To exchange one loan for another; done by ordinary borrowers either on the expiry of the original credit or to take advantage of an alternative loan on better terms. Compare **funding**.

regional bank (Jap.) One of the two categories of Japanese commercial banks. Restricted to local districts, they serve mainly local enterprises. Normally in possession of surplus funds, they are lenders to the **call** market. See also **city bank**.

regional stock exchanges Many major countries have smaller **stock exchanges** in addition to the principal one, and they trade in the **securities** of local organizations as well as in the securities listed on the main exchange. The UK used to have regional exchanges in several cities (see **London Stock Exchange**), while the USA has two major exchanges in New York, the **New York Stock Exchange** and the **American Stock Exchange**, and other regional exchanges that include Boston, Midwest (Chicago) and Pacific (Los Angeles). Although regional exchanges are more important in some countries, notably the **German stock exchanges** and the **Swiss stock exchanges**, in most countries the principal exchange accounts for the vast majority of trading in securities, and recently there has been a tendency for regional exchanges to be integrated under common management. See also **Paris Bourse**, **Tokyo Stock Exchange**.

registrar A person or company appointed by a company to keep a record of the ownership of its **shares** and to communicate with shareholders (US = *transfer agent*, where the registrar is not the company). The *share register* is a list of shareholders' names and addresses and the quantity of stock each one holds.

regular premium See **life assurance**, **unit-linked life assurance**.

regulation Generally, the supervision and control of the activities of private enterprise by government in the interests of efficiency, fairness, health and safety. All **stock exchanges** are regulated (see e.g. **Financial Services Act**, **Securities and Exchange Commission**), as are **banking** and other aspects of finance (see e.g. **consumer credit**, **exchange control**). Regulatory powers may be delegated by government to the financial services industry itself, or they may be exercised directly or through official regulatory agencies. Regulations may act as a barrier to entry and inhibit competition; following the lead of the USA and the UK, there has been a recent trend towards the *deregulation* of stock exchanges in particular, accompanied by some tightening of measures to protect individual investors (see **Big Bang**).

Regulation Q (US) A **Federal Reserve** regulation setting ceilings on rates of interest paid by banks on their deposits. In 1970 and 1973 the application of the regulation was lifted on **certificates of deposit** (CDs) of maturities of 30 to 90 days, and over 90 days, respectively. Regulation Q was an important stimulus to the **Eurodollar** market because it encouraged US banks to bid for funds at higher rates from their branches abroad.

reinstatement The restoration, following payment of a loss, of the original amount of cover pledged in a **reinsurance treaty**; this may be subject to an increase in premium, or a maximum number of reinstatements may be specified in the treaty. Used chiefly in **excess of loss reinsurance** in aviation, marine and property business, and also in catastrophe business.

reinsurance The practice of **insurers** of passing on part of the **risks** they assume to other parties in return for a proportional share of the **premium income**. Although many large insurers themselves undertake reinsurance, the market is also served by large companies specializing in the activity. Reinsurance is essentially an international business. The largest reinsurer in the world is in Munich (Munich Re). Other large reinsurers are Cologne Re, Swiss Re (Zurich), General Re (USA) and the Gerling Group (Germany). **Lloyd's of London** also conducts a substantial proportion of its business in reinsurance.

The reinsurance market grew significantly in the two decades from the 1960s; from a premium income of between $5bn and $6bn, handled by a small number of conservative-minded professional reinsurers, the market then grew to some $56 billion in the early 1980s, handled by many more professional reinsurers, by direct insurers entering into the business and also by **captive insurers**. This strong growth was occasioned by an imbalance of **capacity** as against demand. In the late 1980s, with a revival of profitable direct insurance, reinsurance growth eased. Reinsurance normally accounts for some 10% to 15% of direct business.

reinsurance to close (RITC) (UK) **Lloyd's of London** syndicates have a legal life of one year only, and must reconstitute themselves in order to begin a new year (invariably the membership of the syndicates remains the same). Consequently, a syndicate must, before it closes at the end of the year, provide for the payment of any claims that may subsequently arise from the policies it has written during its life. It therefore reinsures against this with the new syndicate, paying a premium for this into the account of that syndicate. This is known as 'reinsurance to close'. The members of the old syndicate remain formally liable for any subsequent claims, but pass these claims on, under normal reinsurance practice, to the members of the new syndicate. As there may well be some change in membership between the two syndicates, great care is taken to ensure a level of RITC premium that is fair to both sides.

reinsurance treaty A contract between an **insurer** and a reinsurer, whereby **risks** held by the former are assumed by the latter in exchange for a proportional share in the premium income. Reinsurance treaties are binding over the whole range of the risks covered, as compared with **facultative reinsurance**; and the insurers passing on the risks, i.e. ceding insurers, or cedants, are bound to declare their acceptance of all risks covered by such treaties, while reinsurers are bound to accept the cession of all such risks. Variations of reinsurance treaties are **proportional** and **non-proportional treaties**. The former include **quota share treaties**.

REITs See **real-estate investment trusts**.

rendement (Fr.) **1. Yield. 2. Profit**.

Rendite (Ger.) **Yield, profit**.

rente (Fr.) **1**. The flow of **interest** on a **security**. **2**. The interest-bearing security itself. **3**. A government **bond**.

Rente (Ger.) **1**. The rate of **interest**, return on a **security**, or **capital**. **2**. A **pension**. **3**. A **bond**.

Rentenanleihe (Ger.) A government **bond**.

Rentenbank (Ger.) A credit bank.

reorganization See **bankruptcy**.

repayment supplement (UK) Payment by the Inland Revenue

of interest on overpaid tax, paid in respect of the number of years the tax sum was held by the Inland Revenue.

replacement-cost depreciation See **depreciation**.

repo repotate See **repurchase agreement**.

report (Fr.) **Contango.**

reporting accountants A firm of accountants reporting to the **sponsor** of a **new issue** on the financial affairs of a **company**. See also **long form report**.

reporting dealer (US) The official **Federal Reserve** designation for **primary dealer**.

reprise (Fr.) A recovery on the **stock exchange**.

repurchase agreement (repo) Short for *sale and repurchase agreement*. A transaction whereby funds are borrowed through the sale of **short–term securities** on the condition that the instruments are repurchased at a given date. Used principally between the **central bank** and the **money market** as a means of relieving short-term shortages of funds in the money market (perhaps overnight, hence, *overnight repo*) and thus as a means of **monetary control** by the central bank. Interest is paid on the instrument in the meantime. The operation was first developed in the USA and remains widely used as a borrowing method by large corporations and non-banking institutions. The instrument used is normally a US government security, usually **Treasury bills**. A *retail repo* involves a loan to a bank; it differs from a term **deposit** in that early withdrawals may be made without penalty. After the exemption of repurchase agreements from US reserve requirements in 1969, their use as a device for monetary control by the US Federal Reserve became widespread. Reverse repurchase agreements (*reverse repos*), whereby the sale of securities is by the Federal Reserve to the US money market, are also used. Repurchase agreements are also utilized in **open market operations** by other central banks, notably the **Bank of England**, the Banque de France and the **Bundesbank**. An *overnight repo* is held between the closing and opening of the money market.

required reserves (US) **Reserves** required to be held by US banks, prescribed in proportion to **deposits** and other liabilities.

rescription (Fr.) A government short-term **instrument** akin to a **Treasury bill**.

reserve asset ratio The ratio of **reserve assets** to **eligible liabilities** required to be maintained by UK commercial banks under the arrangements for **monetary control** introduced by the Bank of England in 1971, and known as *competition and credit control*. The system was superseded in 1981 by other arrangements under which the reserve asset ratio was abandoned.

reserve assets Holdings of a commercial bank, not used for loans or other transactions, and therefore available for use in the last resort to meet a shortage of funds. In most countries the level and constitution of reserve assets and their ratio to **deposits** (**reserve asset ratio**) are prescribed by the regulatory authorities. See also **liquidity ratio**.

Reserve banks See **Federal Reserve System**.

reserve price The lowest price at which someone is prepared to sell something. Thus a client may instruct a **broker** to sell **securities** or **commodities** at or above a specified reserve price.

reserve requirement (US) The ratio of **reserves** to **deposits**, expressed as a fraction, prescribed by the US regulatory authorities. An alternative form of reference to **required reserves**. See also **liquidity ratio**.

reserves 1. Of countries, the **central bank**'s holdings of gold and foreign currencies and International Monetary Fund **drawing rights**, for the purpose of providing for fluctuations in the country's **balance of payments**; commonly referred to as the gold and foreign currency reserves. 2. Of banks, cash and **short-term claims**, e.g. claims on the central bank, **call money, Treasury bills** and **short-term gilts**, held as backing for the bank's **deposit liabilities**. Commonly referred to as **reserve assets**. 3. Amounts set aside from **profits** in company accounts for an unspecified purpose. Reserves are part of **retained earnings**; i.e. they are undistributed profits and belong to the ordinary shareholders of the company. In the USA the term *reserves* is often used in the UK sense of **provisions**, which are sums set aside for specific anticipated purposes. **4**. Of **insurance**, amounts set aside to meet underwriting liabilities; commonly referred to as *technical reserves*.

reserves maintenance period (US) A period during which banks must hold reserves at least equal on average to **required reserves**; the period is normally of 14 days.

reserves market (US) A term applied to the transactions between the **Federal Reserve open market desk**, banks, securities dealers and **Federal funds** brokers in the **instruments** making up the banking system's reserves. The main effect of such transactions is to regulate bank reserves in accordance with the Federal Reserve's **monetary policy**.

reserves multiplier (US) An indicator used by the **Federal Reserve** to assess the amount of bank deposits that will correspond to a given **reserve** requirement.

reserves pressure (US) A situation brought about by the **open market operations** of the **Federal Reserve** in which the banking system requires to borrow at the **discount window**.

Reskription (Ger.) A **public-sector** short-term **bill**, **discounted** to the banking system, akin to a **Treasury bill**. See also *Schatzwechsel*.

ressources propres (Fr.) **Own resources**.

retail banking See **retail deposit**, **wholesale banking**.

retail deposit **1**. A **deposit** placed by an individual customer, normally in relatively small amounts, with a bank, in contrast to a **wholesale deposit**. **2**. In **money supply** terminology, deposits held for expenditure purposes (*transactions balances*), as against those held for savings (*investment balances*). **3**. In **hire purchase**, funds recruited by **finance houses** from individual investors, rather than from the wholesale **money market**. **4**. In **mortgage** business, funds raised by mortgage banks (building societies) from individual depositors, rather than through wholesale borrowings from the money market or from other sources.

retail price index (RPI) An **index number** measuring changes in the **weighted average** of prices of a basket of goods and services (US = *consumer price index* (CPI)). Intended to measure changes in the cost of living. See also **indexation**.

retail repo See **repurchase agreement**.

retained earnings Undistributed **profits** that may simply be **reserves** or may be used for investment in fixed **assets**. When a company finances its capital expenditure from retained earnings rather than borrowings, it is said to be self-financing.

retrocession The further insurance of **risks** assumed by a reinsurer. See also **reinsurance**.

return on capital employed (ROCE) See **return on investment**.

return on investment (ROI) A **financial ratio** showing **profit** as a percentage of total **assets** or **capital employed** (ROCE) or **shareholders' funds**. The numerator and denomination of the ratio need to be defined carefully, e.g. profit after interest and **depreciation** as a percentage of total assets at *historic cost* (see **costs, historical**).

Reuters A **quoted company** providing screen-based and teletype news, financial information and dealing services worldwide. In financial markets it is particularly strong in the provision of exchange rate quotations. Founded by P. J. Reuter in 1851, it was originally owned by the newspapers that used its services. See **Electronic Broking Service**, **Quotron**, **Telerate**.

Reuters 2000-2 See **Electronic Broking Service**.

revaluation reserve Capital **reserves** created when the book value of existing **assets** is revalued to bring it into line with replacement costs, or when new shares are issued at a **premium** over **par value**.

reversal A fall or rise in the price of a **stock** against a previous trend.

reverse auction The process whereby an issuer of **bonds**, wishing to reduce the number at issue, invites holders to offer prices at which the issuer may repurchase them.

reverse monetization The theory, chiefly propounded by the Princeton University economist Alan S. Binder, that at times of high federal deficits the **Federal Reserve** will tend to restrict bank reserves.

reverse repo See **repurchase agreement**.

reverse yield curve See **yield curve**.

reversionary bonus See **life assurance**.

revolving credit A **loan** facility that is renewed as it is repaid and may therefore be used repeatedly. Also referred to as *open-end credit* (US). **Credit card** loans are a form of revolving credit, since borrowers may make minimum repayments or repayment in full at the end of the account period, provided they remain within the credit limit. Retail *charge accounts*, where regular payments are made and credit is available up to a multiple of the regular payments, are another form of revolving credit.

revolving underwriting facility (RUF) See **note issuance facility** (NIF).

RIE Recognized investment exchange. See **Financial Services Act**.

rights issue An offer of new **shares** to existing shareholders. A company will offer the rights in a certain proportion to existing holdings, depending upon the amount of new **equity** capital it wishes to raise. Thus in a one-for-one rights issue, shareholders will be offered a number of new shares equal to the number they already hold. To ensure that the issue is taken up, the new shares are offered at well below the market price of the existing shares, i.e. at a **discount**, which will usually result in some fall in the price of existing shares. Rights issues are a relatively cheap way of raising **capital** for a quoted company, since the costs of preparing a brochure, **underwriting**, commission and press advertising involved in a new issue are avoided. See **new issue market**.

Riksbanken (Swe.) The **central bank** of Sweden.

ring The trading floor of a **commodity exchange**. The term is also used for the trading session itself.

ring fence A measure to protect members of **Lloyd's of London**, underwriting in the 1994 business year and thereafter, from the effects of **Old Years**. A bylaw of 1993 forbids the acceptance of **reinsurance to close** of any policies issued in any year up to and including 1985. Liabilities of those years were intended in 1993 to be reinsured into **Newco**.

risk Of **insurance**, the contingent loss against which insurance is provided. In insurance contracts the term has the more precise connotation of an uncertainty for which the probability of occurrence is calculable. The term also applies, for insurance purposes, to the whole of the insurance cover provided, rather than to the individual contingencies or **perils** that may arise. See also **dynamic risk**, **static risk**.

risk-adjusted assets **Assets** defined to include **off-balance-sheet** items. Under the **Bank for International Settlements** agreement on **capital adequacy**, the **underwriting** of securitized loans (see **securitization**) creates assets that do not, unlike traditional **loans**, appear on **bank** balance sheets. Risk-adjusted assets make an allowance for these items and under the agreement need to be covered in part by *prudential ratios* for capital reserves.

risk arbitrageur See **corporate raider**.

risk capital Long-term funds invested in enterprises particularly subject to risk, as in small or new ventures. Hence the alternative term **venture capital**, a somewhat more precise term meaning **capital** provided for a new or young business undertaking by people other than the proprietors. Venture capital is provided by **merchant banks** but predominantly by specialized venture capital institutions, including **captives**, and specialized venture capital **funds**.

risk management The identification and acceptance or off-setting of the risks threatening the profitability or existence of an organization. **Insurance** provides protection against death, fire or flood, **hedging** against fluctuations in **exchange rates** and accelerated **depreciation** against the risk of obsolescence of fixed **assets**. Also management by a company of events and activities so as to minimize the degree to which damage or loss may occur, so reducing dependence on insurance.

risk reversal A procedure for minimizing loss, whereby a **call option** sale is combined with a simultaneous *put* option purchase.

risk-weighted assets Assets held by a financial institution to which degrees of risk have been assigned, so that adequate **provisions** can be set aside.

ROCE See **return on investment**.

rodo kinko (Jap.) A banking institution specializing in credit for small businesses.

ROI See **return on investment**.

roll-over In **derivatives**, the transfer from one **delivery month** to another, involving the sale/purchase of the **front month** and of the later delivery month.

roll-over CD An arrangement whereby a **certificate of deposit** (CD) **maturity** is divided into shorter-term periods in respect to which individual CDs are issued, e.g. a three-year CD arrangement is effected through issues of a CD at six-monthly intervals. Purchasers commit themselves to buying the full series but are free to sell any of the individual CDs on the secondary market. Roll-over CDs were first issued in 1976 in the USA. The advantage to bankers is that of securing a longer-term deposit than they might obtain on a less flexible CD. The advantage to purchasers is the avoidance of the need to sell a long-term CD – always more difficult.

roll-over credit A loan by a bank or **syndicate** of banks, usually at **medium term** or longer, the funds for which are raised by the banks themselves through **short-term** borrowing, normally in the **money market** or **interbank market**. The interest then charged to the bank's client fluctuates in accordance with short-term money-market rates, frequently **London interbank offered rate** (LIBOR), to which is added a **spread**.

roll-up funds (UK) Investment schemes involving rolled-up coupon funds, established in centres outside the jurisdiction of the UK Inland Revenue, i.e. abroad or, for example, in the Channel Islands, so enabling the reinvestment of the interest payments without liability to income tax. When eventually repatriated, the funds incur only **capital gains** tax. However, a ruling of the Inland Revenue in 1983 required the **rolled-up coupons** to be assessed as income.

rolled-up coupon An interest payment on a **financial instrument** or **security**, denoted by the **coupon**, which is not passed to the holder but is reinvested in the instrument, so adding to the latter's capital value and enabling, if repeated over time, a compounding of the interest. Most used where the interest can be classed as a capital investment by the holder and not a receipt of income (see **capital gains**), thus enabling the holder to avoid income tax. See **roll-up funds**, **zero coupon bond, fund**.

rolling account See **settlement**.

rolling settlement See **settlement**.

rolling spot contract A **currency derivatives** contract introduced in 1993 by the **Chicago Mercantile Exchange** under which the contract is automatically rolled over each day (see **roll-over**) by the exchange, thus saving the trader the daily settlement costs incurred in normal **spot market** roll-overs.

roly-poly CD See **roll-over CD**.

Room, the (UK) That part of **Lloyd's of London**'s premises in the City of London where **working members** carry on business. Also known as the *underwriting room*.

Roosa bonds (US) **Bonds** issued by the US Treasury during the Kennedy administration of the early 1960s, denominated in currencies other than the US dollar and held by central banks on a non-marketable basis. Roosa bonds enabled financing of the US federal deficit on a long-term basis in conditions of complete exchange security for the lender. In particular, the bonds were designed to induce the former West Germany, then unwilling to increase its dollar holdings, to continue to finance US Treasury needs. The bonds were named after Robert V. Roosa, their creator, then under-secretary at the US Treasury.

rosokuashi (Jap.) A **chartist** technique using box shapes on graphs to depict time periods.

round tripping Occurs when a non-financial company can borrow at lower than current and short-term market **rates of interest** and can therefore borrow and on-lend at a **profit**.

round-up stage (US) The stage at the monthly meeting of the **Federal Open Market Committee** at which comments are called from each of the 19 members.

RP Repurchase **agreement**.

RPB Recognized professional body. See **Financial Services Act**.

Rubber Association of Singapore A major **commodity** market, dealing principally in natural rubber **futures**.

Rücknahmepreis (Ger.) **Redemption price**.

RUF Revolving underwriting facility. See **Euronote facility**.

Rules 535(2) and 535(3) (UK) Formerly Rules 163(2) and 163(3), allowing **brokers** to deal in unlisted securities (see **unlisted securities market**) and mineral exploration **shares** respectively. See also **alternative investment market**.

run-off account (UK) Where a **syndicate** finds, at the end of the three-year accounting cycle for a particular trading year, that it cannot reliably estimate the extent of claims that may still arise on the business of that year, and that it cannot therefore propose an acceptable premium for **reinsurance to close**, then the syndicate must remain open, and its members must retain their liability for such claims, until more certain prospects emerge. The business account for that year is then known as a run-off account.

run to settlement Said of a **commodity** sale contract allowed to run to the date where physical delivery of the commodity is due, i.e. a contract not **liquidated** or **covered** by purchase of an offsetting contract.

running yield See **yield**.

Russia Country Fund A fund set up with the support of the Russian and US governments and of American private institutions, with the purpose of enabling US financial institutions, such as pension funds, to invest directly in private enterprises in Russia and other former Soviet states. The fund is **closed-end** and intends to raise $100m in **project finance** and **venture capital** for new businesses, expansions and **privatization**, with an emphasis on enterprises in the energy and environmental fields. The Russian government will contribute up to $25m. The **Overseas Private Investment Corporation** will provide a $50m **loan guarantee** to protect private institutions supplying the additional capital.

Russian Commodity and Raw Material Exchange A commodity exchange founded in Moscow by Konstantin Borovoi in 1990, planning also to introduce trade in equities.

'S' corporation See **sub-chapter S corporations**.

S&L See **savings and loan associations**.

SA See **société anonyme**.

SAEF See **Stock Exchange Automatic Execution Facility**.

saitori (Jap.) An intermediary in the **stock exchange**, dealing only between members, similar to the **specialists** on the New York Stock Exchange, except that the *saitori* are not allowed to take **positions** for themselves.

sale Cession of ownership of an **instrument** or **bond** against payment of its **face value** with either a **discount** or a **premium**.

sales and repurchase agreement See **repurchase agreement**.

sales tax A tax levied as a proportion of the retail price of a good or service. In contrast to **value added tax**, a sales tax is levied only at the point of sale. Sales taxes are levied in the USA and many other countries.

samurai bond A **foreign bond** issued in Japan by foreign issuers, denominated in yen.

samurai lease An international lease financed by the Japanese leasing industry under subsidy by the Japanese government. The transaction consisted of the purchase of foreign assets for leasing abroad. The practice was most common in the early 1980s and was used by the Japanese government to bring about a temporary increase in import payments.

Sanmekai (Jap.) The committee of **city banks** that determines **short-term rates of interest**.

São Paulo Stock Exchange Bolsas de Valores de São Paulo (BoVeSPa). One of the two largest **stock exchange** in Brazil, regulated by the Commissão de Valores Mobiliaros (CVM) or securities commission. Together with the exchange in Rio de Janeiro, BoVeSPa accounts for the bulk of trading in **securities**, including **futures** and **options**, in Brazil, although there are also exchanges in seven other cities. The BoVeSPa Index is the most widely quoted **share index** for Brazil.

sarakin (Jap.) Finance companies notorious for high interest rates charged to personal customers, frowned on by the government.

Sàrl (Fr.) See **société à responsabilité limitée**.

Saturday-night special (US) A popular reference to 6 October 1979, on the evening of which the **Federal Reserve** announced its decision to abandon its policy of influencing the **Federal funds rate**, in favour of one of influencing the level of bank reserves.

savings Income not spent on consumption. Savings may be accumulated in a **bank deposit account** or **current account** or may be placed in a **building society** or **savings bank** or used to purchase **securities**, including **savings bonds** or **National Savings certificates**. Regular payments into **pensions** schemes or **life assurance** are referred to as contractual savings.

savings account See **deposit account**.

savings and loan (S&L) associations (US) **Savings banks** that, like **building societies**, receive savings **deposits** (see **retail deposit**) and make mortgages. The deregulation of interest rates (see **Depository Institutions Deregulation and Monetary Decontrol Act**) created difficulties for S&Ls because they had commitments for long-term loans at fixed **rates of interest**, so that as deposit rates rose they were sometimes paying more to depositors than they were receiving from their borrowers. Also referred to as *savings and loan institutions* and **thrifts**, they exercise some banking functions, such as operating **cheque accounts** (US = *checking accounts*) and providing **consumer credit** and high-yield investment vehicles. S&Ls are largely **mutual** organizations, though many have incorporated (see **incorporation**) so as to broaden their access to

capital markets. S&Ls are regulated either by the **Federal Home Loan Bank Board** or, in the case of state-**chartered** S&Ls, by the state. See also **Garn–St Germain Act**.

savings bank A bank that accepts **interest**-bearing **deposits** of small amounts. The earliest savings banks were established in the private sector, but later they were set up or supported by governments, to encourage individual savings. In the UK the two main forms of savings bank are the **National Savings Bank** and, before **privatization**, the **Trustee Savings Bank** (TSB). The TSB, however, is now a full bank. The **building societies** share the basic objectives of the savings banks. See also *caisses d'épargne*, **savings and loan associations**, *Sparkassen*.

savings bonds (US) **Bonds** issued by the US government at a **discount** to their *face value* (see **par value**) at which they are redeemed after **maturity**. Investors receive interest and a **capital gain** on maturity. The bonds, which are denominated by letters – E bonds, HH bonds, etc. – are free of state and local taxes and may be exchanged for other bonds so that liability to federal taxation may be deferred.

SBF (Fr.) See **Société des Bourses Françaises**.

SBIC See **small business investment company**.

Schatz bond A term often used in English-speaking markets to mean *Schatzobligation*.

Schatzanweisung (Ger.) See *Schatzwechsel*.

Schatzbrief (Ger.) A **savings bond**.

Schatzobligation (Ger.) A Treasury **bond**.

Schatzschein (Ger.) See *Schatzwechsel*.

Schatzwechsel (Ger.) A **Treasury bill**. Issued by **tap** to the banking system for retention until **maturity**. *Schatzwechsel* are normally for a **term** of 90 days. Sometimes referred to as a *Reskription*.

Scheduled Territories (UK) A term used in UK **exchange**

control, abolished in 1979, to denote areas where sterling is the official **currency** and where the exchange control regulations therefore did not apply. Also known as the *Sterling Area*. Embracing after the First World War the whole of the British Commonwealth, the Scheduled Territories by 1979 included no more than Great Britain, the Channel Islands and the Isle of Man.

Schlussdividende (Ger.) *Final dividend*. See **dividend**.

Schlusskurs (Ger.) **Closing price**.

Schuldschein (Ger.) A **note** in common use for the recruitment of **short-term** funds, used by companies and by government, chief buyers being the insurance companies. Lower costs of issue offset interest rates slightly above the average.

Schuldscheindarlehen (Ger.) A loan based on a *Schuldschein*. The certificates for public-sector loans are traded in the **secondary market**.

Schuldverschreibung (Ger.) A **bond** or a **money-market instrument**, the latter being particularly favoured by banks as a source of **short-term** funds.

scrip issue See **bonus issue**.

SCMC See **Société de Compensation des Marchés Conditionnels**.

SDR See **special drawing right**.

SDR-linked deposit A private bank deposit denominated in **special drawing rights** (SDRs). These are now recognized accounts for the payment of transactions.

SEA See **Single European Act**.

SEAQ See **Stock Exchange Automated Quotation System**.

seasonal borrowings (US) US banks' borrowings from the **Federal Reserve** induced by seasonal fluctuations in credit demand. Seasonal borrowings constitute, together with **adjustment credit**, the **borrowed reserves** of US banks.

SEBI See **Bombay Stock Exchange**.

second marché (Fr.) Second-tier **unlisted securities market** in Paris, with regional markets established in February 1983. The Belgian second-tier market is also called the *second marché*. See also *tweede markt*.

second-tier market See **unlisted securities market**.

secondary bank (UK) A bank (see **banking**) that has relatively few branches and therefore does not play a major role in the payments system as far as the general public is concerned. Included in the term are **merchant banks**, the British **overseas banks** and some **finance houses**. There was a secondary banking crisis in 1973 when the **Bank of England** mounted a lifeboat operation to rescue some of the banks.

secondary market A market in which **securities** or other **assets** are resold and purchased, as distinct from a primary market in which assets are sold for the first time (see **new issue market**). The **stock exchange** is a secondary market, though it is also a primary market. The term is sometimes wrongly used to refer to *second tier* or **unlisted securities markets**.

secured Backed by a **security** (of a loan).

Securities and Exchange Act 1948 (Jap.) Legislation requiring the registration of **broker–dealers** governing **securities** trading in Japan, modelled on the US Securities Exchange Act 1934 (see **Securities and Exchange Commission**). Article 65 of the Act prohibits banks from owning more than 5% of any company or engaging in **share** broking (see **broker**) or acting as an **issuing house**. As in the USA (see **Glass–Steagal Act**), the evolution of international securities markets is resulting in pressures for change in Article 65. Japanese banks do engage in **investment banking** outside Japan through subsidiaries.

Securities and Exchange Commission (SEC) (US) Federal agency for the **regulation** of the markets in **securities**, set up in 1934 to administer the Securities Exchange Acts 1933 and 1934, which require most securities offered for sale to be registered. The

SEC regulates the **stock exchanges** and **brokers**, including those on the **over-the-counter market**, investment advisers and others in industry. See also **Form 10K**.

Securities and Futures Authority See **Financial Services Act**.

Securities and Investment Board See **Financial Services Act**.

Securities Association, The (TSA) (UK) The former self-regulating organization for securities dealing. Formed in 1986 by the amalgamation of the **London Stock Exchange**, now the International Stock Exchange, and the International Securities Regulatory Organization (ISRO), which then regulated dealers in **Eurobonds** and international equities in both registered and **American depository receipt** form. Neither ISRO nor the TSA now exist as such. The TSA merged with the Association of Futures Brokers and Dealers to form the Securities and Futures Authority in 1991. See also **Financial Services Act**.

Securities Exchange of Thailand (SET) Set up in 1975 to succeed the Bangkok Stock Exchange, which in turn dated from 1962. Regulated by the Thai Ministry of Finance.

securities house See **issuing house**.

Securities Industry Automation Corporation See **National Securities Clearing Corporation**.

Securities Investor Protection Corporation (SIPC) (US) A compensation scheme for investors in the event of the failure of **market makers** or **dealers**. All members of the **National Association of Securities Dealers** belong to this scheme.

securitization The substitution of **securities** for bank loans; i.e. a bank may, instead of lending to a customer, purchase or accept (see **acceptance**) a **bill of exchange**, a **note** or other **security** from them. Alternatively a would-be borrower, rather than apply to a bank, may issue a bill of exchange, note or other **debt instrument** to a non-bank purchaser or acceptor. Securitization was in part a revival of the capital markets, much impaired by the economic crisis of the 1970s and early 1980s, and in part a development of short-term security forms that give the lender **negotiable**

instruments and enable banks to raise funds more easily. Securitization also relieves banks of reliance on the traditional interest rate differences on deposits and advances; and it enables them, in times of pressure on capital ratios, to avoid balance sheet additions. In so far as the security issues are managed or **underwritten** by the banks, a fee-earning opportunity is also opened to the banks. Since many of the securities have been short term, with **floating rates** of interest, investors have been more ready to buy them than fixed-rate bonds, whose return or capital value would have fallen with any rise in general market interest rates. See also **disintermediation**.

securitized paper The **instrument** resulting from the conversion of a bank loan into a *marketable* (see **negotiable**) **security**. See **securitization**.

security 1. A pledge of financial or physical property to be surrendered in the event of failure to repay a loan. **2**. Any medium of investment in the money market or **capital market**, e.g. a money-market **instrument**, a **bond**, a **share**, **3**. A term used to refer only to bonds, and shares, as distinct from **money-market assets**.

segundo mercado (Sp.) The markets in unlisted securities (see **unlisted securities market**) in Barcelona (since 1982) and Madrid (since 1987). Also called *bolsa secundaria*.

SEHK See **Hong Kong stock exchanges**.

seiji kabu (Jap.) Literally, a 'political security', i.e. a stock rumoured to be a preferred investment choice of politicians; thus held likely to appreciate. Such stocks are frequent subjects of **ramping**.

Self-Employment Individuals Retirement Act See **Keogh plan**.

self-financing See **retained earnings**.

self-regulating organizations See **Financial Services Act**.

self-select PEP A **personal equity plan** for which the share **portfolio** is selected by the individual investor rather than by a **financial intermediary**; the latter must none the less administer the plan.

senior debt See **subordinated**.

SEPON Stock Exchange Pool Nominee. See **Transfer Accounting, Lodgement for Investors, Stock Management for Jobbers** (TALISMAN).

series Put or call options on the same underlying **instrument**, having the same **striking price** and the same **maturity**.

SERPS State Earnings-Related Pension Scheme. See **pensions**.

services That part of the national economy not concerned with the production of tangible goods, i.e. activities such as insurance, transport, banking, securities and commodity dealing, electricity, gas and other utilities, and telecommunications. In most industrialized countries services account for half or more of all economic activity. The term is also applied in balance of payments terminology to denote the imports and exports of service industries.

servicing Payment of interest on a bank loan.

SES See **Singapore Stock Exchange**.

SESDAQ Stock Exchange of Singapore Dealing and Quotation System. See **Singapore Stock Exchange**.

SET See **Securities Exchange of Thailand**.

settle Of **currency** and **security** transactions, to pay the purchase price.

settlement 1. Payment of an obligation, e.g. payment in cash for **securities**. Hence **account day** on the **London Stock Exchange** is also known as settlement day or the settlement date. Settlement procedures vary. In the UK stockbrokers' accounts fall due at the end of fixed periods (accounts). In the USA payment for securities is usually due on the fifth day after the transaction; this is known as a rolling account or rolling settlement system. This system is soon to be adopted in the UK. 2. The transfer or intended transfer of property after a legal agreement or on the **execution** of a will after death. See also **Transfer and Automated Registration of Uncertified Stock** (TAURUS).

settlement date See **settlement**.

settlement day See **settlement**.

settlement prices See **official prices**.

seven-day money Money placed, i.e. an instrument bought, in the **money market** with a **maturity** of seven days.

Seventh Directive See **consolidated accounts**.

SFE See **Sydney Futures Exchange**.

Shanghai Securities Exchange See **China**.

share One of a number of equal portions in the nominal **capital** of a company, entitling the owner to a proportion of distributed **profits** and of residual value if the company goes into **liquidation**; a form of **security**. Shares may be fully or partly paid (see **paid-up capital**), **voting shares** or non-voting (sometimes called 'A' shares). See also **ordinary shares**, **preference shares**, **stock**.

share certificate A document issued by the **registrar** or their agent confirming legal title to the ownership of a stated number of **equity** shares. Share certificates may one day be replaced by computer entries (see **nominee**).

share exchange scheme Unit trusts, **investment trusts** and other forms of managed **portfolio** investments are often willing to accept investments in the form of **shares** rather than cash. These schemes offer more attractive terms than the alternative of selling shares in the market and paying commission for those who wish to switch from direct ownership of shares into trusts. See also **switching discount**.

share indices **Index numbers** indicating changes in the average prices of **shares** on the **stock exchange**. The indices are constructed by taking a selection of shares and (usually) weighting (see **weighted average**) the percentage changes in prices together as an indication of aggregate movements in share prices. Roughly speaking, a share index shows percentage changes in the market prices of a **portfolio** compared with its value in the base year of the index. See also **Dow-Jones indexes, Financial Times share indices, Hong Kong stock exchanges, Morgan Stanley Capital International**

World Index, NASDAQ OTC Price Index, Nikkei Stock Average, Standard and Poor's Ratings, Toronto Stock Exchange and other national **stock exchange** entries.

share options See **profit-sharing scheme**.

share perks (UK) Benefits for **shareholders** over and above **dividends**, e.g. discounts on company products.

share register See **registrar**.

shareholder The owner of **shares** in a company.

shareholders' equity The total **assets** of a company minus its external **liabilities** (i.e. except those to **equity** shareholders). Put another way, the **balance sheet** will show shareholders' equity as **paid-up capital**, **revaluation reserve** and *undistributed profits* (see **retained earnings**). See also **net assets**.

shelf registration (US) Under Rule 415, larger companies may since 1983 register advance details of **securities** with the **Securities and Exchange Commission** (SEC) without any date of issue, so that when they need to raise capital they may make an issue 'off the shelf' without the delay involved in waiting for clearance of an application to the SEC.

Shenzhen Securities Exchange See **China**.

shibosai (Jap.) The Japanese market for **private placements**.

shibosai **bond** (Jap.) A **samurai bond**, the subject of a *private placing* (see **placing**).

shintaka ginko (Jap.) **Trust bank**.

shinyo kinku (Jap.) A banking institution providing **credit** to small businesses; usually translated into English as a credit association. See also **credit union**.

shinyo kumiai (Jap.) A credit association similar to a *shinyo kinku* but dealing with smaller businesses. See also **credit union**.

shogun bond (Jap.) A **bond** denominated in a **foreign currency**, issued on the Japanese market by a non-resident.

shogun lease An international lease provided by the Japanese leasing industry, the contract being established in yen.

short 1. Of dealings in **currencies**, **securities** and **commodities**, a condition of net indebtedness, either by being liable to discharge a loan of one of these items, or by being committed to supply an amount at a future date, e.g. having sold a **futures** contract; or being committed or liable to supply at a future date at a price below the current rate, as in futures or **options** contracts. See also **position**. **2**. Of dealings in securities and **money-market instruments**, to shift a holding to a shorter-**term** form. **3**. More generally to hold securities, currencies and money-market instruments in reduced quantity.

short covering To **cover** a **short position**.

short-dated securities See **dated securities**.

short hedge A **hedge** effected by the sale of a **futures** contract.

short tail business Insurance business, such as motor insurance, where claims quickly follow losses.

short term 1. Of a **security**, having a short **maturity**, normally up to five years. **2**. Of a bank loan, repayable within three years. **3**. Of a **money-market** instrument, having a maturity of three months or less. **4**. Of **insurance**, business other than life insurance. **5**. See **finance**.

short-term monetary support (STMS) A form of **intervention mechanism** under the **European Monetary System** (EMS) under which the central bank of a country under **exchange rate** pressure due to **balance of payments** difficulties may borrow at three months from the central banks of other member countries; the **term** may be extended, such an extension being known as a *rallonge*. This form of assistance is funded by member country subscriptions based on a quota.

SIAC See **Securities Industry Automated Corporation**.

SIB Securities and Investment Board. See **Financial Services Act**.

SICAV See *société d'investissement à capital variable*.

sight deposit A bank **deposit**, all or part of which may be withdrawn without notice (i.e. on sight). US = *demand deposit*. See also **current account**.

SIMEX See **Singapore International Monetary Exchange**.

simple sum A theory of money measurement that regards all money forms as equal. Also known as the *all-or-nothing* theory.

sine die Indefinitely; of a postponement, or of the fixing of the date of a future event.

Singapore International Monetary Exchange (SIMEX) Deals in financial (especially **Eurodollar**), energy and commodity **futures**. SIMEX was established in 1984 and now has a mutual offset arrangement with the **Chicago Mercantile Exchange**.

Singapore Stock Exchange (SES) In its present form dates from 1973 when the joint **stock exchange** of Singapore and Malaysia were separated. There remain close links between the securities trading activities of the two countries. By 1990 the Malaysian government made its companies delist from the SES, but this was followed by the establishment of the Central Limit Order Book (CLOB) international computerized market in Singapore, which, although not officially recognized by the **Kuala Lumpur Stock Exchange**, lists many Malaysian companies. There is a second tier. The Stock Exchange of Singapore Dealing and Automated Quotation System (SESDAQ) was launched in February 1987 and modelled on the **National Association of Securities Dealers Automated Quotation System** (NASDAQ). The principal **share indices** for **stock** quoted on the SES are the *Straits Times Index* (STI) and the *Stock Exchange of Singapore Index* (SESI).

single capacity A term used to describe a situation where a **market maker** on a **stock exchange** deals only with other professionals and not with the investors. See also **dual capacity**.

single company PEP A **personal equity plan** that is wholly invested in the **shares** of one **quoted company**.

Single European Act See **European Union** (EU).

single premium See **life assurance**.

sinking fund Provision for the repayment of **debt**, including the **redemption** of a **security** by the issuer, by accumulating a fund through regular payments that, with interest, will *amortize* the loan.

SIPC See **Securities Investor Protection Corporation**.

skip day (US) Settlement of the purchase of a **security**, normally in the **money market**, two days after the transaction takes place.

slip The document setting out details of the **insurance risk** to be **covered**, used by **brokers**, particularly at **Lloyd's of London**. Signatures by **insurers** on the slip are evidence of acceptance of the risk.

Small Order Execution System See **National Association of Securities Dealers Automated Quotation System (NASDAQ)**.

small business investment company (SBIC) (US) A company set up with low-cost funds and taxation advantages from the US federal government to invest in small businesses, authorized under the Small Business Investment Act 1958. Similar institutions exist in Japan, while in France and other countries **venture capital** companies and **investment trusts** or their investors may be eligible for tax incentives. See also **Business Expansion Scheme**, **Venture Capital Trust Scheme**.

small loan company See **finance house**.

smaller companies market (SCM) (Ire.) The third-tier **unlisted securities market** (USM) in Ireland. Ireland also has a second-tier USM.

smart card A plastic card incorporating a microchip. Invented in France, where they are called *cartes à mémoire*, smart cards can be used as plastic money a credit facility being drawn down as it is used and recharged by the issuing bank or store; or they may be used at **automatic teller machines** (cash dispensers). See also **credit card**.

SMI See **Swiss stock exchanges**.

SMR See **standard Malaysian rubber**.

Snake see **European Monetary System** (EMS).

SNIF note issuance facility. See **Euronote facility**.

sobashi (Jap.) A speculator, often engaged in **ramping**.

Social Charter See **European Union** (EU).

Social Security Act 1986 (UK) See **pensions**.

sociedad anónima (Sp.) Public limited company. See **incorporation**.

società per azioni (SpA) (It.) Public limited company. See **incorporation**. A private company in Italy has 'Srl' after its name.

société anonyme (SA) (Fr.) Public limited company. See **incorporation**. Also in some non-French-speaking countries, e.g. Greece.

Société Anonyme de la Bourse See **Luxembourg Stock Exchange**.

société à responsabilité limitée (SàRL) (Fr.) Private limited company. See **incorporation**.

Société de Compensation des Marchés Conditionnels Operator of the French equity options market (see **Marché des Options Negotiables de Paris**).

Societé des Bourses Françaises (Fr.) Association of French **stock exchanges**.

société d'investissement à capital variable (SICAV) (Fr.) **Unit trust**.

SOES Small Order Execution System. See **National Association of Securities Dealers Automated Quotation System** (NASDAQ).

SOFFEX See **Swiss Options and Financial Futures Exchange**.

soft commodity A term applied to most **commodities** other than metals, but chiefly referring to agricultural products such as tea, coffee, sugar and wheat, and to raised products such as wool, cotton, hides and skins.

soft currency See **currency**.

soft dollars (US) Payments made for services provided by a **stockbroker** in the form of **commission** to be earned on an agreed future level of trading. For example, a broker might carry out research on the understanding that a given level of trading would be based on the results. Cash payments or fees for research are referred to as *hard dollars*. Also practised in countries other than the USA in local currencies.

sogo bank (Jap.) A bank specializing in housing credit.

sogo shosha (Jap.) A term applying to the large corporations, e.g. Mitsubishi and Mitsui, engaged chiefly in distribution but also in finance and production.

sokai (Jap.) A shareholders' meeting.

sokaiya (Jap.) Literally, a shareholders'-meeting man; hence, a speculator.

sold short See **bear**.

solde (Fr.) **Balance**.

sole proprietorship An **unincorporated business** owned by a single person and not benefiting from limited liability. See **incorporation**.

solvency The ability to pay one's debts in full on the due date. See also **solvency margin**, **solvency ratio**.

solvency margin A required minimum surplus of an insurance company's **assets** over its **liabilities**, the composition of these two aggregates being strictly defined by the supervisory authorities, and varying according to the type of company and the class of business transacted.

solvency ratio Of banks, the relationship of own capital to total **liabilities**.

solvent A condition in which total **assets** exceed total **liabilities**.

sources and uses of funds (UK) Statements of **flows of funds** within a company during a period. Now a required element in the published financial accounts for all but the smallest companies, alongside the **balance sheet** and the **profit and loss account**. Also known as sources of applications (or disposition) of funds and in the USA as statement of *changes in financial position*. There are various forms of flow of funds statements, but typically they show all the **capital** flows of a business between balance sheet dates. *Sources of funds* are **profits** from trading operations, **depreciation** provisions, sales of **assets** and borrowing, including **equity** and other capital issues. *Uses of funds* are purchases of fixed or financial assets, cash and distribution of income.

sovereign A national government in its role, for example, as a lender or borrower; hence **sovereign risk**.

sovereign loan A bank loan to a government, usually of a developing country.

sovereign risk The risk of default on repayment or **servicing** of a **sovereign loan**; of expropriation of assets held in a foreign country; and of licensing or payment restrictions on exports to a foreign country.

SpA (It.) See **società per azioni**.

SPA See **state pension age**.

Sparkassen (Ger.) The oldest network of **savings banks**, dating from the second half of the 18th century. The banks are guaranteed by local authorities.

Special Credit Controls Program (US) A series of emergency counter-inflation measures introduced in March 1980, applying limits to most forms of credit provided by most financial institutions. The programme was abandoned in May of the same year.

special deposits (UK) Deposits required to be placed by UK commercial banks with the **Bank of England**. Special deposits have been used as an instrument of **monetary control** and were first introduced in 1961. The intended effect is broadly to reduce the level of deposits held by the commercial banks and so to reduce their capacity for lending. Special deposits, when called for, are assessed as a proportion of the bank's **eligible liabilities**. Interest is paid on special deposits by the Bank of England at a rate close to **Treasury bill rate**.

special drawing right (SDR) A form of international **reserve** created by the **International Monetary Fund** (IMF) in 1970. The purpose was to assist international **liquidity** by providing a complement to existing reserve vehicles such as gold, the US dollar and UK sterling, supply of the first of which was determined by production factors and of the others by **balance of payments** outturns. SDRs are allocated by the IMF to its member countries in proportion to each country's **quota** and are used, as is the rest of the quota, to acquire other national currencies when needed for balance of payments reasons. SDRs are therefore a universally recognized claim on national currencies and thus have the effect, although not yet all the characteristics, of a new currency.

SDRs were first given a value equal to 0.89 grammes of fine gold, or US$1, which was the then dollar/gold parity. With the subsequent devaluation of the dollar, the value was set to equal the sum of specified national currencies. Since 1981 these currencies, and the amount of each going to the composition of one SDR, are: US$0.54, DM0.46, £0.071, FFr0.74, Y34. SDRs are used as the **unit of account** of the IMF and since 1980 have been the denomination for many **certificates of deposit** and **bond** issues.

special Lombard rate The rate of interest charged by the German **Bundesbank** to the banking system when normal lending against **Lombard rate** has been suspended, and lending proceeds day by day at interest rates fixed each day by the Bundesbank. See **discount window**.

special reserve (UK) An amount that **Lloyd's of London** members may, with relief from taxation, set aside from their **underwriting** profits to meet future tax liabilities. The amount may not exceed a prescribed percentage of the relevant profits, may not be used for any purpose other than payment of tax, and becomes subject again to tax when used.

specialist (US) A member of the **New York Stock Exchange** who makes a market in a number of **stocks** by buying and selling on their own account and for **commission brokers** (see also **order driven**). The role of specialists is similar to that of **jobbers** under the system that operated on the **London Stock Exchange** before the **Big Bang**. A specialist operates from a *trading post*, a location on the **trading floor** where particular securities are bought and sold.

speculation Dealing in a **commodity** or financial **asset** with a view to obtaining a profit on the prospective change in the market value of the item in question.

speculative risk Of insurance, a **risk** arising out of entrepreneurial action, leading to gain or loss in a way not calculable by the **law of large numbers** and therefore not insurable.

split-level trust See **investment trust**.

sponsor See **issuing house**.

spot Immediate or now.

spot month The first month for which **futures** contracts are available.

spot price The present value of an **asset**, as opposed to **futures**, **forward** or **option** prices. It is applied to dealings in **currencies**, **securities** and **commodities**, and synonymous for the latter with *cash*, *physical* or *actual* prices.

spread 1. The difference between the interest rate charged by a bank or banks on a loan and that paid by them for their funds. Most used in connection with syndicated international credits and Euromarket loans. The bank's funding rate is normally assumed to be a reference rate, such as **London interbank offered rate** (LIBOR), *London interbank bid rate* (LIBID) or London interbank mean rate (**LIMEAN**). **2**. The difference between the selling price asked by dealers in foreign exchange or securities and the price at which they have bought them. **3**. Difference between the price at which an underwriter buys securities from an issuer and the price at which they sell them to the general public. **4**. The gap between the highest-valued and lowest-valued currency in the **European Monetary System** (EMS), also termed the *margin*. **5**. The distribution of risks taken on by an insurer. **6**. The sale of a contract in the **commodity**, **options** or **financial futures** market and the purchase at the same time of a contract for a different item, or of a contract with different terms for the same item, the object being to achieve a profit on the movement in prices between the contracts. See also **straddle**. **7**. The difference between the **bid** and **offer** price of units in a **unit trust**.

spreadsheet A (usually) rectangular grid or matrix, setting out large amounts of financial or other data. The data are written or printed in boxes or windows defined by the rows and columns of the sheet, e.g. years along the top and the components of **cash flow** down the left-hand side. Traditionally spreadsheet analysis was carried out on specially ruled paper. Now electronic spreadsheets can be composed on computer screens using proprietary software such as Lotus 1-2-3 that will sum rows and columns quickly after changes are entered in, and produce graphs, subtotals and other calculations at the press of a key.

Square Mile See **City**.

Srl See **società per azioni**.

SRO Self-regulating organization. See **Financial Services Act**.

stag A speculator who subscribes to **new issues**, in the expectation that they will rise to a **premium** over issue price, so that they (the speculator) will be able to sell their allotment of **securities** at a profit when dealings in them begin. Some people make multiple applications where there is a likelihood that the issue will be **oversubscribed** and a ballot or scaling down is expected, though multiple applications may be proscribed and illegal.

stamp duty (UK) A form of **taxation** that involves, or used to involve, the fixing of pre-paid stamps on legal or commercial documents. Stamp duties may be *ad valorem* or specific (see **tax**, *ad* *valorem*). Stamp duty is applied as a percentage of the value of share transactions in the UK.

Standard and Poor's 500 (S&P 500) (US) A **share index** measuring price changes in 500 **securities** quoted on the **New York Stock Exchange** (NYSE); 400 company **stocks**, 40 financial, 20 transportation and 40 public utility issues are included, each weighted in accordance with the number of stocks at issue.

Standard and Poor's Ratings (US) A classification of preferred stocks (see **preference shares**), **bonds** and **common stocks** according to risk. 'AAA' represents the highest-quality investment grade, in which the risk of default is minimal; 'BBB' are medium grade, and 'Bb' predominantly speculative; 'C' are the lowest quality of bond, paying no interest, and 'DDD' are in default or in arrears; 'D' are of questionable value. A similar service is provided by Moody's Investor Services, a subsidiary of Dun & Bradstreet.

standard deviation A measure of the **dispersion** of a group of numerical values from the mean or **average**. The standard deviation is calculated by taking the differences between each number in the group and the arithmetic average, squaring them to give the variance (i.e. multiplying each number by itself), summing them and taking the square root.

standard Malaysian rubber (SMR) A standard product in natural rubber, devised by the Malaysian government in the early 1960s in order to provide homogeneity in competition with synthetic rubber. SMR reduced factory processing time and allowed for quality control through adherence to specification rather than by visual inspection; it also facilitated packing and handling.

standby credit Credit guaranteed in a **note issuance facility** or **Euronote facility**. See also **back-up credit**.

start-up A new independent business venture.

state bank See **national bank**.

State Earnings-Related Pension Scheme (SERPS) See **pensions**.

293

state of the art A doctrine to the effect that producers are not liable for harm caused by their product if, at the time the product was made, the product's potential for harm was unknown to science. This argument was advanced, for instance, to reject liability for the harm caused by asbestos in products manufactured at a time when the noxious characteristics of asbestos had not been discovered.

state pension age The age at which men and women become eligible for **pensions** provided by the state.

statement of changes in financial position See **sources and uses of funds**.

statement week (US) The unit of time in which the **Federal Reserve**'s directions for the average level of bank reserves must be observed. See also **maintenance period**.

static risk Of insurance, a **risk** arising out of natural causes, e.g. fire, earthquake or human frailty such as theft.

stellage (Fr.) **Bourse** transaction conveying the right, against a premium, to sell an underlying security at a given price on or before a stated date; it can also convey the right to buy.

step-lock option See **ladder option**.

sterilization (US) The contention of some theorists, notably R. I. McKinnon of Stanford University, that the US authorities, in not adjusting internal monetary conditions to changes in the dollar's **exchange rate**, neutralize, or sterilize, the effect of growth in the world **money supply**.

Sterling Area See **Scheduled Territories**.

sterling warrant into gilt-edged stock (SWING) Authorized by the **Bank of England** in 1987, an **option** to buy or sell a specific **gilt**. The warrants are issued by the Bank of England, then sold by an appointed dealer.

STI Straits Times Index. See **Singapore Stock Exchange**.

stock 1. A particular type of **security**, usually quoted in units of £100 value rather than in units or proportion of total **capital**, as in

shares. Stock, or stocks, and shares have now become synonymous, and the original distinction between stocks and shares has become blurred. The term 'stock' in UK usage is now coming to mean exclusively a fixed-interest security, e.g. loan stock, but in the USA fixed-interest securities are referred to as **bonds**, while other securities are called 'stocks' as in **common stocks**. **2**. An accumulation of capital. **3**. An accumulation of a **commodity** or of finished or semi-finished goods or materials. See **inventories**.

stock dividend See **bonus issue**.

stock exchange A market in which **securities** are bought and sold. There are stock exchanges in most capital cities, as well as in the larger provincial cities in many countries. The **New York Stock Exchange**, **London Stock Exchange** and **Tokyo Stock Exchange** are the largest in terms of **market capitalization** and **turnover**, although London lists the securities of more companies, particularly overseas companies, than either Tokyo or the NYSE (see table).

Continental European exchanges are often referred to as *bourses* (Fr.). Stock exchanges facilitate **savings** and **investment** by making it possible for investors to dispose of securities quickly if they wish to do so (in the **secondary market**) and for companies, governments and other organizations to raise new **capital** in the primary market (see **new issue market**). Ready marketability requires that: **new issues** should be made and backed by reputable borrowers or institutions; information should be available on existing securities; competition should exist among **market makers**; and there should be adequate **liquidity**. There should be both a legal framework and market rules to prevent fraud and sharp practice (see **regulation**). There are various trading systems on stock exchanges (see **order driven**), but **trading floors** are gradually giving way to **automated screen trading** and telephone markets. These new technologies and deregulation have permitted the development of new systems for trading securities outside of stock exchanges (see **IBIS**, **National Association of Securities Dealers Automated Quotation System**). See also entries for stock exchanges, e.g. **Singapore Stock Exchange**, or country, e.g. **China**, or region, e.g. **Eastern Europe**. See also **unlisted securities market**.

TOP 15 STOCK EXCHANGES 1992

	Market value £m	Total inc. fixed	Number of companies listed	
	Equities	interest	Domestic	Overseas
New York	2,613,286	3,963,429	1,969	120
UK	2,177,144	2,579,339	1,878	514
Tokyo	1,583,463	2,426,683	1,651	117
Osaka	1,583,880	2,406,182	1,163	5
Germany	217,935	1,136,303	425	240
Luxembourg	139,461	937,189	59	162
Toronto	365,317	733,801	1,049	70
Paris	216,947	597,761	515	217
Milan	76,211	493,980	226	3
NASDAQ*	410,723	411,120	3,850	261
Vienna	256,303	311,492	94	47
Switzerland*	129,209	129,209	180	240
Brussels	42,383	287,493	164	154
Amsterdam	113,108	243,573	251	246
Australia	175,916	208,224	1,038	35

*Little or no fixed interest, which in other countries is included in the total.

Source: *Stock Exchange Quarterly*, April–June 1993. Reproduced with permission.

Stock Exchange Alternative Trading Service (SEATS) 1. A system for trading less liquid (see **liquidity**) **securities** introduced on the **London Stock Exchange** on 16 November 1992 to replace the **Company Bulletin Board**, where there is only either a single or no **market maker**. The screen displays the current **quotations** for the market maker (if any) and current public **orders** to provide a central point for business in these illiquid stocks. SEATS complements the **Stock Exchange Automated Quotation System. 2.** An automated screen trading system on the **Australian Stock Exchange**.

Stock Exchange Automated Quotation System (SEAQ) (UK) A screen-based quotation system for **securities** that allows **market makers** on the **London Stock Exchange** to report their price quotes and trading volumes to users of the system. SEAQ was introduced in preparation for the **Big Bang** and has allowed all transactions on the exchange to be carried out by telephone rather than as formerly on the **trading floor**. It feeds into TOPIC (see **Teletext Output of Price Information by Computer**) and is linked into NASDAQ (see **National Association of Securities Dealers Automated Quotation System**). See also **alpha securities**, **normal market size**, **stocks**.

Stock Exchange Automatic Execution Facility (SAEF) (UK) A computerized system for executing small purchase and sales **orders** for **shares** on the **London Stock Exchange**. SAEF automatically routes orders to the **market maker** offering the best price on the **Stock Exchange Automated Quotation System**, executes the order and produces **contract notes**, and enters the transaction into the TALISMAN (see **Transfer Accounting, Lodgement for Investors, Stock Management for Jobbers**) settlement system. TRADE and BEST are competing similar proprietary small order execution systems operated by the London **market maker** houses Barclays de Zoete Wedd and Kleinwort Grieveson Securities respectively. SAEF is similar to the small order execution system operated by the **National Association of Securities Dealers Automated Quotation System**.

Stock Exchange Daily Official List (UK) See **official list**.

Stock Exchange pool nominees See **Transfer Accounting, Lodgement for Investors, Stock Management for Jobbers**.

stock index futures **Futures** contracts based on **share indices**.

stock market See **stock exchange**.

stock split (US) A **bonus issue** of shares that reduces the unit quoted price but not the **yield** or market value of the investor's holding.

stockbroker A member of a **stock exchange** who buys and sells **securities** as an **agent** for clients in return for a **commission** (US = *commission broker*). See also **broker**, **floor broker**, **market maker**.

Stockholm Stock Exchange (SSE) The Stockholm Fondbors, as it is called, is the **stock exchange** of Sweden. The exchange is regulated by the Bank Inspection Board (BIB) and the Riksbanker (**central bank**).

stop-loss 1. The price at which a **security** is automatically sold to protect the investor against further loss. See **orders**. **2.** Insurance against losses on the **Lloyd's of London** market. See **stop-loss insurance**.

stop-loss insurance Insurance by **names** at **Lloyd's of London** against **underwriting** losses, an insurance normally contracted within the market itself.

stop-loss treaty A **non-proportional treaty** (see also **reinsurance**) under which the reinsurer refunds to the insurer the amount of claims paid that exceed a predetermined percentage of premiums received.

stop order See **order**.

stop rate (US) The lowest accepted rate of interest on a **repurchase agreement**.

straddle Used interchangeably in the **commodities**, **options** and **financial futures** markets with the term **spread**. A straddle often signifies the simultaneous sale and purchase of **call** and *put* options or of different **terms** in the same financial futures or commodity market.

straight bond A **bond** at a fixed **rate of interest** without **conversion** (i.e. not replaceable with a new bond or **equity**).

straight-line method See **depreciation**.

Straits Times Index (STI) See **Singapore Stock Exchange**.

strict liability A doctrine in law that a party causing harm or loss is liable, whether or not they acted negligently or with wrongful intent. The doctrine is opposed to that of **state of the art**. Strict liability has increasing adherence in US and German jurisdiction, and legislation on comparable lines is contemplated by the European Commission (see also **European Union**). Limited defences are available under strict liability to defendants, thus distinguishing the concept from *absolute liability*, a rule permitting no exceptions, and one that strict liability has displaced.

striking price, strike price 1. **Offer for sale**. 2. The price paid by the holder of a **call option** or to the holder of a *put* option when the option contract is executed. Normally, for commodities, the current market price at the time of sale of the option.

Structural Adjustment Programme (SAP) See **International Bank for Reconstruction and Development**.

sub-chapter S corporations (US) Under sub-chapter S of the Internal Revenue Code, corporations with 35 or fewer non-corporate shareholders may elect to be subject to **income tax** instead of **corporation tax**. This allows a business to choose whichever tax regime is most favourable to it, e.g. where it would be advantageous to offset losses in the company against other personal income. When a **company** is taxed in the normal way it may be referred to as a *C-corporation*.

subordinated Of a **liability**, ranked below another liability in order of priority for payment. *Junior debt* is ranked after *senior debt* for repayment in the event of **default**.

subsidiary Generally, a company controlled by another, parent company (see **consolidated accounts**). Also referred to as an *affiliate*.

supersaver account (US) See **money-market deposit account**.

supplementary special deposit (SSD) (UK) An additional deposit required to be placed by commercial banks with the Bank of England, over and above **special deposits**. The system, known as 'the corset', was operated by the Bank of England in 1973–5, 1976–7 and 1978–80. It was abandoned permanently in June 1980. The object of the scheme was to reinforce the restraint of banks' deposit taking effected by special deposits. SSDs, which did not qualify for interest, were called in relation to the banks' **interest-bearing eligible liabilities** (IBELs), a higher amount being required as the banks' IBELs exceeded a prescribed rate of growth.

The scheme was largely frustrated by the **bill leak** and by the abolition of exchange control in October 1979.

supply estimates See **supply expenditure**.

supply expenditure (UK) The part of UK central government expenditure that is financed by moneys voted by Parliament, i.e. expenditure not automatically arising from continuing statutory obligations. The parliamentary vote is given in response to detailed presentation of the expenditure needed, in the supply estimates. The moneys arising in this way are frequently referred to as 'the vote'.

surplus ACT See **corporation tax**.

surplus treaty Of **insurance**, a **proportional treaty** (see also **reinsurance**) under which the insurer cedes to the reinsurer that part of the **risk** on which they (the insurer) do not wish to be liable themselves.

sushi bond (Jap.) A foreign-currency **bond** that, when issued by a Japanese institution, is officially classified as a domestic bond. Such bonds are attractive to **trust banks** and insurance companies whose foreign bond holdings are restricted.

swap 1. A transaction whereby a **security** of a certain value is sold to a buyer in exchange for the purchase, from the buyer, of a security having the same value; the purpose being to obtain an improvement, in the eyes of either of the parties, in the quality of the security, or to anticipate a change in yield, e.g. **intermarket spread swap**, **rate anticipation swap**. 2. In **foreign exchange**, the purchase/sale of a currency in the **spot market** against the simultaneous purchase/sale of the same amount of the same currency in the **forward market**. 3. In international monetary relations, the opening by one **central bank** of a **line of credit** in its own currency against the opening of an equivalent line of credit in another currency by the relevant central bank. See also **currency interest rate swap**, **option**.

swap line A **swap** between the **central banks** of different countries in that the borrowing central bank's complementary action is in the form of a **forward** contract, rather than the simultaneous provision of its own currency. An extension of the principle of a **line of credit**.

swap rate The difference between the **forward interest rate** on, say, a **currency** and the **spot** rate expressed as a **discount** or **premium** on the latter.

swaption An **option** to enter into a **swap** contract.

sweep facility An automatic service available on some bank accounts or other **current accounts** that shifts credit balances into a **deposit** account where they will earn interest.

SWIFT Society for Worldwide Interbank Financial Telecommunications. A credit-transfer system between banks operated on a non-profit basis from Brussels. The system links some 1,500 banks in 68 countries.

SWING (UK) See **sterling warrant into gilt-edged stock**.

swing line (UK) An arrangement reconciling different **settlement** dates in domestic and **Euro-commercial paper** markets. Borrowers switching, e.g., from domestic US **commercial paper** with one-day settlement to Euro-commercial paper with two- to three-day settlement first make two- or three-day drawings. With same-day settlement becoming more common in the Euro-commercial paper market, swing lines have more recently become less used.

Swiss Options and Financial Futures Exchange (SOFFEX) An **options** and **futures** market set up by the Basle, Geneva and Zurich stock exchanges, together with five Swiss banks, in May 1988, initial trading being in options on up to 15 first-line Swiss stocks.

Swiss stock exchanges Switzerland has eight **stock exchanges**, the largest being in Zurich, which is followed by Geneva, Basle and Berne. Computerized trading was introduced in 1987, though continuous trading is limited. There is a trade settlement system linking the three big exchanges. A second tier, the *deuxième marché*, for **unlisted companies**, was opened in 1988, and there is also an *avant-bourse* for pre-market trading in other shares. The *Swiss Market Index* (SMI) is the main Zurich exchange index.

switch See **swap**.

switching Of a **commodity**, substituting a contract for delivery at a certain date for one for delivery of the same commodity at another date.

switching discount A **discount** or reduction in the **offer price** of a **unit trust** offered to investors in other unit trusts of the same group.

Sydney Futures Exchange (SFE) Trades **financial futures**, including contracts based on the *All Ordinaries Index*, and other futures and **options**, including **commodity** futures (wool and live cattle).

syndicate 1. A group of banks or other financial institutions formed to provide a **credit** or to **underwrite** or manage an issue of a **security**. 2. The operating unit into which the **Lloyd's of London** insurance market is divided.

syndicated credit See **syndication**.

syndicated lending See **syndication**.

syndication To subject a **credit** or the issue of a **security** to management or **underwriting** by a **syndicate**. This method became common in the international lending market from the 1970s, owing largely to the great increase in funds, available from members of the **Organization of Petroleum Exporting Countries** (OPEC) and demanded by non-OPEC countries, after the oil price rises that began in 1972/3. Syndicated lending, or syndicated credit, also became commonplace in the **Euromarkets**. **Venture capital** companies also syndicate deals so as to spread **risk**.

system repurchase agreement (US) A **repurchase agreement** arranged by the **Federal Reserve** for its own account.

system RP See **system repurchase agreement**.

systematic risk See **alpha coefficient**.

Tafelgeschaft (Ger.) **Over-the-counter** dealing.

Tagesgeld (Ger.) Day-to-day money. See **overnight money**.

Taiwan Stock Exchange Established in 1962 and regulated by the Securities and Exchange Commission. An **over-the-counter market** was launched in 1982.

take-over The acquisition of one company by another. See also **corporate raider**, **merger**, **Take-Over Panel**.

Take-Over Panel (UK) The Panel on Take-Overs and Mergers is a committee responsible for supervising compliance with the City Code on Take-Overs and Mergers, a non-statutory code instituted in 1968 (though with origins earlier) and revised in 1987 . The code is intended to protect the interests of **shareholders** and requires that any company acquiring more than 29.9% of the **shares** in another company must make a full bid at a price not lower than the highest price paid for its shareholding.

taker The buyer of an **option**.

TALISMAN See **Transfer Accounting, Lodgement for Investors, Stock Management for Jobbers**.

tanigata toshi shintaku (Jap.) See *toshi shintaku*.

***tanshi* company** (Jap.) A **market maker** in the **money market** and the **foreign exchange market**.

tap The staged **sale** of a government **money-market instrument** (e.g. a **Treasury bill**) or **bond** over a period of time in response to demand. Also used for staged sales by other issuers.

tap CD An issue of a **certificate of deposit** (CD), normally in very large **denominations**, by arrangement with a specific purchaser.

tap stock (UK) A government **bond** issued formerly by the **government broker** and now by a number of **market makers**. The issue is not made all at once, and its supply can be adjusted like a tap to influence prices in the **gilts** market.

targeting (US) The adoption and application by the **Federal Reserve** of measures to bring about given levels of banking system **reserves**, **credit** growth and **money supply** growth.

tariffs Taxes imposed on imports. They may be levied on an **ad valorem** basis or as a specific amount per unit of imports.

TAURUS See **Transfer and Automated Registration of Uncertified Stock**.

taux d'intérêt (Fr.) **Rate of interest**.

tax, *ad valorem* A tax expressed as a proportion of the price of a good or service; hence it is by *value*. **Value added tax** is an *ad valorem* tax, as is **sales tax**.

tax allowance See **tax credit**.

tax avoidance (UK) Legal means used to take advantage of tax concessions to reduce or eliminate tax liabilities. US = **tax shelter**.

tax credit An amount of tax deemed to have been paid that may be offset against a tax liability or reclaimed by the taxpayer if they have no liability (Fr. = *avoir fiscal*). To be distinguished from a *tax allowance*, the value of which will depend upon the taxpayer's tax bracket or marginal rate of tax. In the UK, tax credits are given on dividends, equivalent to the lower rate of income tax (see also **corporation tax**). Under **double taxation** agreements, a tax credit against US tax liability may be given, for example, to a US citizen who pays UK income tax. See also **capital allowances**, **investment credit**.

tax deposit certificate (UK) Individual or corporate taxpayers may deposit funds with the Inland Revenue in advance of tax liabilities. Interest accrues daily, varying with market rates.

tax haven A financial centre that offers a more favourable tax environment than that enjoyed in their home territory by the non-residents who invest there. Tax havens called offshore financial centres provide a base for offshore funds (e.g. **unit trusts** or other forms of managed **portfolio** investments). Other attractive features of tax havens may include banking secrecy and other favourable aspects of the legal environment. The essential characteristic of offshore banking is that its business is conducted in foreign currencies and on behalf of non-residents. A number of small countries have built up substantial offshore financial business, such as Bermuda, the Cayman Islands, Hong Kong, Singapore, Liechtenstein, Monaco and Luxembourg. The Channel Islands and the Isle of Man are used as tax havens by residents of the UK and other countries.

Tax Reform Act 1986 (US) This important legislation increased thresholds for personal **income tax** and reduced or eliminated various deductions for both personal and business income taxes so as to allow major reductions in income tax and **corporation tax** rates without significantly affecting total tax revenues. The number of personal income tax brackets was reduced from 14, with rates ranging from 11% to 50%, to two rates of 15% and 28% (though the highest effective rate is 33%, because some concessions are withdrawn for high-income taxpayers). The scope for **tax shelters** was greatly reduced, e.g. by the limitation of deduction of interest on borrowings secured by first and second residences; and the exclusion of long-term gains from **capital gains** tax was repealed. Maximum corporation tax rates were reduced from 46% to 34%. The **investment credit** was eliminated. **Depreciation** deductions were revised, and other business deductions reduced or eliminated for both incorporated and **unincorporated business**. Subsequent legislation has affected some of the provisions of the Act.

tax shelter (US) Legal means used to take advantage of tax concessions to reduce or eliminate tax liabilities, e.g. the purchase of tax-free **savings bonds**, the use of **pensions** schemes (see **Keogh plan**) or opting for a corporation to be taxed as a partnership. See also **tax havens, Tax Reform Act**.

taxation A compulsory transfer of money from private individuals, institutions and commercial enterprises to finance government expenditure. It may be levied upon wealth or income, or in the form of a surcharge on prices. In the first case it would then be called a *direct tax* (e.g. **income tax**), and in the second an *indirect tax* (e.g. **value added tax**). See **capital transfer tax, corporation tax, double taxation, excise duty, local taxation, sales tax, stamp duty, tariffs, tax credit, tax deposit certificate, tax shelter, wealth tax**.

taxe d'émission (Fr.) The tax on **security issues**.

taxe professionelle (Fr.) See **local taxation**.

Tea Brokers' Association of London A **physical** commodity market, dealing in tea. Two million chests of 50 kilograms are sold annually on the market, equivalent to half the consumption of the UK, which is itself 40% of world consumption. The association is the main tea trading centre of the world. World tea production was estimated in 1993 at 546m kg.

technical analysis The study and prediction of price movements in **security** and **commodity markets**, based on the analysis of charts of **share prices** and trading volumes; hence the practitioners' title: *chartist*. Contrasted with practitioners of *fundamental analysis*, which involves the study of financial accounts and other information about companies, the chartist tends to believe that all the necessary information is in the share price. See also **efficient market hypothesis**.

technical reserves A collective term used for the various reserves held by insurance companies against claims, namely **unearned premiums reserve, unexpired risks reserve, claims outstanding reserve, incurred but not reported** claims reserve.

teigatu (Jap.) A 10-year deposit certificate issued by the Japanese Post Office, encashable after six months, yielding interest after one year, such interest rising to a higher rate after three years.

Tel Aviv Stock Exchange The largest exchange in the Middle East (there are exchanges in Amman, Kuwait and Tehran; see also **Istanbul Menkul Kiymetter Borsasi**). In its present form dates from 1953. There is also an **unlisted securities market**.

Telefonverkehr (Ger.) See *geregelter Freiverkehr*.

telephone banking The facility to be told of bank account details and to give oral instructions for payments, account movements and other services by telephoning a special telephone number and quoting an identification code. See also **electronic banking**.

Telerate (US) A majority-owned **subsidiary** of the Dow-Jones Corporation, providing news and financial information, to some extent in competition with **Reuters**. Particularly strong in the provision of data on US Treasury **bonds** and **bills**.

teletext See **viewdata**.

Teletext Output of Price Information by Computer (TOPIC) (UK) A **viewdata** system provided by the **London Stock Exchange** for subscribers. It includes company information. See also **Stock Exchange Automated Quotation System**.

10 K See **Form 10K**.

Ten Oever case See **equalization of pensions**.

tender 1. Generally, to offer a payment, as in a written offer to purchase. 2. To offer a service in response to advertisement. 3. To offer to buy Treasury bills (see **Treasury bill tender**) issued by the **Bank of England**. 4. To offer for an issue of **securities** on the **stock exchange** (see also **offer for sale**, **tender offer**). 5. To deliver a **commodity** to the buyer.

tender offer (US) A public offer to purchase **securities** of one company by another at a fixed price, usually at a **premium** over the current market price. Also used to refer to a public **offer for sale** of a specific portfolio of securities, normally for cash.

tender panel See **Euronote facility**.

tenor The **term** or duration to maturity of a **bill of exchange**.

term 1. The period of duration of a **security** until **maturity** or **redemption**. See **long term**, **medium term**, **short term**. 2. An **insurance** policy, particularly in **life assurance**, having a limited period of validity.

term insurance See **insurance**, **life assurance**.

term loan A bank advance for a specific period (normally three to 10 years), repaid, with **interest**, usually by regular periodical payments. Term loans are made by **commercial banks** and other institutions for business finance. For large borrowings the **loan** may be syndicated (see **syndicate**), and it is quite common for loans to large corporations to be unsecured.

terminable annuity An **annuity** whose payment is made for a specified number of years.

terminal bonus See **life assurance**.

terminal date The date of expiry of a **futures** contract in the **commodity market**.

terminal market A **futures** market in **commodities**, so called because futures contracts expire on a **terminal date**.

terzo mercato (It.) The third-tier **unlisted securities market** in Italy.

Texas hedge Any **derivatives** transaction having the effect of increasing risk, e.g. the purchase of two **instruments** adding to each other's risk. The opposite of a true **hedge**.

TGRs See **tigers**.

Third Market (UK) An **over-the-counter market** set up by the **London Stock Exchange** to trade in securities of unlisted companies and with less stringent entry requirements than either the **unlisted securities market** or the **official list** or main market. It opened in January 1987 and was phased out in 1990.

thrifts (US) A general term covering non-bank institutions receiving **deposits** and making loans. See **credit union**, **mutual savings banks**, **savings and loan associations**.

TIBOR (Jap.) Tokyo interbank offered rate. The Japanese equivalent of **London interbank offered rate** (LIBOR).

tick The observed minimum price movement of a **derivative**.

tigers 1. The first four **newly industrialized countries** in Asia: Hong Kong, Singapore, South Korea and Taiwan. See also **dragons**.

2. (US) The colloquial name for Treasury investment growth receipts (TGRs), **zero coupon bonds** issued by the US Treasury.

tighten A **bond** is said to *tighten* in the **aftermarket** if the interest **yield** is lower than the rate at which it was issued (see **issue**).

Tilgung (Ger.) **Redemption**.

till money (UK) Notes and coin held by banks. See also **vault cash** (US).

time and distance policies The practice, chiefly by **Lloyd's of London active underwriters**, and chiefly in respect of **long tail business** where the ultimate claim is uncertain, of taking out an insurance policy maturing at some time in the future, rather than setting aside reserves; and of obtaining a letter of credit in respect of the maturity value of the policy. In this way, the underwriter can meet their **solvency** obligations without the sacrifice of profits for their members that a diversion of funds into reserves would entail. After the major losses of the late 1980s and early 1990s, the practice lost favour.

time deposit See **bank deposit**.

time draft See **banker's acceptance**.

time policy A policy for the **insurance** of a ship, applicable for a fixed period of time, regardless of the movements of the ship.

time value The value of an **option** in relation to its future duration: the longer the remaining life, the higher the time value. Time value and **intrinsic value** together make up the price of the option. See also **discounted cashflow**.

titre (Fr.) A **certificate**, or other documentary title to a **security**; also used to refer to the security itself.

tokkin (Jap.) Literally, 'special investment fund'. A privileged investment fund made available in the late 1980s to Japanese companies having heavy liquidities that they wished to place in the stock market. Such companies already faced large taxable capital gains on existing holdings bought at historically low cost; further investment in such holdings would have added to the tax liability. Companies were therefore permitted to place their new resources in the new *tokkin* funds, valued at current book prices.

Tokyo dollar call market (Jap.) The **call market** in dollar-denominated funds; dealing also in other **currencies**.

Tokyo Grain Exchange A **commodity** market established in 1957 for trade in US and Chinese soya beans and red beans.

Tokyo Round See **General Agreement on Tariffs and Trade** (GATT).

Tokyo Stock Exchange (TSE) One of the three largest **stock exchanges** in the world and one of the three central Japanese exchanges; Osaka and Nagoya are the other two, and there are **regional stock exchanges** in Fukuoka, Hiroshima, Kyoto, Niigata and Sapporo. Tokyo accounts for well over 80% of all the transactions in Japan. Tokyo, Nagoya and Osaka have two main sections – a first section (*ichibu*), which deals in the most actively traded companies, and, since 1961, a second section (*nibu*), which has less stringent listing requirements – as well as a third section for foreign stocks. Some 1,200 companies are listed on the first section and 400 on the second. There is also an **over-the-counter market**, originally based in Osaka, which has an automated quotation system. The main Tokyo Stock Exchange has used an **automated screen trading** system called CORES (Computer-Assisted Order Routing and Execution System) since 1982 on the second section and since 1985 on the first section, but some 200 actively traded shares are still bought and sold on the **trading floor**. Non-Japanese dealing firms were permitted to become members of the exchange in 1986. See also **Nikkei Stock Average**, *saitori*, **Topix**.

tombstone An advertisement recording the details of a **loan** or **new issue**, normally a **Eurobond** or international **bond** issue, with the names of the **underwriters** or **syndicate** members.

TOPIC See **Teletext Output of Price Information by Computer**.

Topix (Jap.) A **share index** of some 1,200 **stocks** quoted on Japanese stock markets. The index is capital weighted and forms the basis of a **futures** contract listed on the **Tokyo Stock Exchange**.

Toronto Stock Exchange (TSE) Incorporated in 1878, the TSE accounts for about 75% of trading **volume** on the Canadian exchanges. Montreal is second in importance, followed by Vancouver, and there are also local exchanges in Calgary and Winnipeg. The Computer-Assisted Trading System (CATS) allows entry and automatic execution of **orders** and carries market information. Reforms that began in 1987 will allow foreign dealers, banks and other financial institutions to own **brokers**. The Toronto 35 Index of leading **stocks** forms the basis for **options** and **futures** contracts. There is also a TSE 300 Composite Index. The TSE is regulated by the Ontario Securities Commission (OSC).

toshi shintaku, tanigata toshi shintaku (Jap.) **Investment trusts**, which may take the same form as in the UK or may, in effect, be **unit trusts**.

touch The difference between the highest **bid price** and the lowest **offer price** in a market for **securities** or **commodities**, i.e. the largest available **spread**.

touch screen A computer monitor screen on which operating instructions can be given by touch as well as by the keyboard. For example, a dealer touches a small square on a video screen, and the computer will dial the number on the square with almost instant connection.

town clearing See **clearing house**.

tradable See **negotiable**, **trade**.

trade 1. To buy and sell, e.g., **negotiable instruments**, **commodities**, **currencies**. **2**. Of the **commodity markets**, business in a particular commodity.

TRADE See **Stock Exchange Automatic Execution Facility**.

trade balance See **balance of payments**.

trade bill A **bill of exchange** accepted by a party other than a bank.

trade credit The **credit** extended by business firms to other businesses, usually arising from the delay of receipts and payments for services performed. See also **factoring**.

trade investments (UK) Shareholdings of one company in another. See also **consolidated accounts**.

traded months Months for which deliveries are quoted in **futures** markets for **commodities**. Standard months in the year are usually set for each market.

traded option See **option**.

trading floor The area of space in a **stock exchange** where members gather to deal face to face in securities. Trading floors operate in most stock exchanges, though no longer on the **London Stock Exchange**, but are gradually giving way to **automated screen trading**.

trading position See **commodity market**, **traded months**.

trading post See **specialist**.

tranche A predetermined section of a financial transaction (from the French, meaning 'slice'). Thus: **1**. Of the **International Monetary Fund** (IMF), instalments of foreign currency that member countries may obtain, in exercise of their **drawing rights**, against their **quota**. **2**. Of the **securities** market, an instalment in the progressive **issue** of a security. **3**. Of the **money market**, a stage in the provision of a loan or in the issue of a money-market **instrument**, such as a **certificate of deposit** (CD).

tranche CD A **certificate of deposit** whose issue is divided into a number of smaller amounts and usually sold through a **placing** by a bank. See **tranche**.

transactions balances See **money supply**.

transfer 1. The passage of money across national frontiers for non-commercial purposes, e.g. for the payment of legacies or pensions. **2**. The physical delivery of certificates attesting ownership following sale of a **security**.

Transfer Accounting, Lodgement for Investors, Stock Management for Jobbers (TALISMAN) (UK) A semi-automated **equity** settlement system for the **London Stock Exchange**. Under the TALISMAN system, **market makers** transfer **shares** that they sell into ownership by a central pool (Stock Exchange Pool Nominees – SEPON) and meet buying orders from the same pool. SEPON therefore provides a clearing system. See also **Transfer and Automated Registration of Uncertified Stock (TAURUS)**.

transfer agent See **registrar**.

transfer pricing The adjustment of prices on sales of material between members of a multi-company group so as to distribute financial burdens between the members in accordance with central financial policy. The term is most common in reference to multinational companies, where transfer pricing is suspected as a method of evading national taxation and customs duties.

Transfer and Automated Registration of Uncertified Stock (TAURUS) (UK) A project for a computerized **share** settlement system that intended to reduce the need for handling **share certificates** on the **London Stock Exchange**. TAURUS, which was abandoned in 1993, acted as a clearing house by making book entry changes in the ownership of shares and issuing confirmation notes to buyer and seller. This would still not have been a full book entry transfer system, since the companies would need to maintain share registers (see **registrar**) and issue share certificates. A new system, CREST, is now under development. CREST is expected to use **nominee** accounts, but shareholders will retain the right not to use the system and to continue to hold share certificates.

transferable See **negotiable**.

transparency The extent to which transaction prices and **volumes** in a **securities** market are visible to all market operators. Transparency is an important condition for full and fair competition. See also **audit trail**, **fiscal transparency**.

Treasury The central economic and finance department of a national government, so named chiefly in the USA and the UK, equivalent to the finance ministry of most other governments. The Treasury has responsibility for the overall economic and financial policy of the government, being chiefly concerned with domestic demand management, the balance of payments, monetary policy, taxation, public expenditure, the budget, government revenue and the issue of government **securities**, usually known as **Treasury bonds** and **Treasury bills**.

Treasury bill A **money-market instrument** issued (sold) by the **central bank**, chiefly in the UK and USA, in principle to supply the government's short-term financial needs, but also as a means of influencing **credit** and the **money supply**. Treasury bills are **negotiable** and in the UK are, at issue, wholly taken up by the **discount houses**. Treasury bills always change hands at a **discount**, the implicit rate of **interest** not being paid. Apart from issue at the **Treasury bill tender**, the bills are also sold through the **tap** but only to foreign government and overseas banks and as special deposits for banks that undertake not to release them to the open market. Treasury bills were first issued, in the UK, in 1877.

Treasury bill rate The implicit **interest** rate at which **Treasury bills** can be bought in the **money market**.

Treasury bill tender (UK) The offer for sale of **Treasury bills** each Friday by the **Bank of England**. The offer is of large quantities, and the bills' **maturity** is normally of three months. By long-established rule the **discount houses** bid (tender) for the whole of the issue, the bills being allotted to the discount houses in relation to the price (i.e. the size of the **discount** in the *face value* of the bills; see **par value**) at which they tender.

Treasury bill tender rate (UK) The implicit interest rate determining the size of the discount at which **discount houses** bid for **Treasury bills** at the weekly **Treasury bill tender**.

Treasury bond A **bond** issued by the US Treasury. Equivalent instruments are issued in France and other countries but not in the UK.

Treasury investment growth receipts (TGRs) (US) See **tigers**.

Treaty of Paris The treaty, signed in 1951, establishing the European Coal and Steel Community. See **European Union** (EU).

Treaty of Rome The treaty, signed in 1957, establishing the European Economic Community. Also, a separate treaty, signed in the same year, establishing the European Atomic Energy Community (Euratom). See **European Union** (EU), **Maastricht Treaty**, **Single European Act**.

treaty reinsurance A form of reinsurance whereby the reinsurer and the *ceding insurer* (see **cedant**) are bound under their contract, or treaty, to accept certain risks. See also **reinsurance treaty**, **facultative reinsurance**.

Treuhandanstalt (Ger.) An agency established by the German government in July 1990 with the task of privatizing large areas of state-owned industry in the former East Germany. Such enterprises were taken into ownership and management by the Treuhandanstalt and thereafter sold to private investors. By May 1992, 7,092 companies had been privatized, for a total payment of DM28bn. Of these, 366 had been acquired by foreign investors, apportioned between France (DM2.3bn), the UK (DM1.6bn), the USA (DM1.5bn) and the Netherlands (DM900m). However, 4,863 companies still awaited privatization.

triple witching hour (US) A familiar expression for the trading sessions when the expiry dates of **stock index futures** contracts, **options** on these contracts and options in individual stock fall together.

troc (Fr.) A **foreign exchange swap**.

TRUF See **Euronote facility**.

trust 1. In general, a legal device under which property, either financial or physical, is placed in the custody of a designated person, or people, named *trustees*, for management on behalf of others; the whole is regulated by a *trust deed* defining the trustee(s), the beneficiaries of the trust and the rights and duties of each. **Unit trusts** and **investment trusts**, as the names imply, are regulated by trust arrangements. **2.** A large US **conglomerate** prevalent in the 19th and early 20th centuries, largely outlawed by anti-trust legislation, the earliest instance of which was the Sherman Act of 1890.

trust bank A category of Japanese bank engaged in both banking and trust activities and also operating as savings institutions for the general public (Jap. = *shintaka ginko*).

trust corporation A corporate body (company) authorized under the legislation to act as trustee.

trust deed See **trust**.

trust letter A document signed by a bank borrower who has pledged goods to the bank as a **security** against the loan. The goods are held by the bank until the customer is due to repay the loan, whereupon the customer can obtain control of the goods, solely to sell to repay the loan, against signature of the trust letter, or trust receipt.

trust receipt See **trust letter**.

trustee See **trust**. Of **bond** issues, a trustee is frequently appointed to supervise the discharge of the borrower's obligation to pay principal, interest and other commitments, and generally to safeguard the interests of the bond holders.

Trustee Savings Bank (TSB) (UK) A **savings bank** movement, originally established in Scotland in 1810 to encourage saving by people with low incomes. It grew to a large number of banks that were eventually amalgamated into a single enterprise. The TSB was floated on the **stock exchange** in 1986 (see **flotation**).

trustee status Of trustees (see **trust**), those authorized in the UK under the Trustee Investments Act 1961 to make designated investments not previously allowed, namely in ordinary shares.

Truth in Lending Act (US) Legislation, implemented by Regulation 2 of the **Federal Reserve**, requiring full disclosure by the lender of the cost of consumer credit, such disclosure to include the **annual percentage rate** (APR) and the nature of the costs involved. The Act also permits the borrower, in the case of **mort-**

gages, to cancel the transaction within three business days of formal completion.

TSA See **Securities Association**.

TSB See **Trustee Savings Bank**.

TSE See **Tokyo Stock Exchange, Toronto Stock Exchange**.

tsuikagata toshi shintaku (Jap.) An open-ended **investment trust**.

turn-round rate A combined charge on a **commodity** transaction, consisting of the **broker**'s **commission** and the **clearing fee**.

turnover 1. The total sales revenue of a business. 2. The value of transactions carried out on a **stock exchange**, defined usually as the value of **securities** changing hands but on the **London Stock Exchange** mainly as the total value of purchases and sales. See also **volume**.

tweede markt (Bel.) The second-tier **unlisted securities market** in Belgium. This is the Flemish name; in French the market is called the *second marché*.

Twelfth Directive See **incorporation**.

24-hour trading The ability to trade in **securities** around the clock. Since some **blue-chip** issues and **bonds** are quoted on several **stock exchanges** in different time zones, it is now possible, using satellite communications, to buy and sell securities at any time. Even though there are gaps in trading hours, many exchanges allow after-hours trading; i.e. **dealers** are allowed to buy and sell outside the official closing time.

Übernahme (Ger.) **1. Take-over. 2.** The **underwriting** by a banking **syndicate** of a **new issue**, the syndicate also being responsible for the sale of the security.

uberrimae fidei Literally, 'in the fullest faith'. The legal principle, especially applicable in **insurance**, that all contracts are made on the basis of the fullest possible disclosure of material facts, regardless of whether this is explicitly stated in the contract.

UBR Uniform business rate. See **local taxation**.

UCITS See **Undertakings for Collective Investment in Transferable Securities**.

ultra vires Outside the legal powers of a company or official.

uncommitted Of an international short-term issue, e.g. **Euro-commercial paper**, not backed by an **underwriting** bank **syndicate**, i.e. with no commitment by banks to underpin the issue.

undated securities (UK) **Government securities** not bearing a **redemption date** or **option**, hence **irredeemable securities**.

Undertakings for Collective Investment in Transferable Securities (UCITS) A **European Union** (EU) **directive** entering into force in 1989 and governing **unit trusts** and **investment trusts**, intended to allow them to be marketed throughout the EU.

undervalued See **purchasing power parity**.

underwrite 1. To guarantee to buy or find buyers for all or part of the issue of a **security**. Normally done in return for a fee by a bank or group (see **syndicate**) of banks to ensure sale of any part of an issue not bought by the public to which it is directed. **2.** To accept on behalf of an insuring firm or syndicate an insurance risk.

underwritten 1. Of a **note**, particularly a **Euronote**, an issue backed by a bank guarantee to buy unsold notes or by a bank **standby credit**. See **note issuance facility**. **2**. Of insurance, a **risk** accepted by the **insurer** and against which a **policy** has been issued.

undistributed profits See **retained earnings**.

unearned income See **income tax**.

unearned premiums reserve (UPR) A fund set aside by an insurance company at the end of its financial year to cover **risks** to be borne in the future, i.e. for the length of time **premiums** will be received in respect of any particular insurance policy.

unexpired risks reserve A fund set aside by an insurance company at the end of its financial year, in addition to its **unearned premiums reserve**, to cover all future **risks** insured under its policies.

unfunded See **pensions**.

Ungeregelter Freiverkehr (Ger.) See *geregelter Freiverkehr*.

ungesichert (Ger.) **Unsecured**.

uniform business rate See **local taxation**.

uniform reserve requirement (US) A requirement that the **reserves** of all financial institutions should conform to the same rule, i.e. broadly that they should be the same percentage of the same aggregate (e.g. deposits). A progressive approach to uniform reserves was prescribed in the **Monetary Control Act** 1980.

unincorporated business A business that has not taken the legal form of a company and may be a **sole proprietorship** or a **partnership**. See **incorporation**.

unit banking See **banking**.

unit-linked life assurance A form of endowment **life assurance** in which **policy**-holders receive, in return for their **premiums**, a portion, or unit, of a fund invested directly by the company in the **stock exchange** or in property or other investment outlets. The merit of the arrangement is seen to be in policy-holders' free choice of, direct knowledge of and, within limits, ability to switch the investment of their premiums, as opposed to their passive position as holders of normal endowment policies. Moreover, the existence in the UK until 1984 of tax relief on all life assurance premiums (*life assurance premium relief* – LAPR), together with the concessionary level of **corporation tax** paid by the life company on the income from the investment, produced considerable tax advantages for policy-holders, particularly those at higher levels of income tax. With the abolition of premium tax relief, an advantage only to higher-rate taxpayers remained.

Unit-linked life assurance has made major use of the *single-premium* technique, the policies then being generally known as *bonds*. Unit-linked assurance emerged in the UK in the 1960s, the pioneer company being Abbey Life, directed by Mark Weinberg (later Sir Mark Weinberg), who subsequently transferred his activities to Hambro Life, a company eventually renamed Allied Dunbar.

unit of account 1. In economic theory, one of the functions of money, i.e. a generally accepted unit of value, available to establish the price of goods, e.g. a pound, a dollar or a franc. 2. The standard unit, usually an intangible creation, used normally by international financial organizations to measure their financial activities. Thus the **special drawing right** (SDR) has been adopted as the unit of account of the **International Monetary Fund** (IMF), and the **European Currency Unit** (ECU) as the unit of account of the **European Monetary System** (EMS).

unit trust (UK) An investment organization that invests funds subscribed by the public in **securities** and in return issues units that it will repurchase at any time. The units, which represent equal shares in the trust's investment **portfolio**, produce income and fluctuate in value according to the **interest** and **dividends** paid and the **stock exchange** prices of the underlying securities. The subscriber to a unit trust does not, unlike the shareholder in an **investment trust**, receive any of the **profits** of the organization managing the trust. Management derives its income from a regular service charge as a percentage of the income of the trust's investments (normally less than $\frac{1}{2}$% p.a.), and the difference (see **spread**) between the (bid) price at which it buys in units and the (offer) price at which it sells them, which includes an initial charge. The trust is regulated by a trust deed, the trustees being separate from the management. Unit trusts are free to invest in any type of security and in recent years have tended to specialize, e.g. in small companies or **blue-chip** shares, others in **commodities** or foreign companies or countries. Some are designed to maximize income, others **capital** growth. Many unit trusts offer the option of distributed or reinvested income (*accumulation units*), and there are also trusts incorporating **life assurance** that can be subscribed to by regular payments. Unit trusts in the UK first appeared in the 1930s, were based upon the principle of **mutual funds** in the USA, and in 1993 had £75bn under management. (Fr. = *société d'investissement à capital variable* (SICAV).) See also **open-ended fund.**

unitary taxation (US) Under the unitary tax system some states in the USA assess **corporation tax** not only on **profits** arising from operations within the state but on total income, including the income of subsidiaries in other states or even overseas.

United Nations Monetary and Financial Conference 1944 See **Bretton Woods**.

United Sugar Terminal Market The London market in sugar **futures**, established in 1888, closed during the First and Second World Wars, last reopened in 1957. A paper market only; i.e. physical deliveries are not made. The market fixes the London daily price, used by a number of producer countries as a reference for their physical contracts. The market is a member of the **International Commodities Clearing House**. The London market is about the same size as the New York market and considerably larger than the other world-ranking market, in Paris. Dealing has for long been dominated by sucessive International Sugar Agreements establishing quotas.

unitized property market See **property income certificate**.

universal banking See **banking**.

unlisted company A company whose **shares** are not admitted for trading on a major **stock exchange**. Unlisted companies, also referred to as *unquoted companies*, may none the less have their shares quoted and traded on **unlisted securities markets**. See also **over-the-counter market**.

unlisted securities market(s) (USM(s)) 1. Generally, the markets for shares of public companies (see **incorporation**) not included in the official list for the main market (or first tier) of the **stock exchange**. Most of the larger industrialized countries have organized and regulated lower-tier markets as well as informal *placing markets* in which unlisted shares are traded. These lower stock market segments are less stringently regulated and perform an important function in providing a stepping-stone to the main markets. See also **National Association of Securities Dealers Automated Quotation System**, **over-the-counter market**, *second marché*. 2. Specifically, a market set up in 1980 by the **London Stock Exchange** to trade in designated unlisted securities. **Shares** in well over 400 companies were dealt with by **market makers** on the USM in the early 1990s but by 1993 the number listed had fallen to 275, and the market is to close in 1996 and to be replaced by the proposed **alternative investment market**. Changes in admission and other requirements for the main market of the London Stock Exchange following the implementation of European Community/Union directives had reduced the differences between the two markets and lessened the appeal of the USM.

unquoted company See **unlisted company**.

unrelieved corporation tax See **corporation tax**.

unsecured Of a loan, not backed by a **security**.

unsecured debt A loan made without **collateral** or any charge on the **assets** of the borrower. Unsecured notes are **securities** issued by a company, involving no **charge** on the assets of the company in the event of default.

unvalued policy An **insurance** policy in which the sum to be paid in respect of loss of the subject of the contract is not stated but a maximum sum payable is usually stated.

unweighted See **weighted average**.

up-and-in call/put option An **option** that has no value until the price of the underlying security rises above a certain level.

up-and-out call/put option An **option** becoming valueless when the price of the underlying security rises above a certain level.

UPR See **unearned premiums reserve**.

Uruguay Round See **General Agreement on Tariffs and Trade** (GATT).

valeur (Fr.) **1**. The price of a **security** or value of a number of securities. **2**. The security itself.

valeur à revenu fixe (Fr.) A **fixed–interest security**.

valeur à revenu variable (Fr.) A **variable rate security**.

valeur au porteur (Fr.) A bearer bond. See **bearer security**.

valeur marchande (Fr.) The market value of a **security**.

valeur non-cotée (Fr.) An **unlisted security**.

value Of **foreign exchange** transactions, the date on which a transaction must be paid for. See also **settle**.

value added tax (VAT) A general tax on consumption applied at each point of exchange of goods or services from primary production to final consumption. It is levied on the difference between the sale price of the goods and services (outputs) and the cost of bought-in inputs. At each point of exchange the tax is passed on in the form of higher prices. Businesses do not bear any VAT included in the invoices for the inputs that they buy from suppliers. Being at the final point in the chain of exchange, the final consumer bears the whole of the tax in the same way as if it were a **sales tax** levied at the retail level. VAT was introduced in the UK in 1973 because it is the form of indirect **taxation** applied in the European Union (EU) and is the basis of contribution to the Union budget. It is levied in all 12 EU member states, in Japan and in many other countries but not in Australia or the USA, which have sales taxes.

variable life insurance (Jap.) **Life assurance** where the sum payable varies in relation to inflation or **exchange rates**.

variable rate security A **security** for which the **rate of interest**

is not fixed but varies with rates on short-term securities, such as **Treasury bills**, according to a specified formula that adjusts rates, say, every six months. The UK government issued variable rate stock in 1977, but such issues are common in the **Eurobond** market and in the USA, where they are known as **floating rate notes** (FRNs) or, more generally, *floaters*.

variabler Kurs (Ger.) The continuous quotation allowable for large company **shares** on the **German stock exchanges**. See *Einheitskurs*.

variation margin The losses and gains attributable to **derivatives** in the light of their **mark-to-market** values.

vault cash (US) Money held at banks in the form of banknotes and coins (UK = *notes and coin*).

velocity Of **money supply**, the rate at which the **money stock** circulates within the economy. The figure for velocity is obtained by dividing the money stock into the **gross domestic product** (GDP). See also **monetary school**, **money**.

vendor placing Where a **listed company** issues **shares** to the sellers of another company as full or partial settlement of the acquisition price, the sellers may ask a **stockbroker** to dispose of the shares by placing them with clients. This is known as vendor placing and may be preferable to selling them on the market, where the offer of a large line of stock might depress the price.

vente à découvert (Fr.) An uncovered sale of a **security**, a **currency** or a **commodity**. See **cover**.

venture capital **Finance** provided by a specialized institution to an entrepreneur, **start-up** or developing business, where a fairly high degree of risk is involved. Strictly, venture capital includes **equity** capital, and this is often provided in a package including **subordinated** or other **loans**. See also **risk capital**, **development capital**, **mezzanine**.

Venture Capital Trust Scheme (VCTS) (UK) A scheme announced in November 1993 to give tax-free **dividends** and **capital gains** for pooled investments in qualifying unquoted trading companies (see **unlisted companies**). The VCTS is expected to operate from 1995 onwards.

Verfall (Ger.) **Redemption date**.

Verkehrswert (Ger.) Market value.

vertical spread A combination of **options**: a **long call option** combined with a **short** call option, both with the same expiry date. Similarly a combination of long and short *put* options.

VIBOR The Vienna interbank offered rate; the Austrian equivalent of **London interbank offered rate** (LIBOR).

videotext See **viewdata**.

viewdata The provision of selected information, e.g. on **share** prices, through television screens. One example is **Teletext Output of Price Information by Computer** (TOPIC). There are two types of viewdata system: **1**. In *teletext* or *videotext* the viewer calls up pages of information by keying in numbers selected from a directory on the screen via a keyboard. Ceefax and Oracle are provided by the BBC and the Independent Broadcasting Authority respectively and are transmitted to the set by television signal. **2**. Prestel, operated by British Telecom, enables viewers to select pages of information stored on a central computer via telephone lines using their television set as a terminal. TOPIC uses this system. Viewers may also access information about their bank account and buy or sell shares (see **electronic banking**).

visible balance See **balance of payments**.

visible trade See **balance of payments**.

volatility, price The extent to which security prices fluctuate, usually measured by hourly percentage changes in a **share index**.

volume 1. The amount of any aggregate when unaffected by price changes, i.e. expressed in terms of a given period, taking no account of price changes; e.g. the volume of UK company profit margins, expressed in terms of 1980, rose by 21% between 1980 and 1987. See also **inflation**, **nominal**, **real**. **2**. An indicator of **turnover** on a **stock exchange**. Volume is usually measured by the number of transactions in a **security** or in all securities during a period, e.g. a day; but on the **London Stock Exchange** volume is measured by the total number of sales and purchases – a figure twice as high.

vorläufig Dividende (Ger.) Interim dividend. See **dividend**.

Vorstand (Ger.) Board of directors.

vostro account A bank account maintained by a **correspondent bank** on behalf of a depositing bank in another country; *vostro* (It.) meaning 'your'. The depositing bank will refer to *nostro account*, meaning 'our account'.

vote See **supply expenditure**.

voting shares **Equity** shares entitling holders to vote in the election of directors of a company. Normally all **ordinary shares** are voting shares, but sometimes a company may create a class of non-voting ordinary shares if the holders of the equity wish to raise more equity capital but exclude the possibility of losing control of the business. Bearer shares (see **bearer security**) are commonly used to raise capital in some countries. Most Swiss companies register only shares held by Swiss citizens, although this is changing.

voyage policy A policy of **insurance** of a ship, applicable only for the duration of one voyage.

Wall Street See **New York Stock Exchange**.

Wandelobligation (Ger.) A **convertible bond**.

warrant, warehouse warrant (UK) See **warrant of settlement**.

warrant of settlement A document showing title to a specific quantity of a **commodity** in storage, conveying responsibility for warehouse charges and insurance.

warrants **Securities** giving the holder a right to subscribe to a **share** or a **bond** at a given price and from a certain date. Warrants, which are commonly issued 'free' alongside the shares of new **investment trusts** when launched, and carry no income or other rights to **equity**, immediately trade separately on the **stock exchange** but at a price lower than the associated security. This provides the investor in warrants with an element of **gearing**, since, if the associated share or bond price ultimately rises above the subscription price, it will have a value corresponding to the difference between the subscription price at which the warrant rights may be exercised and the market price of the share or bond. See also **dilution, dividend warrant**, **option**.

warranty The confirmation by the **insured** party to an insurance contract that the details given as to the subject of the insurance are correct.

Warsaw Stock Exchange See **Eastern Europe**.

wash sale (US) The sale and purchase of a **block** of **securities** by a single investor (or investors in collusion) simultaneously or within a short period. The objective may be to establish a loss or gain or to create a false impression of **volume** and **turnover** in a security. See also **bed and breakfast**.

wealth tax An annual tax on the net value of **assets** of an individual, levied above a threshold. There are wealth taxes in a number of countries, including Denmark, Germany, the Netherlands and Spain, but not in the UK, Japan or the USA.

weighted average An **average** calculated by assigning weights to each item to reflect their relative importance. For example, the weighted average for a share price index calculated in this way could be arrived at by multiplying the prices of **securities** by their traded **volumes** (weights), adding them together and dividing by the sum of the weights. This weighted average could then be expressed as a percentage of the weighted average calculated in a similar way for an earlier, base year, to give a percentage change in prices. An *unweighted* average or index gives all its constituents an equal value. See also **share indices**.

weights See **weighted average**.

Wertpapier (Ger.) A **security**.

Wertzuwachs (Ger.) **Capital gain**.

Wertzuwachssteuer (Ger.) Capital gains tax. See **capital gain**.

Wheat Trade Convention (WTC) See **International Wheat Agreement** (IWA), **International Wheat Council** (IWC).

white knight A company subject to an unwelcome or hostile bid (see **corporate raider**) may invite a second bid from a friendly company as an alternative to succumbing to a **take-over**. That company is a white knight.

whole life policy See **life assurance**.

wholesale banking The making of loans or acceptance of deposits between banks and other **financial institutions**, especially in the **interbank market**. As distinct from *retail banking*, a term for the activities of the **commercial banks** carried out with the general public and business enterprises.

wholesale deposit A **deposit**, normally of a large amount, obtained by a bank from other banks, or from large companies or institutions, i.e. not a deposit placed directly by an individual client.

wholesale market Of banks, the **money market** that operates between banks, dealing in interbank short-term loans in large amounts. See **interbank market**.

Wig Index See **Eastern Europe**.

winding up See **liquidation**.

window A term used to describe a period, normally short, in which particular funds are available. Also applied to special lending by a **central bank**. See **discount window**.

window dressing Financial adjustments made solely for the purpose of accounting presentation, normally at the time of auditing of company accounts. For example, a bank may wish to show large holdings of cash at the **balance sheet** date and may in advance of that date sell **securities**, only to repurchase them immediately afterwards.

window guidance (Jap.) Informal direction by the Bank of Japan in respect of bank lending policies.

with-profits life assurance See **life assurance**.

withdrawable repurchase agreement (US) A **repurchase agreement** that can be cancelled by the dealer giving notice of termination to the **Federal Reserve** by 1.30 p.m. on the day of intended cancellation.

withdrawable RP Withdrawable **repurchase agreement**.

withholding tax Taxation deducted from payments to non-residents, usually in the form of a standard rate of **income tax** applied to **dividends** or other payments by companies. May be reclaimable under **double taxation** agreements.

working capital The excess of current **assets** over current **liabilities**; that part of current assets financed from long-term funds. The ratio of current liabilities to the current assets of a business, the current ratio, is sometimes used as a measure of **liquidity**.

working member A professional member of **Lloyd's of London**

carrying on the actual business of Lloyd's, either as an underwriter or as a broker.

World Bank See **International Bank for Reconstruction and Development**.

World Gold Council An international non-profit association of gold producers with the task of stimulating demand for gold in major end-use markets. Founded in 1987 by 16 gold-mining companies from four countries, in 1993 the council had 50 member companies from nine countries, representing about half of world gold production. In 1992, among other activities, the council established the Central Bank Advisory Board to promote understanding of the role of central banks in the gold market and began publication of the quarterly review *Gold Demand Trends* for the use of market analysts and commentators.

world indices See **Morgan Stanley Capital International World Index**.

writer The seller of a **derivative**, i.e. the person who must sell or buy at the instance of the buyer, or holder.

writing-down allowance See **capital allowances**.

written back See **provisions**.

written off See **provisions**.

WTC Wheat Trade Convention. See **International Wheat Agreement** (IWA), **International Wheat Council** (IWC).

xd See **ex-dividend**.

yankee bond (US) A dollar-dominated **bond** issued in the USA by foreign banks and corporations. A **foreign bond**.

year of account A business year of a **Lloyd's of London** syndicate.

yearling bond (UK) **Stock** issued by municipal authorities with **maturity** within a year.

Yellow Book (UK) A publication of the **London Stock Exchange**, setting out the regulations governing admission to the **official list** and subsequent procedures for reporting. See also **Green Book**.

yellow sheets See **pink sheets**.

yield The income from a **security** as a proportion of its current market price. This is the *current yield*. The *dividend yield* is the current **dividend** as a percentage of the market price of a security. The *earnings yield* is a theoretical figure, based on the last dividend paid as a percentage of the current market price. For **fixed-interest securities**, the *running yield*, *interest yield* or *flat yield* is the interest rate as a percentage of the price paid for the **stock**. For example, a **bond** with a nominal or issued value of £100, but bought for £50, and with an interest rate of 5%, has a running yield of 10%. Where it is a **redeemable security** the return will also include any **capital gain** on **redemption**. This is the *redemption yield*, which takes into account the purchase price, the interest payments, the redemption value and the time remaining to maturity. The initial yield is the estimated income that an investor in a new **unit trust** or other form of managed investment, such as an **investment trust**, may expect to receive. It is based upon the present yield of the underlying investments and expressed as a percentage of the **offer price**.

yield curve The normal tendency of **yields** to rise with the increasing **maturity** of the **security**. When the opposite effect occurs, this is described as a *reverse yield curve*.

zaibatsu (Jap.) A large interlocking grouping of Japanese companies, similar to a **US trust** or a German *Konzern*; dominated by a bank, holding controlling interests in the other members of the group. The *zaibatsu* have been largely outmoded by legislation since the Second World War, their place being taken by the *keiretsu*.

zaitech (Jap.) Sophisticated financial management, normally that of the surplus funds of industrial companies; the term used to contrast financial profits with industrial profits.

zero coupon bond, zero coupon fund A **bond** issued at a discount (i.e. below **par value**), earning no **interest** but redeemable at its par value, thus providing a guaranteed **capital gain**. See also **rolled-up coupon**.

zero dividend preference shares **Preference shares** that pay no **dividend** but a fixed sum at a **redemption date**.

Zins (Ger.) **Interest**.

Zinssatz (Ger.) **Rate of interest**.

Zinsschein (Ger.) **Coupon**.

Zurich Stock Exchange See **Swiss stock exchanges**.

Zwischenhandler (Ger.) Intermediary, **broker**.

READ MORE IN PENGUIN

In every corner of the world, on every subject under the sun, Penguin represents quality and variety – the very best in publishing today.

For complete information about books available from Penguin – including Puffins, Penguin Classics and Arkana – and how to order them, write to us at the appropriate address below. Please note that for copyright reasons the selection of books varies from country to country.

In the United Kingdom: Please write to *Dept. EP, Penguin Books Ltd, Bath Road, Harmondsworth, West Drayton, Middlesex UB7 ODA*

In the United States: Please write to *Consumer Sales, Penguin USA, P.O. Box 999, Dept. 17109, Bergenfield, New Jersey 07621-0120.* VISA and MasterCard holders call 1-800-253-6476 to order Penguin titles

In Canada: Please write to *Penguin Books Canada Ltd, 10 Alcorn Avenue, Suite 300, Toronto, Ontario M4V 3B2*

In Australia: Please write to *Penguin Books Australia Ltd, P.O. Box 257, Ringwood, Victoria 3134*

In New Zealand: Please write to *Penguin Books (NZ) Ltd, Private Bag 102902, North Shore Mail Centre, Auckland 10*

In India: Please write to *Penguin Books India Pvt Ltd, 706 Eros Apartments, 56 Nehru Place, New Delhi 110 019*

In the Netherlands: Please write to *Penguin Books Netherlands bv, Postbus 3507, NL-1001 AH Amsterdam*

In Germany: Please write to *Penguin Books Deutschland GmbH, Metzlerstrasse 26, 60594 Frankfurt am Main*

In Spain: Please write to *Penguin Books S. A., Bravo Murillo 19, 1° B, 28015 Madrid*

In Italy: Please write to *Penguin Italia s.r.l., Via Felice Casati 20, I–20124 Milano*

In France: Please write to *Penguin France S. A., 17 rue Lejeune, F–31000 Toulouse*

In Japan: Please write to *Penguin Books Japan, Ishikiribashi Building, 2–5–4, Suido, Bunkyo-ku, Tokyo 112*

In Greece: Please write to *Penguin Hellas Ltd, Dimocritou 3, GR–106 71 Athens*

In South Africa: Please write to *Longman Penguin Southern Africa (Pty) Ltd, Private Bag X08, Bertsham 2013*

READ MORE IN PENGUIN

BUSINESS

READ MORE IN PENGUIN

BUSINESS AND ECONOMICS

North and South   David Smith

'This authoritative study ... gives a very effective account of the incredible centralization of decision-making in London, not just in government and administration, but in the press, communications and the management of every major company' – *New Statesman & Society*

I am Right – You are Wrong   Edward de Bono

Edward de Bono expects his ideas to outrage conventional thinkers, yet time has been on his side, and the ideas that he first put forward twenty years ago are now accepted mainstream thinking. Here, in this brilliantly argued assault on outmoded thought patterns, he calls for nothing less than a New Renaissance.

Lloyds Bank Small Business Guide   Sara Williams

This long-running guide to making a success of your small business deals with real issues in a practical way. 'As comprehensive an introduction to setting up a business as anyone could need' – *Daily Telegraph*

The *Economist* Economics   Rupert Pennant-Rea and Clive Crook

Based on a series of 'briefs' published in the *Economist* , this is a clear and accessible guide to the key issues of today's economics for the general reader.

The Rise and Fall of Monetarism   David Smith

Now that even Conservatives have consigned monetarism to the scrap heap of history, David Smith draws out the unhappy lessons of a fundamentally flawed economic experiment, driven by a doctrine that for years had been regarded as outmoded and irrelevant.

Understanding Organizations   Charles B. Handy

Of practical as well as theoretical interest, this book shows how general concepts can help solve specific organizational problems.

READ MORE IN PENGUIN

BUSINESS AND ECONOMICS

The Affluent Society   John Kenneth Galbraith

Classical economics was born in a harsh world of mass poverty, and it has left us with a set of preoccupations hard to adapt to the realities of our own richer age. Our unfamiliar problems need a new approach, and the reception given to this famous book has shown the value of its fresh, lively ideas.

Lloyds Bank Tax Guide   Sara Williams and John Willman

An average employee tax bill is over £4,000 a year. But how much time do you spend checking it? Four out of ten never check the bill – and most spend less than an hour. Mistakes happen. This guide can save YOU money. 'An unstuffy read, packed with sound information' – *Observer*

Trouble Shooter II   John Harvey-Jones

The former chairman of ICI and Britain's best-known businessman resumes his role as consultant to six British companies facing a variety of problems – and sharing a new one: the recession.

Managing on the Edge   Richard Pascale

Nothing fails like success: companies flourish, then lose their edge through a process that is both relentless and largely invisible. 'Pascale's analysis and prescription for "managing on the edge" are unusually subtle for such a readable business book' – *Financial Times*

The Money Machine: How the City Works   Philip Coggan

How are the big deals made? Which are the institutions that really matter? What causes the pound to rise or interest rates to fall? This book provides clear and concise answers to a huge variety of money-related questions.

READ MORE IN PENGUIN

REFERENCE

The Penguin Dictionary of Literary Terms and Literary Theory
J. A. Cuddon

'Scholarly, succinct, comprehensive and entertaining, this is an important book, an indispensable work of reference. It draws on the literature of many languages and quotes aptly and freshly from our own' – *The Times Educational Supplement*

The Penguin Spelling Dictionary

What are the plurals of *octopus* and *rhinoceros*? What is the difference between *stationery* and *stationary*? And how about *annex* and *annexe*, *agape* and *Agape*? This comprehensive new book, the fullest spelling dictionary now available, provides the answers.

Roget's Thesaurus of English Words and Phrases
Edited by Betty Kirkpatrick

This new edition of Roget's classic work, now brought up to date for the nineties, will increase anyone's command of the English language. Fully cross-referenced, it includes synonyms of every kind (formal or colloquial, idiomatic and figurative) for almost 900 headings. It is a must for writers and utterly fascinating for any English speaker.

The Penguin Dictionary of English Idioms
Daphne M. Gulland and David G. Hinds-Howell

The English language is full of pitfalls for the foreign student – but the most common problem lies in understanding and using the vast array of idioms. *The Penguin Dictionary of English Idioms* is uniquely designed to stimulate understanding and familiarity by explaining the meanings and origins of idioms and giving examples of typical usage.

The Penguin Wordmaster Dictionary
Martin H. Manser and Nigel D. Turton

This dictionary puts the pleasure back into word-seeking. Every time you look at a page you get a bonus – a panel telling you everything about a particular word or expression. It is, therefore, a dictionary to be read as well as used for its concise and up-to-date definitions.

READ MORE IN PENGUIN

REFERENCE

Medicines: A Guide for Everybody Peter Parish

Now in its seventh edition and completely revised and updated, this bestselling guide is written in ordinary language for the ordinary reader yet will prove indispensable to anyone involved in health care – nurses, pharmacists, opticians, social workers and doctors.

Media Law Geoffrey Robertson QC and Andrew Nichol

Crisp and authoritative surveys explain the up-to-date position on defamation, obscenity, official secrecy, copyright and confidentiality, contempt of court, the protection of privacy and much more.

The Slang Thesaurus Jonathon Green

Do you make the public bar sound like a gentleman's club? The miraculous *Slang Thesaurus* will liven up your language in no time. You won't Adam and Eve it! A mine of funny, witty, acid and vulgar synonyms for the words you use every day.

The Penguin Dictionary of Troublesome Words Bill Bryson

Why should you avoid discussing the *weather conditions*? Can a married woman be celibate? Why is it eccentric to talk about the aroma of a cowshed? A straightforward guide to the pitfalls and hotly disputed issues in standard written English.

The Penguin Dictionary of Musical Performers Arthur Jacobs

In this invaluable companion volume to *The Penguin Dictionary of Music* Arthur Jacobs has brought together the names of over 2,500 performers. Music is written by composers, yet it is the interpreters who bring it to life; in this comprehensive book they are at last given their due.

The Penguin Dictionary of Third World Terms Kofi Buenor Hadjor

Words associated with the Third World are rarely subject to analysis and definition. Yet many of these terms are loaded with assumptions and cultural attitudes. As a result, discussion of the Third World can be bogged down in bias, prejudice – and Western self-interest.

READ MORE IN PENGUIN

DICTIONARIES

Abbreviations
Archaeology
Architecture
Art and Artists
Astronomy
Biology
Botany
Building
Business
Challenging Words
Chemistry
Civil Engineering
Classical Mythology
Computers
Curious and Interesting Numbers
Curious and Interesting Words
Design and Designers
Economics
Electronics
English and European History
English Idioms
Foreign Terms and Phrases
French
Geography
Historical Slang

Human Geography
Information Technology
Literary Terms and Literary Theory
Mathematics
Modern History 1789–1945
Modern Quotations
Music
Musical Performers
Physical Geography
Physics
Politics
Proverbs
Psychology
Quotations
Religions
Rhyming Dictionary
Saints
Science
Sociology
Spanish
Surnames
Telecommunications
Troublesome Words
Twentieth-Century History